DUNGEONS & DRAGONS

ESSENTIALS™

RULES COMPENDIUM™

ROLEPLAYING GAME CORE RULES

Rob Heinsoo ✦ Andy Collins ✦ James Wyatt ✦ Jeremy Crawford

CREDITS

Rules Compendium™ Design and Compilation
Jeremy Crawford

D&D 4th Edition Design
Rob Heinsoo, Andy Collins, James Wyatt

Additional Design
Stephen Schubert, Mike Mearls

Editing
Jennifer Clarke Wilkes (lead), Greg Bilsland

Managing Editing
Kim Mohan, Michele Carter

D&D R&D/Book Publishing Director
Bill Slavicsek

D&D Creative Manager
Christopher Perkins

D&D Design Manager
James Wyatt

D&D Senior Creative Art Director
Jon Schindehette

D&D Brand Team
Liz Schuh, Kierin Chase, Laura Tommervik, Shelly Mazzanoble, Chris Lindsay, Hilary Ross

Art Director
Mari Kolkowsky

Graphic Designer
Mari Kolkowsky

Cover Illustration
Mike May (front), Adam Paquette (back)

Interior Illustrations
Alexey Aparia, Eric Belisle, Kerem Beyit, Julie Dillon, Emrah Elmasli, Jason A. Engle, Ralph Horsley, Goran Josic, Howard Lyon, David Martin, Lee Moyer, Jim Nelson, William O'Connor, Adam Paquette, Steve Prescott, Eva Widermann, Ben Wootten, James Zhang

Cartographers
Jason A. Engle, Mike Schley

D&D Script Design
Daniel Reeve

Publishing Production Specialist
Angelika Lokotz

Prepress Manager
Jefferson Dunlap

Imaging Technician
Carmen Cheung

Production Manager
Cynda Callaway

Building on the Design of Previous Editions by
E. Gary Gygax, Dave Arneson, David "Zeb" Cook, Jonathan Tweet, Monte Cook, Skip Williams, Richard Baker, Peter Adkison

U.S., CANADA, ASIA, PACIFIC, & LATIN AMERICA
Wizards of the Coast LLC
P.O. Box 707
Renton WA 98057-0707
+1-800-324-6496

EUROPEAN HEADQUARTERS
Hasbro UK Ltd
Caswell Way
Newport, Gwent NP9 0YH
GREAT BRITAIN
Please keep this address for your records

WIZARDS OF THE COAST, BELGIUM
Industrialaan 1
1702 Groot-Bijgaarden
Belgium
+32.070.233.277

987654321
First Printing: September 2010
620-24753000-001 EN   ISBN: 978-0-7869-5621-0

VISIT OUR WEBSITE AT WWW.DUNGEONSANDDRAGONS.COM

CONTENTS

INTRODUCTION

This book presents the core rules of the DUNGEONS & DRAGONS® GAME, the premier roleplaying game of fantasy adventure. Whether you're new to the game or a veteran, you'll find rules, guidelines, and examples herein that will help you and your friends play through tales of high fantasy.

The game is vast, as are its rules. This book focuses on the rules that nearly all groups need, and it is structured so that you can read it front to back or hop from one topic to another using the index. Intended for both players and Dungeon Masters, the rules collected in the following chapters are the most up-to-date versions, reflecting refinements since the current edition was released in 2008.

> *Whether you're new to the game or a veteran, you'll find rules, guidelines, and examples that will help you and your friends play.*

These rules are in service to your group's fun. Experiment with them, and make them your own. In the 1979 *Dungeon Master's Guide*® rulebook, Gary Gygax, the game's cocreator, introduced the main principles of the rules, many of which have been evident in all of the game's editions. What he said about the game still applies today:

> As a realistic simulation of things from the realm of make-believe, or even as a reflection of medieval or ancient warfare or culture or society, it can be deemed only a dismal failure. Readers who seek the latter must search elsewhere. Those who desire to create and populate imaginary worlds with larger-than-life heroes and villains, who seek relaxation with a fascinating game, and who generally believe games should be fun, not work, will hopefully find this system to their taste.

A ROLEPLAYING GAME

The DUNGEONS & DRAGONS game is a roleplaying game. In fact, this game invented roleplaying games and started an industry.

A roleplaying game is a storytelling game that has elements of the games of make-believe that many of us played as children. However, a roleplaying game provides form and structure, with robust gameplay and endless possibilities. While the DUNGEONS & DRAGONS game uses dice and miniatures or other tokens, the action takes place in the imagination. There, players have the freedom to create anything they can imagine, with an unlimited special-effects budget and the technology to make anything happen.

In the DUNGEONS & DRAGONS game, each player creates a hero (also called a character or an adventurer), teams up with other adventurers (played by friends), explores a magical world, and battles monsters. One player takes on the role of the Dungeon Master (DM), the game's lead storyteller and referee. The DM creates adventures for the characters and narrates the action for the players. Having a DM makes the DUNGEONS & DRAGONS game infinitely flexible; he or she can react to any situation—any twist suggested by the players—to make each adventure vibrant, exciting, and unexpected.

An adventure is the heart of the DUNGEONS & DRAGONS game. It's like a fantasy movie or novel, except that the players' group of characters (often referred to as the adventuring group, or the party) are the stars of the story. The DM sets the scene, but no one knows what's going to happen until the adventurers do something, and then anything can happen! The group might explore a dark dungeon, a ruined city, a lost temple deep in a jungle, or a lava-filled cavern beneath a mysterious mountain. The adventurers can solve puzzles, talk with other characters, battle all kinds of fantastic monsters, and discover fabulous magic items and other treasure.

The DUNGEONS & DRAGONS game is a cooperative game in which a group of friends works together to complete each adventure and have fun. It's a storytelling game where the only limit is a player's imagination. It's a fantasy-adventure game, building on the traditions of the greatest fantasy stories of all time.

The game has no real end; when one story or quest wraps up, another one can begin, woven in an ongoing story called a campaign. Many people who play the game keep their campaigns going for months or years, meeting with their friends every week or so to pick up the story where they left off. The adventurers grow in might as the game continues. Each monster defeated, each adventure completed, and each treasure recovered not only adds to the continuing story, but also earns the adventurers new powers and other abilities. This increase in might is reflected by an adventurer's level.

There's no winning and losing in the DUNGEONS & DRAGONS game—at least, not the way those terms are usually understood. The DM and the players

TRY IT!

When you play an adventurer, you put yourself into his or her boots and make decisions as if you were that person. You decide which door your adventurer opens next. You decide whether to attack a monster, to negotiate with a villain, or to attempt a dangerous quest. You can make these decisions based on your adventurer's personality, motivations, and goals, and you can even speak in character if you like. Within the boundaries set by the Dungeon Master, you control what your adventurer can do and say in the game.

Your hero can attempt anything you can think of. Want to talk to the dragon instead of fighting it? Want to disguise yourself as an orc and sneak into the foul lair? Go ahead and give it a try. An adventurer's actions might work, or they might fail spectacularly, but either way the player contributed to the unfolding story and had fun.

participate together in an exciting story of bold adventurers confronting deadly perils. Sometimes an adventurer might come to a grisly end, torn apart by ferocious monsters or done in by a nefarious villain. Even so, the other adventurers can search for powerful magic to revive their fallen comrade, or the player might choose to create a new character to carry on. The group might fail to complete an adventure successfully, but if everyone had a good time and created a memorable story, they all win.

A Fantastic World

The world of the DUNGEONS & DRAGONS game is a place of magic and monsters, of brave warriors and spectacular adventures. It begins with a basis of medieval fantasy and then adds the creatures, places, and powers that make the DUNGEONS & DRAGONS world unique.

The world of the DUNGEONS & DRAGONS game is ancient, built upon and beneath the ruins of past empires, leaving the landscape dotted with places of adventure and mystery. Legends and artifacts of past empires still survive—as do terrible menaces. Although minor realms exist, they are widely scattered points of light in the surrounding darkness that shrouds the world. Monsters and supernatural creatures prowl the dark spaces. Some are threats, others are willing to aid the adventurers, and many fall into both camps and might react differently depending on how the adventurers approach them.

ADAM PAQUETTE

THE HISTORY OF THE GAME

Before roleplaying games, before computer games, before trading card games, there were wargames. Using metal miniatures to simulate famous battles from history, wargamers were the original hobby gamers. In 1971, Gary Gygax created *Chainmail*®, a set of rules that added fantastic creatures and magic into the traditional wargame. In 1972, Dave Arneson approached Gygax with a new take on the subject; instead of controlling an army, each player would play a single character, a hero. Instead of fighting each other, the heroes would cooperate to defeat villains and gain rewards. This combination of rules, miniatures, cooperation, and imagination created a totally new entertainment experience, and in 1974 Gygax and Arneson published the first set of roleplaying game rules with TSR Hobbies, Inc.: the DUNGEONS & DRAGONS® roleplaying game.

In 1977, the rules were rewritten and repackaged into a new form with the DUNGEONS & DRAGONS Basic Set, and suddenly the game was on its way to becoming a phenomenon. A year later, the first edition of the ADVANCED DUNGEONS & DRAGONS game was published in a series of hardcover books.

Throughout the 1980s, the game experienced remarkable growth. Novels, a cartoon series, computer games, and the first campaign settings (GREYHAWK®, FORGOTTEN REALMS®, and DRAGONLANCE®) were released, and in 1989 the second edition of the AD&D game took the world by storm. The 1990s started out strong, with the release of more campaign settings (including RAVENLOFT®, DARK SUN®, and PLANESCAPE™), but as the decade was drawing to a close, the DUNGEONS & DRAGONS juggernaut was losing steam. In 1997, Wizards of the Coast purchased TSR and moved its creative staff to Seattle to begin work on the third edition of the game.

In 2000, the third edition of DUNGEONS & DRAGONS was released, and it was hailed as an innovation in game mechanics. During this period, DUNGEONS & DRAGONS reached new heights of popularity, celebrated its thirtieth anniversary, and published a vast collection of rulebooks, supplements, and adventures.

In 2008, the DUNGEONS & DRAGONS game reached a new milestone with its latest edition. This edition builds on what has gone before, introducing and refining various game elements.

Over the years, DUNGEONS & DRAGONS has grown and made its mark on popular culture. It has inspired multiple generations of gamers, writers, computer game designers, filmmakers, and more with its ability to expand the imagination and inspire creativity. Whether you were with it from the beginning or just discovered it today, the DUNGEONS & DRAGONS game is your key to a world of fantasy and adventure.

Magic is everywhere. People believe in and accept the power that magic provides. True masters of magic, however, are rare. At some point, all adventurers rely on magic. Wizards and warlocks draw power from the fabric of the universe. Clerics and paladins call down the wrath of their gods to sear their foes with divine radiance, or they invoke their gods' mercy to heal wounds. Fighters and rogues don't use magical powers, but their expertise with magic weapons makes them masters of the battlefield. At the highest levels of play, even nonmagical adventurers perform deeds that no mortal could dream of doing without magic.

WHAT'S IN A GAME

All DUNGEONS & DRAGONS games have several basic components: at least one player (five players works best), a Dungeon Master, an adventure, and game books and accessories, including dice.

Players

DUNGEONS & DRAGONS players fill two distinct roles in the game: controlling the players' characters—also called adventurers—and acting as the Dungeon Master. These roles aren't mutually exclusive, and a player can roleplay an adventurer today and run an adventure for the other players tomorrow. Although everyone who plays the game is technically a player, this book usually refers to players as those who run the adventurers.

Each player creates an adventurer, part of a team that delves into dungeons, battles monsters, and explores the world's dark wilderness. Like the protagonists of a novel, a movie, or a video game, adventurers stand at the center of the game's action.

The Dungeon Master

The Dungeon Master controls the pace of the story and referees the action along the way. Every DUNGEONS & DRAGONS game needs a DM. The DM has several parts to play in the game.

+ **Adventure Builder:** The DM creates adventures, or selects published ones, for the other players to experience.

+ **Narrator:** The DM sets the pace of the story and presents the various challenges and encounters that the other players must overcome.

+ **Monster Controller:** The DM controls the monsters that the adventurers confront, choosing the monsters' actions and rolling dice for them.

+ **Referee:** The DM decides how to apply the game rules and guides the story. If the rules don't cover a situation, the DM determines what to do. At times, the DM might alter or even ignore the result of a die roll if doing so benefits the story.

Many players find that being the Dungeon Master is the best part of the game. The Dungeon Master role isn't necessarily a permanent post; each player in the group can take turns being the DM from adventure to adventure.

COOPERATION, NOT OPPOSITION

Even though as the DM you control the monsters in an adventure, you aren't the other players' adversary and don't want them to fail. Your job is to provide a framework for the whole group to enjoy an exciting adventure. That means challenging the adventurers with interesting encounters and tests, keeping the game moving, and applying the rules of the game fairly. Your goal is to make success taste its sweetest by presenting challenges that are just hard enough that the other players have to work to overcome them, but not so hard that victory or escape is impossible.

The Adventure

Adventurers need adventures. A DUNGEONS & DRAGONS adventure consists of a series of linked events. As the players decide which way to go next and how their characters deal with the resulting encounters and challenges, they turn the adventure into an exciting story about their characters. All DUNGEONS & DRAGONS adventures feature action, combat, mystery, magic, challenges, conversation, and lots of monsters.

Adventures come in three forms.

✦ **Ready-to-Play:** The DM can buy or obtain professionally written, ready-to-play adventures from a number of sources, including a local game store and www.dndinsider.com.

✦ **Adventure Hooks and Components:** Most DUNGEONS & DRAGONS products offer pieces of adventures—story ideas, maps, interesting monsters—that the DM can assemble into an adventure.

✦ **Homemade:** Many DMs choose to create their own adventures, building challenging encounters and stocking them with monsters and treasures from products such as the *Monster Vault* and the *Dungeon Master's Kit*.

An adventure can be a simple "dungeon crawl," a series of rooms filled with monsters and traps that has little story to explain why the adventurers are facing those challenges. It can be as complex as a murder mystery or a tale of political intrigue, or it can be but one chapter in an epic tale related to the fate of the world. An adventure can last for a single game session or stretch out over many sessions of play. For instance, exploring a haunted castle (which takes a few hours or days in the game world) might involve half a dozen game sessions over the course of a couple of months of real time.

When the same group of adventurers plays with the same Dungeon Master through multiple adventures, the result is a campaign. The story of the heroes doesn't end with a single adventure but continues on for as long as desired, just as in an ongoing comic book, television, or novel series.

Game Books and Accessories

The action of the game takes place mostly in the imagination, but a few products are necessary to play the DUNGEONS & DRAGONS game. The following DUNGEONS & DRAGONS Essentials™ products provide a great place to start.

Essential Products for Players and Dungeon Masters

✦ DUNGEONS & DRAGONS *Fantasy Roleplaying Game Starter Set.* This boxed set contains everything a group of players needs to start playing the DUNGEONS & DRAGONS game. It contains rules, dice, maps, tokens, and an adventure that takes characters from 1st to 2nd level.

✦ DUNGEONS & DRAGONS *Rules Compendium*™. This comprehensive book contains the essential rules of the game collected in one place, taking a campaign from 1st to 30th level.

✦ DUNGEONS & DRAGONS Roleplaying Game Dice Set. The DUNGEONS & DRAGONS game, as well as other games using the D&D® game system, require a special set of dice (see the "Game Dice" sidebar). Pick up extra dice so that every player has a set.

Essential Products for Players

The Essentials player books feature the fundamental elements of the game from a player's point of view.

✦ *Heroes of the Fallen Lands*™. This volume contains rules for several classes: cleric, fighter, rogue, and wizard. It also describes several races: dwarf, eladrin, elf, halfling, and human.

✦ *Heroes of the Forgotten Kingdoms*™. This volume contains rules for several classes: druid, paladin, ranger, and warlock. It also describes several races: dragonborn, drow, half-elf, half-orc, and tiefling.

Essential Products for Dungeon Masters

✦ *Dungeon Master's Kit*™. This product features game rules, advice, adventures, maps, tokens, and a DM screen—all useful tools for a Dungeon Master. Many Dungeon Masters like to use a screen to keep the other players from seeing dice rolls for the monsters and from spotting secrets in the DM's notes.

✦ *Monster Vault*™. This product features a collection of monsters for use in any DUNGEONS & DRAGONS game, from 1st level to 30th level, and includes monster tokens and an adventure.

✦ *Dungeon Tiles Master Sets.* Three master sets of Dungeon Tiles (*The Dungeon, The City,* and *The Wilderness*) enable you to create encounter areas for any adventure, using DUNGEONS & DRAGONS tokens and miniatures. The tiles let you easily create a battle map for a combat encounter. Tokens and miniatures are placed on the map to keep track of where adventurers and monsters are positioned as the encounter unfolds.

Other Useful Ingredients for Play

A Place to Play: The bare minimum of space needed to play the DUNGEONS & DRAGONS game is room for everyone in the group to sit. Most likely, everyone will also want a table to sit around. A table holds the battle grid and tokens or miniatures, gives players a place to roll dice and write on character sheets, and holds piles of books and papers. People can pull chairs around a dining table or sit in chairs or sofas by a coffee table. It's possible to run a game without a table for the battle grid, but combat runs more easily if everyone can see where everything is positioned.

Paper and Pencils: Everyone should have a pencil and paper. During every round of combat, players need to keep track of hit points, bonuses and penalties, the use of powers, the consequences of various conditions, and other information. Someone in the group typically takes notes about what has happened in the adventure, and players need to make note of experience points and treasure their characters acquire. Alternatively, players can do a lot of this note-taking digitally, using a computer or a smart phone.

GAME DICE

The game uses polyhedral dice with different numbers of sides, as shown here. You can find dice like these in game stores and in many bookstores.

In these rules, the different dice are referred to by the letter "d" followed by the number of sides: d4, d6, d8, d10, d12, and d20. For instance, a d6 is a six-sided die (the typical cube that many games use).

When you need to roll dice, the rules tell you how many dice to roll, what size they are, and what modifiers to add. For example, "3d8 + 5" means you roll three eight-sided dice and add 5 to the total.

The same "d" notation appears in the expressions "1d3" and "1d2." To simulate the roll of 1d3, roll a d6 and divide the result by 2. To simulate the roll of 1d2, roll any die and assign a result of 1 or 2 to the roll depending on whether it was odd or even.

HOW TO PLAY

Basically, the DUNGEONS & DRAGONS game consists of a group of heroes taking on an adventure presented by the Dungeon Master. Each adventure is made up of encounters—various challenges that the characters face.

In a board game, you have a piece, or pieces, to move around. Your "piece" in the DUNGEONS & DRAGONS game is your adventurer if you're a player and an adventure's monsters and other characters if you're the DM. Often the action of an adventure takes place in your imagination only, but if you use tokens or miniatures, you literally move pieces around on the table.

Basics of Play

Here's a summary of the basic rules of the game.

Every creature has powers, skills, and special features tied to one of six ability scores. The abilities are Strength, Constitution, Dexterity, Intelligence, Wisdom, and Charisma. Each creature also has **hit points**, which are reduced when the creature takes damage, most often as the result of a **damage roll**.

A creature does things in the game by performing **actions**. Actions are resolved by making different kinds of **checks**. A check is rolling a twenty-sided die (a **d20**), adding modifiers based on the type of action, and announcing the result.

Example: An adventurer might make a melee basic attack, using the character's Strength modifier and a modifier based on the weapon used to make the attack (totaling 5). The player rolls a d20 and adds 5, getting a 12 on the die and announcing a result of 17 (12 + 5 = 17).

The three basic checks that are used all the time are **attack rolls, skill checks**, and **ability checks**. Players usually make checks against a target number, but sometimes a check is compared to another character's check. This is an **opposed check**.

WILLIAM O'CONNOR

A **modifier** is any number that adds to or subtracts from a die roll. A character's ability scores, for example, provide modifiers that apply to many actions in the game. A **bonus** is a positive modifier (such as a +2 bonus). A **penalty** is a negative modifier (for example, a -1 penalty).

In any task, a creature's modifiers represent training, competence, and natural talent. The d20 roll, on the other hand, reflects luck and the unpredictable nature of action and adventure.

The Dungeon Master compares a check result against a target number, the **Difficulty Class (DC)** of the task being attempted or the **defense** against which an attack is being made. Most target numbers are set for the DM, such as a monster's defense numbers or the DC for climbing a dungeon wall. Other times, the DM estimates the difficulty of a task that isn't specifically covered by the rules. To do this, the DM makes use of advice and tables provided in adventures, the *Dungeon Master's Kit*, or this book.

Chapter 1 goes into more detail about the basic rules of the game.

Encounters

Encounters are the action scenes in an adventure, various kinds of challenges that the adventurers must face and overcome. Encounters come in two types.

✦ **Combat encounters** are battles against nefarious foes. In a combat encounter, adventurers and monsters take turns attacking until one side or the other is defeated.

✦ **Noncombat encounters** include deadly traps, difficult puzzles, and other obstacles to overcome. Sometimes the adventurers prevail in noncombat encounters by applying their skills or with clever use of magic, and sometimes the players have to puzzle them out with nothing but their wits. Noncombat encounters also include social interactions, such as attempts to persuade, bargain with, or obtain information from a character played by the DM.

Adventurers have an array of tools at their disposal to help them overcome the challenges in encounters, including attack powers—such as a wizard's *fireball* or a fighter's *power strike*—that deal damage and produce other effects against enemies in combat. Adventurers also have utility powers, skills, and other features that can be useful in both combat and noncombat encounters.

Exploration

Between encounters, the adventurers explore the world—or whatever limited segment of the world the DM's adventure presents them with. The players make decisions about which way their characters travel and what they try to do next. Exploration is the give-and-take of the players saying what they want their characters to do, and the DM telling the players what happens when their characters do it.

For instance, let's say the adventurers have just climbed down into a dark chasm. The DM tells the players that their characters see three tunnels leading from the chasm floor into the gloom. The players decide which tunnel their characters venture into first, and they indicate which way their characters are heading. That's exploration. The players might have their adventurers try almost anything: finding a place to hide and set an ambush in case monsters come by, shouting "Hello, any monsters here?" as loud as they can, or searching the chasm floor carefully in case there's anything interesting lying amid the boulders and moss. That's all exploration too.

Decisions the characters make as they explore eventually lead to encounters. One tunnel might open into a cave full of goblins. If the characters decide to go that way, they're heading into a combat encounter. Another tunnel might lead to a door sealed by a magic lock that they have to break through—a noncombat encounter.

The Dungeon Master decides whether something the adventurers try actually works. Some actions automatically succeed (characters can usually move around without trouble); some actions require one or more checks (breaking down a locked door, for example); and some actions simply can't succeed. Adventurers are capable of any deeds a strong, smart, agile, and well-armed human action hero can pull off. They can't punch their way through a door of 3-inch-thick iron plate with their bare hands, for example—not unless they have powerful magic to help them out!

Chapters 4 and 6 give the information that a group needs to determine whether the characters can succeed at the tasks they attempt. "Making Checks," page 22, spells out the details of making each kind of check.

Exploration

While exploring an adventure location, the adventurers might try to do any of the following actions:

+ Move down a hallway, follow a passage, or cross a room
+ Have conversations with DM-controlled characters
+ Listen by a door to determine if they hear anything on the other side
+ Try a door to see if it's locked
+ Break down a locked door
+ Search a room for treasure
+ Pull levers or push statues or furnishings around
+ Pick the lock of a treasure chest
+ Jury-rig a trap

Taking Turns

In exploration, players don't usually need to take turns. The DM might prompt the players by asking, "What do you do?" The players answer, and then the DM tells them what happens. The players might break in with questions, offer suggestions to other players, or bring up a new action any time they like.

Combat encounters work differently: The adventurers and the monsters all take turns in a fixed rotation, called the initiative order. See Chapter 6 for how combat works.

Example of Play

Here's an example scene in a typical game session. The adventurers are exploring the ruins of an old dwarven stronghold infested by monsters. There are four
players in this session:

+ Chris, the Dungeon Master
+ Justin, playing the human fighter Shara
+ Mike, playing the halfling rogue Uldane
+ Jennifer, playing the eladrin wizard Albanon

Chris (*DM*): Old stone steps climb about 30 feet or so into the mountain, along-
side a cold stream that splashes through the cave. The steps end at a landing
in front of a big stone door carved with the image of a bearded dwarf face.
The door stands open about a foot or so. There's a bronze gong hanging from a
bracket in the wall nearby. What do you do?

Mike (*Uldane*): I'll creep up and peek through the opening.

Jennifer (*Albanon*): I want to take a closer look at the gong.

Justin (*Shara*): I'm going to hang back and keep watch, in case Uldane gets into
trouble.

Mike (*Uldane*): Not a chance, I'm a pro.

Chris (*DM*): OK, first Albanon: It's a battered old bronze gong. There's a small
hammer hanging beside it.

Justin (*Shara*): Don't touch it!

Jennifer (*Albanon*): I wasn't going to! It looks like the doorbell to me. No sense
telling the monsters we're here.

Chris (*DM*): Now for Uldane. Since you're trying to be sneaky, Mike, make a
Stealth check.

Mike (*rolls a Stealth check for Uldane*): I got a 22.

Chris (*DM*): Uldane is pretty stealthy.

*Chris compares Uldane's Stealth check result to the Perception check result of the
monsters he knows are in the next room. Mike's roll beats the Perception check, so the
monsters don't know the halfling is there.*

Jennifer (*Albanon*): So what's in there?

Chris (*DM*): You're by the gong, remember? Uldane, you peek through the door's
opening, and you see a large stone hall with several thick pillars. There's a
large fire pit in the center of the room filled with dimming embers. You see
four beastlike humanoids with hyena faces crouching around the fire pit, and

a big animal—like a hyena, but much bigger—dozing on the floor nearby. The hyena-men are armed with spears and axes.

Justin (*Shara*): Gnolls! I hate those guys.

Jennifer (*Albanon*): Looks like we'll have to fight our way in. Can we take them?

Mike (*Uldane*): No problem—we've got the drop on 'em.

Chris (*DM*): So are you going through the door?

The players all agree that they are.

Chris (*DM*): Show me where your characters are standing right before you go in.

The players arrange their characters' tokens on the Dungeon Tiles that Chris has prepared for the encounter. They're now on the landing just outside the room with the gnolls.

Justin (*Shara*): All right, on the count of three . . .

Mike (*Uldane*): Is that on three or right after three?

Jennifer (*Albanon*): Uldane!

Mike (*Uldane*): What? I'm just asking for clarification!

Justin (*Shara*): One . . . two . . . three!

Chris (*DM*): You have surprised the gnolls! Everybody roll initiative, and we'll see if you can take these monsters down or not.

What happens next? Can Shara, Uldane, and Albanon defeat the gnolls? That depends on how the players play their characters, and how lucky they are with their dice.

THE BASICS

The DUNGEONS & DRAGONS game offers many sorts of adventures, including a descent into a monster lair, back-alley investigation in a bustling city, an expedition into an enchanted forest, a battle under dragon-filled skies, intrigue in the court of lords and ladies, the exploration of a haunted castle, and a confrontation with the forces of the gods themselves. The adventurers who face the game's challenges are as varied as the stories they help to shape.

Because the possibilities for adventure are so vast, the game's rules must be able to guide play in many different situations, both in combat and outside it. A few basic rules form the foundation of play—the focus of this chapter. After mastering these basics, any player can understand how most of the game works.

The game offers many sorts of adventures ... a descent into a monster lair, an expedition into an enchanted forest, a battle under dragon-filled skies, a confrontation with the forces of the gods themselves.

This chapter covers the following topics.

✦ **Creatures and Levels:** The rules of play often refer to "creatures," "characters," and "adventurers." This section explains the differences between those key terms. As well, many of the game's rules depend on a creature's level or tier, which are discussed here.

✦ **Making Checks:** The core mechanic of the DUNGEONS & DRAGONS game is making a check (rolling a d20 and adding modifiers, then comparing to a target number). This section goes into more detail about the three kinds of checks in the game: attack rolls, skill checks, and ability checks.

✦ **Table Rules:** Putting together a play group and keeping the game running smoothly require a few table rules, which guide how the group conducts its game sessions. This section provides a few suggestions.

✦ **Improvisation:** This game is all about imagination. Players are free to try anything they can think of for their characters to do, and DMs should be flexible enough to respond to unexpected player choices. This section provides tips on "winging it."

✦ **The DUNGEONS & DRAGONS World:** Because this is a storytelling game at its heart, understanding the setting where the game's rules come to life is important.

WILLIAM O'CONNOR

CREATURES AND LEVELS

The main participants in a DUNGEONS & DRAGONS adventure are creatures. Some of them are the adventurers. The rest of them are the monsters and peoples of the world that are controlled by the Dungeon Master.

KEY TERMS

The following terms appear again and again in the game's rules.

creature: A being in the game world. Both adventurers and monsters are creatures. See Chapter 2 for rules about creature statistics.

character: Another term for a creature. The term is usually used to refer to a person who is not monstrous: either an adventurer or a DM-controlled individual (sometimes called a nonplayer character, or NPC).

adventurer: The character controlled by a player other than the Dungeon Master. An adventurer is sometimes called a player character.

monster: A creature controlled by the Dungeon Master. The term is usually used to refer to creatures that are hostile to the adventurers (often including DM-controlled characters).

If a creature is going to be involved in combat or some other encounter that requires game statistics, it has a character sheet if the creature is an adventurer, or a statistics block (often called just "stat block") if the creature is a monster or a DM-controlled character. It might have a full complement of statistics (such as ability scores, powers, and skills) or only the few statistics needed for the encounter in which the creature appears.

Many creatures are simply part of an adventure's background and have no game statistics at all. For instance, the DM might describe the proprietor of an inn and have that character appear in multiple sessions of play, but the proprietor probably never has game statistics, unless the DM plans to have him join a battle. He is simply a name and perhaps a sentence or two on a page, though he might be a beloved figure in the campaign.

A creature that has game statistics typically has a level. A creature's level represents how powerful it is compared to everything else in the game. For instance, a 2nd-level creature is substantially less powerful than a 30th-level creature. After adventurers complete encounters and quests, the DM awards experience points to them, and each gains a new level (or "levels up") whenever he or she reaches a certain number of points. It takes about eight to ten encounters to advance from one level to the next.

See Chapter 2 for information on the game statistics of creatures, including how to make a character and how to advance that character in level.

Tiers of Play

Heroes in the DUNGEONS & DRAGONS game and most of the threats they face have levels, which reflect their relative power. Levels are grouped into three tiers: the heroic tier (levels 1-10), the paragon tier (levels 11-20), and the epic tier (levels 21-30).

When adventurers leave one tier and cross the threshold into a new one, they experience a major increase in power and simultaneously face more lethal threats. As a campaign progresses through the three tiers, its story and the style of its encounters also evolve.

Heroic Tier
Even 1st-level characters are heroes, different from common folk because of exceptional aptitudes, learned skills, and the hint of a great destiny. At the start of their careers, adventurers rely on their own abilities and powers, and they quickly acquire magic items.

The fate of a village might hang on the success or failure of heroic tier adventurers. Heroes in this tier navigate dangerous terrain and explore haunted crypts, where they can expect to fight sneaky goblins, savage orcs, ferocious wolves, giant spiders, evil cultists, and flesh-seeking ghouls. If the heroes face a dragon, it is a young one that might still be searching for a lair and has not yet found its place in the world. One, in other words, that is much like themselves.

Paragon Tier
By 11th level, heroes are shining examples of courage and determination, set well apart from the masses. Paragon tier adventurers are more versatile than they were at lower levels.

The fate of a nation or even the world might depend on momentous quests that heroes in this tier undertake. Such heroes explore uncharted regions and delve into long-forgotten dungeons, and they confront monsters such as savage giants, cruel beholders, bloodthirsty vampires, and devious mind flayers. They might face a powerful adult dragon that has established a lair and a role in the world.

Epic Tier
By 21st level, characters have truly superheroic capabilities, and ordinary people can hardly dream of such power. The heroes' deeds become the stuff of legend.

Epic adventures have far-reaching consequences, possibly determining the fate of the natural world and even planes beyond. Epic characters navigate otherworldly realms and explore never-before-seen caverns of wonder. They fight demon lords, mind flayer masterminds, terrible archdevils, lich archmages, and even the gods themselves. The dragons they encounter are ancient wyrms of earthshaking power, whose sleep troubles kingdoms and whose waking threatens the world.

MILESTONES AND QUESTS

As adventurers move from one encounter to another on their way to gaining the next level, they reach milestones and complete quests.

Milestones: When the adventurers complete two consecutive encounters without stopping for an extended rest (page 172), they reach a milestone. Each time they reach a milestone, each adventurer gains an action point (page 235). The DM might provide additional rewards, depending on the adventure and the style of the campaign.

Quests: Quests are the fundamental story framework of an adventure—the reason the adventurers want to get involved. They are why an adventure exists, and they indicate what the adventurers need to do to resolve the situation the adventure presents.

A quest connects a series of encounters into a meaningful story. The simplest adventures revolve around a single major quest, usually one that gives everyone in the group a motivation to pursue it. For example, a group's major quest might be to put an end to the goblin raids on a local village, to rescue a kidnapped merchant, or to recover an ancient relic lost in the nearby ruins.

Most adventures, however, involve multiple quests. An adventure might have two or more major quests. For example, the goblin raiders might also be responsible for kidnapping an important merchant. Adventures often also include minor quests that relate to individual characters' goals or backgrounds. Sometimes these quests can conflict with each other, presenting characters with interesting choices about which quests to pursue.

When the group completes a quest, each character earns experience points and possibly other kinds of rewards, depending on the quest. See Appendix 2 for typical rewards for completed quests.

Each published adventure usually includes one or more quests appropriate to that adventure. The *Dungeon Master's Kit* includes guidelines for creating quests.

MAKING CHECKS

Does a sword swing hurt the dragon or just bounce off its iron-hard scales? Will the ogre believe an outrageous bluff, or can a character swim across a raging river? The DUNGEONS & DRAGONS game relies on die rolls, called checks, to determine success or failure in these kinds of situations.

Making a check is the core mechanic of the game. It follows a few simple steps.

1. Roll a twenty-sided die (d20). The higher the result, the better.

2. Add any relevant modifiers, whether bonuses or penalties.

3. Compare the result to a target number. If the result equals or exceeds the target number, the check is a success. Otherwise, it's a failure.

This simple rule governs most Dungeons & Dragons play. Three types of checks come up in most sessions of the game: attack rolls, skill checks, and ability checks. No matter what type of check a creature is making, modifiers come into play: bonuses, penalties, or both.

Check Modifiers

Modifiers of some sort apply to every check. A creature's innate advantages and disadvantages affect its chance of success, and the circumstances surrounding the check might contribute bonuses or penalties.

The following kinds of modifiers can affect a check.

✦ **One-Half Level:** No matter which type of check a creature is making, the creature's level affects how much of a chance it has to succeed. This fact is represented by a bonus that a creature gains to every check equal to one-half the creature's level, rounded down. The modifiers in a monster's stat block already include this bonus, whereas an adventurer applies the bonus to every check that he or she makes (most players record this bonus on their character sheets and adjust it whenever their characters reach an even-numbered level).

Example: The level of a 1st-level adventurer contributes no bonus to his or her checks, since half of 1 is 0 after rounding down. In contrast, the level of a 7th-level adventurer contributes a +3 bonus to all of the adventurer's checks.

- ✦ **Ability Modifier:** A typical creature has six abilities—Strength, Dexterity, Constitution, Intelligence, Wisdom, and Charisma—each of which has a score representing how strong the creature is in that ability. Each score has a modifier associated with it (see the Ability Modifiers table, page 63). For instance, a score of 14 in an ability grants a +2 modifier to checks using that ability. In other words, if a character has a Strength of 14, he or she gains a +2 bonus to any check using Strength. A monster's ability modifiers are already included in its statistics, but an adventurer applies the appropriate modifier whenever he or she makes a check (most players record this bonus on their character sheets).

- ✦ **Persistent Modifiers:** Creatures have various modifiers that persist from one encounter to another. One adventurer might have a feat that gives him a +1 bonus to attack rolls whenever he uses a particular type of weapon, whereas another adventurer might take a -1 penalty to all of her checks because of a powerful curse. Almost every creature has a bonus to a skill or two as the result of skill training (page 124). Magic items (page 275) and weapon proficiencies (page 273) also grant persistent bonuses. Monsters have fewer persistent bonuses than adventurers do, since monsters don't have feats or weapon proficiencies and rarely benefit directly from magic items.

- ✦ **Temporary Modifiers:** Powers, circumstances, feats, conditions, and other effects cause many bonuses and penalties in play. For instance, a creature's target might have partial cover, causing the creature to take a -2 penalty to the attack roll it makes against the target. Or an adventurer might use a power that grants a temporary bonus to all of her companions' defenses. Temporary modifiers are extremely varied and are specified in many different parts of the game.

Attack Rolls

An attack roll is a kind of check that occurs in every battle, where the target number for the check is the defense of a target.

Attack rolls are often described using a shorthand notation:

[Ability name] vs. [Defense]   *or*   **[Modifier] vs. [Defense]**

The ability (or other modifier) as well as the defense involved are specified in the attack used. The four defenses are Armor Class (AC), Fortitude, Reflex, and Will. (See "Defenses," page 65, for more information.) If the result of the attack roll is equal to or higher than the target's defense, the attack hits. A monster's attack roll modifier already includes the modifier for one-half its level and the relevant ability modifier.

For instance, an adventurer's attack power might include the following attack roll notation: "Strength vs. Fortitude." The adventurer makes a check (adding his

THE DM'S BEST FRIEND

As the Dungeon Master, you're frequently faced by unusual circumstances in the game, since the players often come up with unexpected things for their characters to do—acts the rules don't cover. Other times, the adventurers do something that is covered by the rules, but neither you nor the players can remember the relevant rule.

In such cases, you can fall back on the following rule of thumb, known as the "DM's best friend": An especially favorable circumstance gives a +2 bonus to a check, and a particularly unfavorable circumstance gives a -2 penalty.

This rule of thumb can be used in encounter after encounter, and it can save a group from spending too much time trying to recall a forgotten rule. Can't remember if there's a rule for the effect of strong winds on attack rolls with ranged weapons? Just apply a -2 penalty and keep playing. In the end, what matters is crafting a vivid scene so that everyone has fun, not focusing on a minor rule of the game.

or her Strength modifier, one-half his or her level, and any other modifiers) and compares the result to the target's Fortitude. The power specifies what happens if the adventurer hits and might even specify something that happens on a miss.

In contrast, a monster might use an attack power that specifies "+10 vs. Reflex" for the attack roll. The monster makes a check, adding 10 plus any other modifiers, and compares the result to the target's Reflex.

The modifiers to an attack roll include temporary modifiers, such as a +2 bonus for having combat advantage or a -2 penalty if the target has partial cover.

Players use the information in player books such as *Heroes of the Fallen Lands* and *Heroes of the Forgotten Empires* to determine the attack modifiers for their powers. The Dungeon Master most often uses the numbers provided for monsters in sources such as the *Monster Vault*.

Attack rolls are described in more detail in Chapter 6.

Skill Checks

Skill checks occur both in combat and outside it. Such checks test a creature's aptitude in a particular field: athletic ability (represented by the Athletics skill), knowledge of history (represented by the History skill), a knack for making the improbable seem believable (represented by the Bluff skill), and so on. An adventurer begins play with training in a handful of skills, the number of which is determined by the adventurer's class. A typical monster has training in only one or two skills. Training in a skill gives a creature a +5 bonus to checks involving that skill.

Skill checks sometimes use a shorthand notation:

[DC] [Skill name] check

The target number for a skill check—called its Difficulty Class, or DC—is determined by the DM. Published adventures and rulebooks (including this one) provide many target numbers for the DM to use, but he or she has the final say on what number is appropriate in a particular situation (see the Difficulty Class by Level table, page 126, for target numbers that are appropriate for different levels of play).

For instance, a published adventure might include the following skill check notation: "Make a DC 20 Athletics check." The adventurer makes a check (adding his or her Strength modifier, one-half his or her level, the bonus for training in Athletics if applicable, and any other modifiers) and compares the result to the target DC. The check is successful if the result equals or exceeds the DC.

If a monster attempts the same DC 20 Athletics check, it adds either the Athletics check modifier in its stat block or its Strength modifier, plus any other modifiers, and compares the result to the DC.

Sometimes the DC for a creature's skill check is the result of another creature's skill check. In that situation, the creatures are said to be making opposed checks. Whoever gets the higher result succeeds.

A successful skill check usually just means that the character accomplishes what he or she set out to do, but the results can be more subtle than that. If a character attempts a Perception check while pressing her ear against a door, hoping to hear signs of what might lurk on the other side of the door, it's up to the DM to describe the sounds she hears if her check meets or beats the DC set by the DM. If a character makes an Athletics check in an attempt to jump over a chasm, however, a successful check probably just means that he cleared the chasm and landed safely on the other side.

Chapter 4 gives complete rules on making skill checks.

Ability Checks

Attack rolls and skill checks account for most of the checks that a creature makes, but sometimes the DM wants a creature to make a check when none of the creature's skills or powers apply. In that situation, the DM has the creature make an ability check, using the most appropriate ability modifier of the creature. For instance, an adventurer might try to hold a door closed against an orc, and the DM decides that's a test of raw strength: a Strength check (another DM might decide that the Athletics skill is appropriate in the same situation).

Ability checks often use a shorthand notation similar to that for a skill check:

[DC] [Ability name] check

Ability checks follow the rules for skill checks in Chapter 4, including the rules for opposed checks and aiding another creature. The main difference between ability checks and skill checks is that a creature uses an ability modifier for an ability check instead of a skill modifier.

Bonuses and Penalties

Checks, as well as other die rolls, are modified by bonuses and penalties.

Bonuses

There's one important rule for bonuses: Don't combine bonuses of the same type to the same roll or score. If a creature has two bonuses of the same type that apply to the same roll or score, use the higher one. For instance, if a character has a +2 power bonus to attack rolls and gains a +4 power bonus to attack rolls, the character has a +4 power bonus, not a +6 power bonus.

Monsters don't have feats and don't use proficiency bonuses, and they rarely wield or use magic items. In general, all the relevant bonuses to a monster's check are included in its stat block.

Each of the bonus types in the game is described below.

Armor Bonus: Granted by armor, this bonus applies only as long as a creature wears the armor.

Enhancement Bonus: This bonus improves attack rolls and damage rolls or defenses. An adventurer gains an enhancement bonus to Armor Class when wearing magic armor, an enhancement bonus to attack rolls and damage rolls when wielding a magic weapon or implement, and an enhancement bonus to Fortitude, Reflex, and Will when wearing a magic item that occupies the neck item slot (such as an enchanted cloak). An adventurer can benefit from a magic weapon, magic armor, and a magic cloak at the same time, since their enhancement bonuses add to different rolls or scores.

Feat Bonus: Granted by a feat, this bonus applies only as long as a creature has the feat.

Item Bonus: Granted by a magic item, this bonus applies only as long as a creature wears or wields the item.

Power Bonus: Granted by powers and class features, power bonuses are usually temporary.

Proficiency Bonus: Gained from proficiency with a weapon, this bonus applies to attack rolls with that weapon. An adventurer gains the proficiency bonus only when wielding the weapon and using powers that have the weapon keyword.

Racial Bonus: This bonus is granted by a racial trait, such as the elf's Group Awareness trait.

Shield Bonus: Granted by a shield, this bonus applies to AC and Reflex only as long as a creature uses the shield. Some powers, feats, and magic items provide a shield bonus; these typically help only characters who aren't using shields.

Untyped Bonus: Some bonuses have no type ("a +2 bonus," for instance). Most of these bonuses are situational and combine with other bonuses, including other untyped bonuses. However, untyped bonuses from the same named game element (such as a power or a feat) are not cumulative; only the highest applies, unless otherwise noted.

ACTION TYPES

As the adventurers explore the world and interact with its inhabitants, game play is usually free-form, guided by the roleplaying of the players and the DM. When the adventurers enter combat, though, the game becomes very structured.

The creatures involved in combat each take a turn over the course of a round. A creature can take a limited number of actions each round, and each action has a type. During some rounds, a creature spends its entire allotment of actions, and during other rounds, it might not take a single action.

A creature gets the following three actions on its own turn.

✦ **Standard Action:** A standard action requires more effort than any other type of action and is usually the main action of a creature's turn. Making an attack almost always requires a standard action.
✦ **Move Action:** A move action involves movement from one place to another.
✦ **Minor Action:** A minor action involves a simple activity of some kind, such as opening a door or picking up an item.

A creature's allotment of actions includes some actions that it can take on others' turns.

✦ **Immediate Action:** An immediate action is always in response to a trigger on another creature's turn (such as an action or an event), and either interrupts the trigger or reacts to it. A creature can take only one immediate action per round.
✦ **Opportunity Action:** An opportunity action is like an immediate action, but it always interrupts its trigger. Also, a creature can take a single opportunity action on each turn except its own.

The one type of action that is rarely limited is the appropriately named free action.

✦ **Free Action:** A creature can take free actions on its own or anyone else's turn. Because most free actions require at least a small amount of time, the DM can restrict the number of free actions a creature can take during a round.

Chapter 6 has more about actions in combat.

Penalties Unlike bonuses, penalties don't have types. Penalties are added together, unless they're from the same named game element. For instance, if two monsters attack an adventurer with the same power and each causes the adventurer to take a penalty to a particular roll or score, the adventurer doesn't add the penalties together but instead takes the worst penalty.

A penalty might be neutralized by a bonus, and vice versa. For instance, if a creature gains a +2 bonus to attack rolls and takes a -2 penalty to attack rolls at the same time, it ends up with a +0 modifier.

Two Principles to Keep in Mind

This rulebook presents the general rules of the DUNGEONS & DRAGONS game. While reading these rules, remember the two principles discussed below.

1. Specific Beats General

Powers, class features, racial traits, feats, magic items, monster abilities, and other game statistics usually include some element that breaks the general rules in some way. The element creates an exception to how the rest of the game works. Remember this: If a specific rule contradicts a general rule, the specific rule wins.

Exceptions and contradictions to the rules are often minor. For instance, most adventurers don't have proficiency with longbows, but every elf adventurer does because of a racial trait. That trait creates a minor exception in the game. Other examples of rule-breaking are more conspicuous. For instance, a creature can't normally enter an enemy's space during combat, but the creature might gain a power that lets it enter several enemies' spaces in the same turn. Similarly, a creature's melee basic attack normally requires a standard action to use, but many powers allow the use of a melee basic attack as a free action instead. Powers often create major exceptions to the rules.

Many of the exceptions in the game last for but a moment. For instance, a power might grant a character the ability to move up to his or her speed as a free action. Moving that far usually requires a move action, but the power breaks that general rule for an instant. Once the power's moment has passed, the character must again follow the general rule. Other exceptions, such as the elf's proficiency with longbows, are persistent for certain creatures.

2. Always Round Down

The game does require calculations now and then, which sometimes end up in a fraction. Unless instructed otherwise, always round down even if the fraction is ½ or larger. For instance, this rule comes into play when calculating one-half a character's level for making a check. If the level is an odd number, always round down to the next lower whole number.

TABLE RULES

While setting up a DUNGEONS & DRAGONS game, every gaming group needs to establish some table rules, which outline everyone's responsibility to keep the game fun. Some table rules deal with the conflict between the needs of the game and the realities of life, such as when players are unable to attend a game session. Others are about coming to agreement on special situations, such as how to treat strange die rolls.

Respect: Be there, and be on time. Don't let disagreements escalate into loud arguments. Don't bring personal conflicts to the gaming table. Don't hurl insults or dice across the table. Don't touch other players' dice if they're sensitive about it.

Distractions: If the DM runs a casual, lighthearted game, it might be fine to have players wandering away from the table and back. Most groups, though, come together to focus on playing. Turn off the television, ban portable video games, and get a babysitter if necessary. By reducing distractions everyone has an easier time getting in character, enjoying the story, and focusing on playing the game.

Food: Come to a consensus about food for a session. Should everyone eat before arriving, or eat together? Does one player want to play host? Do all players chip in for takeout? Who provides snacks and drinks?

Character Names: Agree on some ground rules for naming adventurers. In a group consisting of Sithis, Travok, Anastrianna, and Kairon, the human fighter named Bob II sticks out—especially when he's identical to Bob I, who was killed by kobolds. If everyone takes a lighthearted approach to names, that's fine. If the group would rather take the adventurers and their names a little more seriously, Bob's player should come up with a better name.

Player character names should match the flavor of the campaign world, as should the names that the DM makes up for nonplayer characters and for places. Travok and Kairon might feel out of place visiting Gumdrop Island or talking to the enchanter Tim.

Missing Players: How does the group deal with the absence of missing players? Consider these options:

+ *Have another player run the missing player's character.* Don't do this without the permission of the missing player. The player running the extra character should make an effort to keep the character alive and use his or her resources wisely.

+ *Have the DM play the character.* Doing this can sometimes be too much to handle, given all of the DM's other tasks during a session, but it can work. The DM needs to play the character reasonably, as the missing player would.

- *Decide the character's not there.* The DM might be able to provide a good reason for the character to miss the adventure, perhaps by having him or her linger in town. Make sure there's a way for the character to rejoin the adventuring group when the player returns.
- *Have the character fade into the background.* This solution requires everyone to step out of the game world a bit and suspend disbelief, but it's the easiest solution. The group acts as if the character is absent, but without any explanation for the absence. When the player returns, the character reappears, also without explanation.

Multiple Characters: Most of the time, each player controls one character. The game plays best that way, since the player can devote his or her full attention to that character. However, if the group is small, one or more players might want to take on playing two characters. One character could be the mentor or employer of the other, giving the player a good reason to focus on roleplaying one of the characters.

Another situation in which multiple characters can be a good idea is in a game with a high rate of character death. If the group is willing to play such a game, each player might want to keep one or two additional characters on hand, ready to jump in whenever the current character dies. Each time the main character gains a level, the backup ones do as well.

JAMES ZHANG

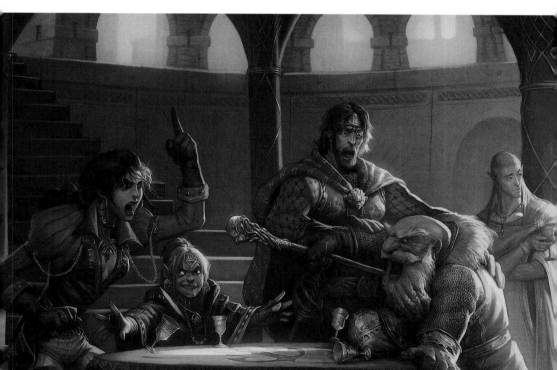

Table Talk: It's a good idea to set some expectations about how players converse at the table.

+ Who's speaking—the character or the player (out of character)?
+ Can a player offer advice if his or her character isn't present or is unconscious?
+ Can a player give other players information such as how many hit points they have left?
+ If a player immediately regrets the action chosen for his or her character, can the player pick a different action before any consequences occur?

Being Ready: Every round of combat is an exercise in patience. Everyone wants to take a turn. If a player isn't ready when his or her turn comes up, the others can get impatient. The DM should encourage the players to consider their actions before their turns and let them know the consequences of holding up the game. For instance, if a player takes too long to make a decision, the DM might decide that the player's character is considered to be delaying (page 241).

Rolling Dice: Establish some basic expectations about how players roll dice. Rolling in full view of everyone is a good starting point. If a player consistently makes checks and scoops the dice up before anyone else can see the result, the DM might nudge that player to be less cagey. This is a cooperative game, after all.

What about strange die rolls? When a die falls on the floor, does it count, or should the player reroll it? When it lands cocked against a book, should the player pull the book away and see where the die lands, or reroll?

Rules Discussions: Set a policy on rules discussions at the table. Some groups don't mind putting the game on hold while they hash out different interpretations of the rules. Others prefer to let the DM make a call and get on with things. If the group does gloss over a rules issue in play, make a note of it (a good task to delegate to someone other than the DM) and get back to it later at a natural stopping point.

Metagame Thinking: Players get the best enjoyment when they preserve the willing suspension of disbelief. A roleplaying game's premise is that it is an experience of fictional people in a fictional world. Metagame thinking means thinking about the game *as a game*. It's like a character in a movie knowing he's in a movie and acting accordingly. "This dragon must be a few levels higher than we are," a player might say. "The DM wouldn't throw such a tough monster at us!" Or, "The read-aloud text spent a lot of time on that door—let's search it again!"

The DM can discourage this sort of thinking by giving a gentle verbal reminder: "But what do your *characters* think?"

DM'S GUIDE TO DICE ROLLS

If you're the DM, you can make your die rolls where the others can see them, or you can hide the rolls behind your *Dungeon Master's Screen*. It's up to you, but consider the following.

Rolling behind a screen keeps the players guessing about the strength of the opposition. When a monster hits all the time, is it of a much higher level than the players, or are you just rolling a string of high numbers?

Rolling behind the screen lets you fudge if you want to. If two critical hits in a row would kill an adventurer, you might want to change the second critical hit to a normal hit, or even a miss. Don't do this sort of thing too often, though, and don't let on that you're doing it. Otherwise the other players might feel as though their characters don't face any real risk—or worse, that you're playing favorites.

If you roll where everyone can see, they know that you're playing fair. You're not going to fudge the dice either in their favor or against them.

You need to make some rolls behind the screen no matter what. If a player thinks there might be someone hiding in a room and makes a Perception check, roll a die behind the screen, as though making a Stealth check, even if no one is hiding. If you didn't roll a die at all, the player would know no one is hiding. If you rolled in front of your screen, the player would have some idea how hidden the opponent was, and be able to make an educated guess about whether someone was there at all. Rolling behind the screen preserves the mystery.

Sometimes you need to make a roll for an adventurer, because the player shouldn't know how good the check result is. If the adventurer suspects the baroness might be charmed and wants to make an Insight check, you should make the roll behind the screen. If the player rolled it and got a high result, but didn't sense anything amiss, he or she would be confident that the baroness wasn't charmed. If the roll was low, a negative answer wouldn't mean much. A hidden die roll allows some uncertainty.

IMPROVISATION

Improvisation, the fine art of making things up on the fly, is one of the most enjoyable and compelling parts of the DUNGEONS & DRAGONS game. No one ever knows exactly what twist or turn a session of play might take.

One aspect of the game—an aspect that has helped keep it going for over thirty-five years—helps improvisation more than any other: the Dungeon Master. A session of play is never an exercise in reading from a script, following a linear path from one place to the next, or walking through a static plot toward a predetermined ending. This is a dynamic game, primarily because the DM—a person—adjudicates the action.

Other types of games (such as video games, board games, and card games) rely on the specific options and choices built into them by their designers. A player can never decide to go in a direction or take an option that isn't built into the game. In the DUNGEONS & DRAGONS game, the DM can change the game's direction on the fly, often in reaction to the decisions of the other players.

WHEN PLAYERS DO THE UNEXPECTED

Let's say you're the DM and the adventurers in your campaign have tracked an evil priest to an old castle deep in the forest. When you mapped out the castle and designed the encounters that you expected to take place there, you assumed that the group of gung-ho, battle-ready characters would kick in the front gate and storm the place.

As it happens, the players have chosen a different path. Convinced that the group is outnumbered, and remembering that the priest is trying to negotiate an alliance with the sleazy Baron Haldar, they decided that their adventurers are disguising themselves as the baron's diplomats. Now, the adventurers have tracked the evil priest, Kolden, to his castle. You have to decide the fairest way to handle this unexpected twist.

With the right preparation, this kind of improvisation is easy to run at the table. If you didn't think ahead of time about the opposing characters' personalities and the relationships between them, your task would be much harder. If you treated each of your encounters solely as a chance for a fight, that's all you would be ready for. In this case, you can take the time to name a few important opponents and work out some story details that cement their relationships.

The players' plan does make sense. Kolden wants to ally with the baron, and his eagerness filters down to his followers. The guards are likely to err on the side of believing the adventurers' story.

However, the adventurers shouldn't be able to just walk into the castle. You need a complication. Perhaps the captain of the guard, an ogre named Oldek, plans to betray Kolden. He wants to ally with Haldar, so rather than bring the adventurers directly to the priest, the guards bring them to Oldek.

Oldek isn't the smartest guy in the world. He's an ogre, after all. Kolden has spies watching him. If the adventurers ally with Oldek, they might fall into the trap that Kolden has set for him.

You can easily note that Oldek wants to usurp Kolden's power, while Kolden is spying on the ogre. If the adventurers had simply attacked the castle, those relationships might not have come up. However, even during a fight they can inform the action. Oldek might surrender rather than fight to the death. He might even attack Kolden, using the adventurers' assault as his chance to eliminate a rival.

As you can see, improvisation works both ways. The players will never know that the sudden, dramatic turn in the game was improvised. By taking a little time to prepare, you create your own opportunities for twists and turns that you might not have seen coming.

DMs and Improvisation

The DM's job includes telling a story, playing monsters, and building dungeons for the adventurers to explore. Those activities are part of the job, but they aren't everything. Once everyone sits down to play, the DM takes on another, very important role: making spot judgments on the other players' ideas, plans, and tactics. Such improvisation requires a DM to make decisions in the space of a few seconds. This job might sound hard, but it's actually fairly simple.

A good DM rolls with the players' ideas, judging them in a fair manner, applying the rules even-handedly, and letting the players succeed when they have ideas that seem particularly clever, entertaining, or both. By the same token, a DM never simply gives the players what they want. If a player has an idea that seems ill-conceived or short-sighted, the DM might assign a high DC to it, add an extra complication, or let the adventurers stumble into a perilous situation.

5 Rules for DM Improvisation

+ Keep the action moving forward.
+ Add complications.
+ Be fair.
+ Be prepared.
+ Failure isn't an end point.

Five Rules for DM Improvisation

Anyone who has ever participated in improv theater or comedy should find the following rules familiar. Good improvisation requires a little practice and perhaps a change in adventure preparation, but most people can grasp these principles quickly.

1. **Keep the Action Moving Forward.** When the players come up with an improvised plan or action, try to avoid saying no unless the plan is truly terrible, nonsensical, or impossible. The DM shouldn't give the players the world on a platter, but the game should remain open to improvisation. After all, if the players wanted a scripted experience, they could play some other game. Letting them take the adventure in an unexpected direction encourages them to be engaged by the action.

2. **Add Complications.** The players aren't masters of the campaign. That's the DM's job! When they have a good idea for improvisation, add some personalized spin or complication to it. Ideally, this complication takes what might have been an easy route around a problem and makes it a little more difficult or tense.

3. **Be Fair.** The DM's role is to adjudicate the rules, so be fair and consistent in handling them. When it comes to improvisation, such decisions usually boil down to choosing DCs, deciding what sort of skill or attack makes sense, and so forth, relying on the Difficulty Class by Level table (page 126) for guidance. Don't favor one player over another, or punish the players with high DCs just because the story is heading in an unexpected direction.

4. **Be Prepared.** A DM can be tempted to plot out every detail of an adventure ahead of time. Knowing where things are going makes it easier to keep the action moving. But when planning sessions, the DM should avoid focusing on one path or course of action. Consider the DM-controlled characters in general terms of how they think and act for easier roleplaying in a variety of situations. Add layers of conflict between them: rivalries, secret hatreds, and jealousies. When building dungeons or other locations, focus on details beyond combat. What sort of daily routine do the inhabitants engage in? When they aren't expecting an attack, what do they do? It doesn't take much effort to come up with such details, but they help a lot when it comes to making judgments on the fly.

5. **Failure Isn't an End Point.** Every improvised action or plan should have a chance for failure, but that failure should lead to more action and new challenges. The players might think of how their plan will succeed, but the DM needs to think about what happens when they fail. The adventurers shouldn't be stuck in the same position that they started in. Instead, their failure should have consequences that change the situation, making it harder but possibly more interesting.

THE IMPROV MINDSET

As a player, it's easy to let the DM set up all your options, but where's the fun in that? You don't have to constantly think up crazy plans, but it helps to keep your eyes open for the opportunity to do something interesting and inventive.

The easiest approach is to put yourself in your character's shoes. If you faced a problem in real life, what would you do? What would your character do? If you were in your enemy's shoes, what's the one thing you wouldn't want your character to do? Consider your character's surroundings and how they might be turned to your advantage. Think about an opponent's personality and goals, and try to come up with ways you can take advantage of them.

Improvisation makes life easier for your character. It also happens to be a fun way to approach the game. When battling an evil wizard atop a castle tower, it's easy but boring to fall back on making melee attack after melee attack—but a good, hard shove might send that wizard over the parapet and into the moat. When goblins stream over a rope bridge high in the mountains, turn your weapon to hacking at the bridge. A *sleep* spell might send a group of guards into a deep slumber, allowing you and your friends to walk into an enemy castle.

Chapter 4 contains improvisation suggestions for using the various skills available to characters in the game. Look there for inspiration. Above all, pay attention, immerse yourself in the game, and enjoy!

Players and Improvisation

In the DUNGEONS & DRAGONS game, the players' imagination is the primary limit on options available to their characters. The open-ended nature of the game makes things interesting and fun. If the adventurers must get into an evil cleric's castle, they might storm the gate—or they could decide to dig a secret tunnel under the outer wall, disguise themselves as mercenaries and talk their way past the guards, or sneak over the wall under the cover of night.

> ### 3 Rules for Player Improvisation
> ✦ Be engaged.
> ✦ Help out.
> ✦ Respect the DM.

Rather than assuming that the characters would fight their way in, a good DM recognizes that they might find other ways into the castle.

Just as a good DM is ready to improvise and serve as a fair judge of the players' ideas, the players need to be active participants in the game. A good player is a creative thinker, always looking for a clever plan to overcome an obstacle. A good player also respects the effort needed to be a good Dungeon Master. The players have as much of a responsibility for making the game enjoyable as the DM does.

Three Rules for Player Improvisation

Players' responsibilities rest mostly in remaining open to interesting ideas, supporting other players' suggestions, and keeping the action moving.

1. **Be Engaged.** Players should pay attention during the game, looking for details that can be used for interesting actions or plans, and taking notes. By leaving it up to the DM to think of every option, players miss out on a big part of the game's fun. Likewise, a player who spends the entire session texting friends or engaged in side conversations won't know enough about what's going on and will miss out on chances to improvise.

2. **Help Out.** If one player has an idea for an improvised action or plan, the others can help by adding their own ideas or filling in details. Try to make all the characters part of the action in a way that shares the spotlight.

3. **Respect the DM.** The DM has a lot of things to handle. When players improvise, he or she needs to make a lot of decisions in a short time. When the DM makes a ruling on a plan's chances of success, save any disagreements for outside the game.

THE DUNGEONS & DRAGONS WORLD

As mentioned in the introduction, the world of the DUNGEONS & DRAGONS game is a place of magic and monsters, of heroes and adventure. Place names, creatures' origins, and other features of the game's background depend on a few basic assumptions about the world in which adventures take place.

A Dark World. The current age has no all-encompassing empire. The world is shrouded in a dark age, caught between the collapse of the last great empire and the rise of the next, which might be centuries away. Minor realms do prosper: baronies, holdings, city-states. But each settlement is a point of light in the widespread darkness, an island of civilization in the wilderness that covers the world. Adventurers can rest in settlements between adventures, but no settlement is entirely safe. Adventures break out within (and beneath) such places as often as not.

The World Is a Fantastic Place. Magic works, servants of the gods wield divine power, and fire giants build strongholds in active volcanoes. The world might be based on reality, but it's a blend of real-world physics, cultures, and history with a heavy dose of fantasy. For the game's purposes, it doesn't matter what historical paladins were like—only what paladins are like in this world. Adventurers visit the most fantastic locations: wide cavern passages cut by rivers of lava, towers held aloft by ancient magic, and forests of twisted trees draped in shimmering fog.

The World Is Ancient. Empires rise and empires crumble, leaving few places that have not been touched by their grandeur. Ruin, time, and natural forces eventually claim all, leaving the DUNGEONS & DRAGONS game world rich with places of adventure and mystery. Ancient civilizations and their knowledge survive in legends, artifacts, and the ruins they left behind, but chaos and darkness inevitably follow an empire's collapse. Each new realm must carve a place out of the world rather than build on the efforts of past civilizations.

The World Is Mysterious. Wild, uncontrolled regions abound and cover most of the world. City-states of various races dot the darkness, bastions in the wilderness built amid the ruins of the past. In some of these settlements, adventurers can expect peaceful interaction with the inhabitants, but many more are dangerous. No one race lords over the world, and vast kingdoms are rare. People know the area they live in well, and they have heard stories of other places from merchants and travelers, but few know what lies beyond the mountains or in the depths of the great forest.

Monsters Are Everywhere. Most monsters of the world are as natural as bears or horses are on Earth, and monsters inhabit civilized parts of the world as well as the wilderness. Griffon riders patrol the skies over dwarven cities,

THE NENTIR VALE

The Nentir Vale is a region of the DUNGEONS & DRAGONS world, built on the assumptions outlined in this chapter. It's the setting for various published adventures and novels.

Up until four centuries or so ago, the Moon Hills and the surrounding Nentir Vale were thinly settled borderlands, home to quarrelsome human hill-chieftains and remote realms of nonhumans such as dwarves and elves. Giants, minotaurs, orcs, ogres, and goblins plagued the area. Ruins such as those in the Gray Downs and the Old Hills date back to those days, as do stories of the hero Vendar and the dragon of the Nentir Falls.

With the rise of the empire of Nerath to the south, human settlers began to move up the Nentir River, establishing towns such as Fastormel (now a ruin), Harkenwold, and Winterhaven. A Nerathan hero named Aranda Markelhay obtained a charter to build a keep near the Nentir Falls. She raised a simple tower at the site of Moonstone Keep 310 years ago. Under the tower's protection, the town of Fallcrest began to grow.

Over the next two centuries, Fallcrest became a small but prosperous city. It was a natural crossroads for trade, and the Markelhay family ruled it well. When the empire of Nerath began to crumble about a century ago, Fallcrest continued to flourish—for a time. About ninety years ago, a fierce horde of orcs known as the Bloodspears descended from the Stonemarch and swept over the vale. Fallcrest's army was defeated in a rash attempt to halt the horde on Gardbury Downs. The orcs burned and pillaged Fallcrest and went on to wreak havoc in the region.

In the decades since the Bloodspear War, Fallcrest has struggled to reestablish itself. The town is a shadow of the former city; little trade passes up and down the river these days. The countryside for miles around is dotted with abandoned homesteads and manors from the days of Nerath. Once again the Nentir Vale is a thinly settled border-land where few folk live. This is a place in need of heroes.

domesticated behemoths carry trade goods over long distances, a yuan-ti empire holds sway just a few hundred miles from a human kingdom, and a troop of ice archons from the Elemental Chaos might suddenly appear in the mountains near a major city.

Adventurers Are Exceptional. The players' characters are the pioneers, explorers, trailblazers, thrill seekers, and heroes of the DUNGEONS & DRAGONS game world. Although other characters might have classes and gain power, they do not necessarily advance as adventurers do, and they exist in the game for a different purpose. A human veteran might have survived numerous battles and still not be a 3rd-level fighter; an army of elves is made up of soldiers, not members of the fighter class.

The Civilized Races Band Together. The great races of the world—humans, dwarves, eladrin, elves, and halflings—drew closer together during the time of the last great empire, which was dominated by humans. They are the civilized races, the ones found living together in the towns and cities of the world. Other races, including dragonborn and tieflings, are in decline, heirs of ancient empires long forgotten. Goblins, orcs, gnolls, kobolds, and similar savage races were never part of that human empire. Some of them, such as the militaristic hobgoblins, have cities, organized societies, and kingdoms of their own.

Magic Is Not Everyday, but It Is Natural. No one is superstitious about magic, but neither is the use of magic trivial. People might see evidence of magic every day, but it's usually minor: a fantastic monster, a visibly answered prayer, a wizard flying by on a hippogriff. However, true masters of magic are rare. Many people have access to a little magic, which helps those living within settlements to maintain their communities. Many people have access to a little magic, but those who have the power to shape magical energy the way a blacksmith shapes metal are as rare as adventurers and might be friends or foes to them.

Gods and Primordials Shaped the World. The primordials, elemental creatures of enormous power, shaped the world out of the Elemental Chaos. The gods gave it permanence and warred with the primordials for control of the new creation in a great conflict known as the Dawn War. The gods eventually triumphed, and primordials now slumber in remote parts of the Elemental Chaos or rage in hidden prisons.

Gods Are Distant. At the end of the Dawn War, the mighty primal spirits of the world exerted their influence, forbidding gods and primordials alike from directly influencing the world. Now exarchs act in the world on behalf of their gods, and angels undertake missions that promote the agendas of the gods they serve. Gods are extremely powerful, compared to mortals and monsters, but they aren't infallible. They provide access to the divine power source for their clerics and paladins, and their followers pray to them in hopes that they or their exarchs will hear them and bless them.

The Planes

The world occupies a special place at the center of the universe. It's the middle ground where the conflicts between gods and primordials, and among the gods themselves, play out through their servants both mortal and immortal. But other planes of existence surround the world, nearby dimensions where some power sources are said to originate and powerful creatures reside, including demons, devils, and the gods.

Before the world existed, the universe was divided into two parts: the Astral Sea and the Elemental Chaos. Some legends say that those two were once one realm, but even the gods can't know that for certain, for they had their origin in the Astral Sea.

The Astral Sea

The Astral Sea floats above the world, an ocean of silvery liquid with the stars visible beneath the shallow sea. Sheets of shimmering starlight like gossamer veils part to reveal the dominions, the homes of the gods, like islands floating in the Astral Sea. Not all the gods live in astral dominions—the Raven Queen's palace of Letherna stands in the Shadowfell, and Lolth's home, the Demonweb Pits, is located in the Abyss. Avandra, Melora, and Torog travel the world, and both Sehanine and Vecna wander the whole cosmos.

Arvandor is a realm of natural beauty and arcane energy that echoes the Feywild. It's the home of the god Corellon and sometimes of Sehanine. Arvandor seems to be as much a part of the Feywild as of the Astral Sea, and travelers claim to have reached it through both planes.

The Bright City of Hestavar is a vast metropolis where the deities Erathis, Ioun, and Pelor make their homes. Powerful residents of all the planes travel to the Bright City to buy and sell exotic goods.

WILLIAM O'CONNOR

The Astral Sea

Pandemonium

Pluton

Kalandurren

Tytherion

Carceri

Arvandor

Tu'narath

Shom

The Nine Hells

Hestavar

Chernoggar

Celestia

Sigil

Letherna

Shinaclestra

Gloomwrought

Avaellor

Senaliesse

Moil

Plain of
Sighing Stones

Nachtur

Cendriane

Mag Tureah

The Murk Sea

The Mortal World

The Shadowfell

The Feywild

The Elemental Chaos

The City
of Brass

Zerthadlun

The Ninth
Bastion

The Keening
Delve

The
Abyss

Tytherion, called the Endless Night, is the domain that the dark gods Tiamat and Zehir share. No light can pierce its darkest depths, and both serpents and dragons haunt its otherworldly wilderness.

The Iron Fortress of Chernoggar is Bane's stronghold in the Astral Sea. It's a mighty stronghold of rust-pitted iron, said to be impregnable to attack. Even so, Gruumsh makes his home on an eternal battlefield outside the fortress's walls, determined to raze it to the ground one day. Immortal warriors fight and die on both sides of this conflict, returning to life with every nightfall.

Celestia is the heavenly realm of Bahamut and Moradin. Upon parting a veil to enter Celestia, a traveler arrives on the lower reaches of a great mountain. Behind, the mountains disappear into silvery mist far below. Kord also spends a good deal of time on the mountain's slopes because of an old friendship with the other gods, but his tempestuous nature keeps him from calling it home.

The Nine Hells is the home of Asmodeus and the devils. This plane is a dark, fiery world of continent-sized caverns ruled by warring princelings, though all are ultimately under the iron fist of Asmodeus.

Creatures native to the Astral Sea and its dominions are known as immortals, since they do not age or die of natural causes, though none are truly deathless. They include the gods themselves, their angel servitors, and the devils, who were themselves once angels but were transformed into their current form as punishment for the deicide committed by their lord, Asmodeus. The pirate race called githyanki also haunts the Astral Sea, striking from sleek astral vessels against targets at the outskirts of the divine dominions, and often raiding into the world as well to secure supplies and plunder.

The Elemental Chaos and the Abyss

At the foundation of the world, the Elemental Chaos churns like an ever-changing tempest of clashing elements—fire and lightning, earth and water, whirlwinds and living thunder. Just as the gods originated in the Astral Sea, the first inhabitants of the Elemental Chaos were the primordials, creatures of raw elemental power. They shaped the world from the raw material of the Elemental Chaos, and if they had their way, the world would be torn back down and returned to raw materials. The gods have given the world permanence, a quality utterly alien to the primordials' nature.

The primordials are no longer a major power in the Elemental Chaos. In the wake of the Dawn War against the gods, most primordials were imprisoned or otherwise diminished, and others were slain. In their stead, titans—the mighty giants who served as the primordials' laborers in crafting the world—rule over tiny domains scattered across the Elemental Chaos, and the evil fire spirits called efreets lord over fortresses and even cities, such as the fabled City of Brass. Their subjects include an assortment of elementals, creatures formed of raw elemental matter and animated to life and some measure of sentience. Among the most fearsome elemental creatures are archons—humanoid soldiers formed of a pure elemental substance.

JASON A. ENGLE

SIGIL, THE CITY OF DOORS

Somewhere between the planes, neither adrift in the Astral Sea nor rooted in the Elemental Chaos, spins the City of Doors, the bustling metropolis of Sigil. Planar trade flows freely through its streets, facilitated by a tremendous number of portals leading to and from every known corner of the universe—and all the corners yet to be explored. The ruler of the City of Doors is the enigmatic Lady of Pain, whose nature is the subject of endless speculation.

The Elemental Chaos approximates a level plane on which travelers can move, but the landscape is broken up by rivers of lightning, seas of fire, floating earthbergs, ice mountains, and other formations of raw elemental forces. However, it is possible to make one's way slowly down into the lower layers of the Elemental Chaos. Near its bottom, it turns into a swirling maelstrom that grows darker and deadlier as it descends.

At the bottom of that maelstrom is the Abyss, the home of demons. Before the world was finished, Tharizdun, the Chained God, planted a shard of pure evil in the heart of the Elemental Chaos, and the gods imprisoned him for this act of blasphemy. The Abyss is as wild as the Elemental Chaos where it was planted, but it is actively malevolent, where the rest of the Elemental Chaos is simply untamed. The demons that infest it range from the relatively weak and savage carnage demons and dretches to the demon princes, beings of nearly godlike power whose names—Orcus, Demogorgon, Baphomet—strike terror into mortal hearts.

The World and Its Echoes

The world has no proper name, but it goes by a wide variety of prosaic and poetic names among those people who ever find need to call it anything but "the world." It's the creation, the middle world, the natural world, the created world, or even the first work.

The primordials formed the world from the raw materials of the Elemental Chaos. Looking down on this work from the Astral Sea, the gods were fascinated with the world. Creatures of thought and ideal, the gods saw endless room for improvement in the primordials' work, and their imaginings took form and substance from the abundance of creation-stuff still drifting in the cosmos. Life spread across the face of the world, the churning elements resolved into oceans and landmasses, diffuse light became a sun and moon and stars. The gods drew upon astral essence and mixed it with the tiniest bits of creation-stuff to create mortals to populate the world and worship them. Elves, dwarves, humans, and others appeared in this period of spontaneous creation. Resentful of the gods' meddling in their work, the primordials began the Dawn War that shook the universe, a series of battles that raged across the cosmos for millennia. The gods slowly gained the upper hand, working together to imprison or banish individual primordials. However, this war threatened the very existence of the world.

In the last days of the Dawn War, a new force made itself known in the cosmos: the spiritual expression of the world itself. These primal spirits declared an end to the conflict, asserting that the world would no longer be a battleground for the two opposing forces. The gods and the primordials were banished to their home planes, and the primal spirits of the world decreed a balance: The world would remain a place where matter and spirit mingled freely, where life and death proceeded in an orderly cycle, where the seasons changed in their unending wheel without interference. The gods and the primordials could still influence the world, but they could not rule it.

As the world took shape, the primordials found some pieces too vivid and bright, and hurled them away. They found other pieces too murky and dark, and flung them away as well. These discarded bits of creation clustered and merged, and formed together in echoes of the shaping of the world. As the gods joined in the act of creation, more ripples spread out into those echo realms, bringing creatures to life there as reflections of the world's mortals. Thus the world was born with two siblings: the bright Feywild and the dark Shadowfell.

The Shadowfell is a dark echo of the world. It touches the world in places of deep shadow, sometimes spilling out into the world and other times drawing hapless travelers into its dark embrace. The plane is not wholly evil, but everything in the Shadowfell has its dark and sinister side. When mortal creatures die, their spirits travel first to the Shadowfell before moving on to their final fate. Undead creatures have

GORAN JOSIC

strong ties to the Shadowfell, and monsters of raw shadow stalk in the darkness there, hunting anything that lives. The shadar-kai, gray-skinned servitors of the Raven Queen, are the most populous race of the Shadowfell, but even they are hardly common.

The Feywild is an enchanted reflection of the world. Arcane energy flows through it like streams of crystal water. Its beauty and majesty are unparalleled in the world, and every creature of the wild is imbued with a measure of fantastic power. Eladrin are far more common in the Feywild than in the world, though they war frequently with the monstrous giants known as fomorians and their cyclops servitors, which inhabit the subterranean depths of the Feywild known as the Feydark. Even plants in the Feywild can manifest sentience and deep wisdom, as evidenced by the majestic treants.

And Beyond Scholars claim that the universe described here is not all there is—that something else exists beyond the Astral Sea and the Elemental Chaos. Evidence for this idea appears in the form of the most alien creatures known: aberrant monsters such as the beholder, the mind flayer, and even more bizarre beings. These creatures don't seem to be a part of the world or any known realm, and where they live in the world, reality alters around them. This fact has led sages to postulate the existence of a place they call the Far Realm, where the laws of reality work differently from how they function in the known universe. Mad sorcerers and aberrant monsters themselves sometimes attempt to open portals to this Far Realm or make contact with the godlike beings that inhabit it, with disastrous consequences in the world.

In addition, the souls of the dead, though they travel first to the Shadowfell, pass beyond that realm after a time. Some souls are claimed by the gods and carried to the divine dominions, but others pass to another realm beyond the knowledge of any living being.

The Gods

The deities of the DUNGEONS & DRAGONS game world are powerful but not omnipotent, knowledgeable but not omniscient, widely traveled but not omnipresent. They alone of all creatures in the universe consist only of astral essence. The gods are creatures of thought and ideal, not bound by the same limitations as beings of flesh.

The gods wear myriad different faces, and artwork depicting them shows them in a variety of forms, but their true nature is beyond any physical form. Corellon is often depicted as an eladrin, but he is no more an eladrin than he is a fey panther; he is a god, and he transcends the physical laws that bind even angels to their concrete forms.

This transcendence allows the gods to perform deeds that physical creatures can't. They can appear in the minds of other creatures, speaking to them in dreams or visions, without being present in physical form. They can appear in multiple places at once. They can listen to the prayers of their followers (but they don't always). But they can also make physical forms for themselves with a moment's effort, and they do so when the need arises—when presumptuous mortal adventurers dare to challenge them in their own dominions, for example. In these forms, they can fight and be fought, and they can suffer terrible consequences as a result. However, to destroy a god requires more than merely striking its physical form down with spell or sword. Gods have killed other gods (Asmodeus being the first to do so), and the primordials killed many gods during their great war. For a mortal to accomplish this deed would require performing rituals of awesome magical power to bind a god to its physical form—and then a truly epic battle to defeat that form.

Some deities are good or lawful good, some are evil or chaotic evil, and many are unaligned. Each has a vision of how the world should be, and the agents of that god seek to bring that vision to life in the world. Even the agents and worshipers of deities who share an alignment can come into conflict. Except for those who are chaotic evil (Gruumsh, Lolth, and Tharizdun), the gods are enemies of demons, which would rather destroy the world than govern it.

The most powerful servants of the gods are their exarchs. Some exarchs are angels whose faithful service has earned them this exalted status. Others were once mortal servants who won the station through their mighty deeds. Asmodeus has devils as exarchs, and both Bahamut and Tiamat have granted that status to powerful dragons. Every exarch is a unique example of its kind, empowered with capabilities far beyond those of other angels, mortals, or monsters.

THE DEITIES

Deity	Alignment	Areas of Influence
Asmodeus	Evil	Power, domination, tyranny
Avandra	Good	Change, luck, trade, travel
Bahamut	Lawful good	Justice, honor, nobility, protection
Bane	Evil	War, conquest
Corellon	Unaligned	Arcane magic, spring, beauty, the arts
Erathis	Unaligned	Civilization, invention, laws
Gruumsh	Chaotic evil	Turmoil, destruction
Ioun	Unaligned	Knowledge, prophecy, skill
Kord	Unaligned	Storms, strength, battle
Lolth	Chaotic evil	Spiders, shadows, lies
Melora	Unaligned	Wilderness, sea
Moradin	Lawful good	Creation, artisans, family
Pelor	Good	Sun, summer, agriculture, time
The Raven Queen	Unaligned	Death, fate, winter
Sehanine	Unaligned	Trickery, moon, love, autumn
Tharizdun	Chaotic evil	Annihilation, madness
Tiamat	Evil	Wealth, greed, vengeance
Torog	Evil	Underdark, imprisonment
Vecna	Evil	Undeath, secrets
Zehir	Evil	Darkness, poison, serpents

Asmodeus

Asmodeus is the evil god of tyranny and domination. He rules the Nine Hells with an iron fist and a silver tongue. Aside from devils, evil creatures such as rakshasas pay him homage, and evil tieflings and warlocks are drawn to his dark cults. His rules are strict and his punishments harsh:

✦ Seek power over others, that you might rule with strength as the Lord of Hell does.

✦ Repay evil with evil. If others are kind to you, exploit their weakness for your own gain.

✦ Show neither pity nor mercy to those who are caught underfoot as you climb your way to power. The weak do not deserve compassion.

Avandra

The good god of change, Avandra delights in freedom, trade, travel, adventure, and the frontier. Her temples are few in civilized lands, but her wayside shrines appear throughout the world. Halflings, merchants, and all types of adventurers are drawn to her worship, and many people raise a glass in her honor, viewing her as the god of luck. Her commandments are few:

✦ Luck favors the bold. Take your fate into your own hands, and Avandra smiles upon you.

✦ Strike back against those who would rob you of your freedom and urge others to fight for their own liberty.

✦ Change is inevitable, but it takes the work of the faithful to ensure that change is for the better.

Bahamut

Called the Platinum Dragon, Bahamut is the lawful good god of justice, protection, nobility, and honor. Lawful good paladins often revere him, and metallic dragons worship him as the first of their kind. Monarchs are crowned in his name. He commands his followers thus:

✦ Uphold the highest ideals of honor and justice.

✦ Be constantly vigilant against evil and oppose it on all fronts.

✦ Protect the weak, liberate the oppressed, and defend just order.

Bane

Bane is the evil god of war and conquest. Militaristic nations of humans and goblins serve him and conquer in his name. Evil fighters and paladins serve him. He commands his worshipers to:

- Never allow your fear to gain mastery over you, but drive it into the hearts of your foes.
- Punish insubordination and disorder.
- Hone your combat skills to perfection, whether you are a mighty general or a lone mercenary.

Corellon

The unaligned god of spring, beauty, and the arts, Corellon is the patron of arcane magic and the fey. He seeded the world with arcane magic and planted the most ancient forests. Artists and musicians worship him, as do those who view their spell-casting as an art, and his shrines can be found throughout the Feywild. He despises Lolth and her priestesses for leading the drow astray. He urges his followers thus:

- Cultivate beauty in all that you do, whether you're casting a spell, composing a saga, strumming a lute, or practicing the arts of war.
- Seek out lost magic items, forgotten rituals, and ancient works of art. Corellon might have inspired them in the world's first days.
- Thwart the followers of Lolth at every opportunity.

Erathis

Erathis is the unaligned god of civilization. She is the muse of great invention, founder of cities, and author of laws. Rulers, judges, pioneers, and devoted citizens revere her, and her temples occupy prominent places in most of the world's major cities. Her laws are many, but their purpose is straightforward:

- Work with others to achieve your goals. Community and order are always stronger than the disjointed efforts of lone individuals.
- Tame the wilderness to make it fit for habitation, and defend the light of civilization against the encroaching darkness.
- Seek out new ideas, new inventions, new lands to inhabit, new wilderness to conquer. Build machines, build cities, build empires.

Gruumsh

Gruumsh is the chaotic evil god of destruction, lord of marauding barbarian hordes. Where Bane commands conquest, Gruumsh exhorts his followers to slaughter and pillage. Orcs are his fervent followers, and they bear a particular hatred for elves and eladrin because Corellon put out one of Gruumsh's eyes. The One-Eyed God gives simple orders to his followers:

- ✦ Conquer and destroy.
- ✦ Let your strength crush the weak.
- ✦ Do as you will, and let no one stop you.

Ioun

Ioun is the unaligned god of knowledge, skill, and prophecy. Sages, seers, and tacticians revere her, as do all who live by their knowledge and mental power. Corellon is the patron of arcane magic, but Ioun is the patron of its study. Libraries and wizard academies are built in her name. Her commands are also teachings:

- ✦ Seek the perfection of your mind by bringing reason, perception, and emotion into balance with one another.
- ✦ Accumulate, preserve, and distribute knowledge in all forms. Pursue education, build libraries, and seek out lost and ancient lore.
- ✦ Be watchful at all times for the followers of Vecna, who seek to control knowledge and keep secrets. Oppose their schemes, unmask their secrets, and blind them with the light of truth and reason.

Kord

Kord is the unaligned storm god and the lord of battle. He revels in strength, battlefield prowess, and thunder. Fighters and athletes revere him. He is a mercurial god, unbridled and wild, who summons storms over land and sea; those who hope for better weather appease him with prayers and spirited toasts. He gives few commands:

- ✦ Be strong, but do not use your strength for wanton destruction.
- ✦ Be brave and scorn cowardice in any form.
- ✦ Prove your might in battle to win glory and renown.

Lolth

Lolth is the chaotic evil god of shadow, lies, and spiders. Scheming and treachery are her commands, and her priests are a constant force of disruption in the otherwise stable society of the evil drow. Though she is properly a god and not a demon, she is called Demon Queen of Spiders. She demands that her followers:

- ✦ Do whatever it takes to gain and hold power.
- ✦ Rely on stealth and slander in preference to outright confrontation.
- ✦ Seek the death of elves and eladrin at every opportunity.

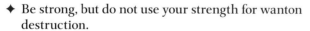

Melora

Melora is the unaligned god of the wilderness and the sea. She is both the wild beast and the peaceful forest, the raging whirlpool and the quiet desert. Rangers, hunters, and elves revere her, and sailors make offerings to her before beginning their voyages. Her strictures are these:

- ✦ Protect the wild places of the world from destruction and overuse. Oppose the rampant spread of cities and empires.

- ✦ Hunt aberrant monsters and other abominations of nature.

- ✦ Do not fear or condemn the savagery of nature. Live in harmony with the wild.

Moradin

Moradin is the lawful good god of creation and patron of artisans, especially miners and smiths. He carved the mountains from primordial earth and is the guardian and protector of the hearth and the family. Dwarves from all walks of life follow him. He demands these behaviors of his followers:

- ✦ Meet adversity with stoicism and tenacity.

- ✦ Demonstrate loyalty to your family, your clan, your leaders, and your people.

- ✦ Strive to make a mark on the world, a lasting legacy. To make something that lasts is the highest good, whether you are a smith working at a forge or a ruler building a dynasty.

Pelor

The good god of the sun and summer, Pelor is the keeper of time. He supports those in need and opposes all that is evil. As the lord of agriculture and the bountiful harvest, he is the deity most commonly worshiped by ordinary humans, and his priests are well received wherever they go. Paladins and rangers are found among his worshipers. He directs his followers thus:

- ✦ Alleviate suffering wherever you find it.

- ✦ Bring Pelor's light into places of darkness, showing kindness, mercy, and compassion.

- ✦ Be watchful against evil.

The Raven Queen

The name of the unaligned god of death is long forgotten, but she is called the Raven Queen. She is the spinner of fate and the patron of winter. She marks the end of each mortal life, and mourners call upon her during funeral rites, in the hope that she will guard the departed from the curse of undeath. She expects her followers to abide by these commandments:

+ Hold no pity for those who suffer and die, for death is the natural end of life.

+ Bring down the proud who try to cast off the chains of fate. Punish hubris where you find it.

+ Watch for the cults of Orcus and stamp them out whenever they arise. The Demon Prince of the Undead seeks to claim the Raven Queen's throne.

Sehanine

The unaligned god of the moon and autumn, Sehanine is the patron of trickery and illusions. She has close ties to Corellon and Melora and is a favorite deity among elves and halflings. She is also the god of love, who sends shadows to cloak lovers' trysts. Scouts and thieves ask for her blessing on their work. Her teachings are simple:

+ Follow your goals and seek your own destiny.

+ Keep to the shadows, avoiding the blazing light of zealous good and the utter darkness of evil.

+ Seek new horizons and new experiences, and let nothing tie you down.

Tharizdun

Tharizdun is the chaotic evil god who created the Abyss. His name is rarely spoken, and even the fact of his existence is not widely known. A few scattered cults of demented followers revere him, calling him the Chained God or the Elder Elemental Eye. Tharizdun doesn't speak to his followers, so his commands are unknown. But his cults teach their members to:

+ Channel power to the Chained God, so he can break his chains.

+ Retrieve lost relics and shrines to the Chained God.

+ Pursue the obliteration of the world, in anticipation of the Chained God's liberation.

Tiamat

Tiamat is the evil god of wealth, greed, and envy. She is the patron of chromatic dragons and those whose lust for wealth overrides any other goal or concern. She commands her followers thus:

- Hoard wealth, acquiring much and spending little. Wealth is its own reward.
- Forgive no slight and leave no wrong unpunished.
- Take what you desire from others. Those who lack the strength to defend their possessions are not worthy to own them.

Torog

Torog is the evil god of the Underdark, patron of jailers and torturers. Common superstition holds that if his name is spoken, the King that Crawls burrows up from below and drags the hapless speaker underground to an eternity of imprisonment and torture. Jailers and torturers pray to him in deep caves and cellars, and creatures of the Underdark revere him as well. He teaches his worshipers to:

- Seek out and revere the deep places beneath the earth.
- Delight in the giving of pain, and consider pain that you receive as homage to Torog.
- Bind tightly what is in your charge, and restrain those who wander free.

Vecna

Vecna is the evil god of undead, necromancy, and secrets. He rules that which is not meant to be known and that which people wish to keep secret. Evil spellcasters and conspirators pay him homage. He commands them to:

- Never reveal all you know.
- Find the seed of darkness in your heart and nourish it; find it in others and exploit it to your advantage.
- Oppose the followers of all other deities so that Vecna alone can rule the world.

Zehir

Zehir is the evil god of darkness, poison, and assassins. Snakes are his favored creation, and the yuan-ti revere him above all other gods, offering sacrifice to him in pits full of writhing serpents. He urges his followers thus:

- Hide under the cloak of night, that your deeds might be kept in secret.
- Kill in Zehir's name and offer each murder as a sacrifice.
- Delight in poison, and surround yourself with snakes.

It's the DM's World

The preceding sections sum up the basics of what the game assumes about the DUNGEONS & DRAGONS world. Within those general parameters, though, there's a lot of room for the DM to fill in the details. Each published campaign setting describes a different world that adheres to some of those core assumptions, alters others, and then builds a world around them. Any DM can do the same to create a unique, personalized world.

Altering Core Assumptions

One definition of speculative fiction (of which fantasy and science fiction are two branches) is that it starts with reality as we know it and asks, "What if some aspect of the world was different?" Most fantasy starts from the question "What if magic was real?"

The assumptions sketched out on these pages aren't graven in stone. They make for an exciting world full of adventure, but they're not the only set of assumptions that do so. Anyone can build an interesting campaign concept by altering one or more of those core assumptions, asking, "What if this wasn't true in my world?"

The World Is Not a Fantastic Place. What if magic is rare and dangerous? What if the campaign is set in a version of historical Europe?

The World Is Not Ancient. What if the world is brand-new, and the player characters are the first heroes to walk the earth? What if there are no ancient artifacts and traditions, no crumbling ruins?

The World Has No Secrets. What if it's all charted and mapped, right down to the "Here there be dragons" notations? What if great empires cover huge stretches of countryside, with clearly defined borders between them?

Monsters Are Rare. What if monsters are scarce but terrifying?

Adventurers Are Everywhere. What if the cities of the world are crowded with adventurers, buying and selling magic items in great markets?

The Civilized Races Live Apart. What if, to use a fantasy cliché, dwarves and elves don't get along? What if hobgoblins live side by side with the other races?

Magic Is Pervasive. What if every town is ruled by a powerful wizard? What if magic item shops are common?

Primordials Rule the World. What if the primordials won the Dawn War, and hidden cults dedicated to a handful of surviving deities are scattered through a shattered world that echoes the Elemental Chaos?

Gods Are Among Us. What if the gods regularly walk the earth? What if the adventurers can challenge them and seize their power? Or what if even exarchs and angels never sully themselves by contact with mortals?

FILLING IN THE DETAILS

Where the DUNGEONS & DRAGONS rulebooks talk about the world, they drop names that exemplify core assumptions—such as the tiefling empire of Bael Turath and the *Invulnerable Coat of Arnd*. Just as you can alter names in published adventures to suit the flavor of your campaign, you can change the names of these assumed parts of the world. For example, you might decide that the tieflings of your world have a culture reminiscent of medieval Russia, and call their ancient empire Perevolochna.

Aside from these changeable assumed details, most of the specifics of the world are left to your own invention. Even if you begin your campaign in the town of Fallcrest (page 39) and lead the characters on to Winterhaven and Hammerfast, eventually the adventurers will explore new lands of your own creation.

If you follow the core assumptions of the game, sketching out the world beyond your starting area is a simple matter. Great tracts of wilderness separate civilized areas. South of Fallcrest, the adventurers might travel through a forest on an old, overgrown road they've been told leads to the city-state of Ironwood. You can throw adventures in their path along the way, then draw them into another grand dungeon adventure when they arrive in what turns out to be the gnoll-infested ruins of Ironwood.

You can draft a map of the whole continent at or near the beginning of your campaign. You don't have to, of course, but even if you do, it's a good idea to keep it sketchy. As the campaign progresses, you'll find that you want certain terrain features in specific places, or perhaps an element of the campaign story will lead you to fill in details of the map in ways you couldn't have anticipated at the start of the campaign. Just as when you prepare an adventure, don't overprepare your campaign. Even in a published campaign, the large-scale maps of regions and continents don't detail every square mile of land. You can and should feel free to add details where you need them—and alter them when your campaign suggests it.

DUNGEONS & DRAGONS Worlds

A number of official campaign settings are available, and getting involved with the community of DUNGEONS & DRAGONS players will reveal many more incredible fantasy worlds—all products of the fertile imaginations of Dungeon Masters everywhere.

To start, you can explore the world in greater depth through DUNGEONS & DRAGONS *Gazetteer: The Nentir Vale*. This product covers the Nentir Vale itself, exploring the region in more detail than the *Dungeon Master's Kit* could contain. You can also learn more about the Nentir Vale and surrounding regions by reading novels in the new DUNGEONS & DRAGONS line, starting with *The Mark of Nerath* by Bill Slavicsek.

The Forgotten Realms

The FORGOTTEN REALMS world is a classic fantasy setting that stays close to the game's core assumptions. For almost twenty-five years, it has been the backdrop for a host of adventures, novels, computer games, and comic books.

The world is defined largely by the powerful forces that threaten it. An undead necromancer named Szass Tam rules the dreaded land of Thay and commands hordes of undead minions and evil Red Wizards in his campaign to expand the borders of his nightmare land of death. The ancient empire of Netheril has been reborn under the reign of the shadow-infused Twelve Princes of Shade to become a growing threat to the lands of the north. Creatures of the Underdark, including drow and a recent threat, the Abolethic Sovereignty, are a terrible threat to even the surface world.

The world of the Realms is both infused with and horribly scarred by the powerful forces of magic. Magic flows through the land and pools in places of power, but nearly a hundred years ago, the death of the god of magic sent a Spellplague raging across the land. Throughout the history of the world, ancient empires have been brought low by the abuse of powerful magic, and pockets of uncontrolled magical energy created in their downfall still dot the landscape.

One key alteration to the game's core assumptions lies in the world's distant past, at the end of the Dawn War. As the Dawn War between the gods and the primordials reached a fever pitch, the world was twinned, creating two separate worlds—one ruled by the gods, the other by the primordials. The tumult of the Spellplague threw the worlds back together, mingled their lands and cultures, and then separated them once more.

You can learn more about this world in the *FORGOTTEN REALMS Campaign Guide* and the *FORGOTTEN REALMS Player's Guide*. If you want to get started reading novels set in the world, any of the books in the *Ed Greenwood Presents Waterdeep* series is a great place to begin. This series showcases all that the most famous city of the Realms has to offer, and you can read the books in the series in any order. Also check out the popular novels by R.A. Salvatore featuring the character Drizzt Do'Urden.

Dark Sun

The burnt world of the DARK SUN campaign is another classic setting for games and novels, originally introduced in 1991. DARK SUN presents a significantly different vision of fantasy from that set forth in the core assumptions of the game, echoing the swords-and-sandals adventure of early pulp fantasy writers more than the sweeping epics of more traditional fantasy. Here, adventurers might be enslaved gladiators, nomadic elves, or even savage halflings from one of the world's few remaining forests. They come together to adventure in Athas, a bleak landscape wasted by arcane magic gone horribly awry, a region dominated by city-states under the iron-fisted rule of evil sorcerer-kings.

The most significant departure in the DARK SUN setting from the core assumptions of the game is in its idea that the primordials won the Dawn War, banishing and imprisoning the gods so that their influence is virtually unknown in the world. This story accounts for the harsh nature of life in Athas's deserts, where the elements themselves are as much a hazard as the terrible monsters that haunt the wilds. Athas has no real "points of light" to ameliorate the darkness; the greatest places of civilization in the world are fully under the control of the sorcerer-kings and their templar servitors.

The DARK SUN Campaign Setting provides a wealth of knowledge about the world, and the DARK SUN Creature Catalog™ presents a look into the varied and deadly monsters that dwell in its wilderness. You can learn more about the world of Athas in the setting's novels, including a new series of stand-alone novels beginning with *City Under the Sand* by Jeff Mariotte.

Eberron
The most recent addition to the multiverse of DUNGEONS & DRAGONS worlds, the EBERRON® campaign setting is a blend of classic high fantasy adventure with the grittier sensibilities of film noir, marked by scheming and mystery. Set in the years immediately following a terrible war, this milieu ties together themes of prophecy, ongoing conflict and intrigue among nations, dungeon delving and urban intrigue, and the growing power of a mercantile class empowered with magical dragonmarks.

Eberron is a world with powerful nations, though the borders of those kingdoms still encompass plenty of wilderness grown increasingly dangerous after a century of war. The nations include the goblin kingdom of Darguun, the monstrous nation of Droaam (ruled by three hags), and the distant nation of Riedra, ruled by the sinister forces of the Inspired. One of the nations at the heart of civilization was utterly annihilated during the Last War and is now the desolate and deadly Mournland—a wasteland ripe for exploration and adventure.

In Eberron, magic is an everyday thing, and it has been used to create conveniences that seem almost modern—from the continent-spanning lightning rail to airships that carry passengers and freight through the skies. A working class of minor mages called artificers uses magical skill to provide energy and other necessities in towns and cities. The culmination of the artificer's art is the sentient race of constructs known as the warforged.

The EBERRON Campaign Guide and the EBERRON Player's Guide serve as a great starting point for adventures in this world. If you're interested in delving into novels about Eberron, consider seeking out the *Draconic Prophecies* trilogy, starting with *Storm Dragon* by James Wyatt.

CHAPTER 2

ADVENTURERS AND MONSTERS

The DUNGEONS & DRAGONS world is filled with creatures. Some—such as humans, elves, and dwarves—are humanoid and once had great civilizations. Others stand upright like humans but are almost always savage, malevolent, or both: goblins, orcs, gnolls, and other humanoids. Certain creatures are animate but lack the spark of life: vampires, liches, zombies, and other undead. Others are mythical beasts, such as dragons, unicorns, and griffons. And some creatures arise from celestial or infernal realms: angels, demons, devils, and titans.

> *The DUNGEONS & DRAGONS world is filled with creatures ... savage, malevolent, or both.*

Whatever a creature's nature, the creature is an adventurer, a monster, or a DM-controlled character (also called a nonplayer character, or NPC). Adventurers and monsters always have game statistics, whereas other characters usually have them only if those characters participate in a battle.

The chapter includes the following information.

✦ **Creature Statistics:** Most creatures that appear in the game have statistics that describe their abilities in combat, their role in the world, and other details. This section summarizes that information.

✦ **Creating an Adventurer:** A step-by-step guide to generating the numbers and inventing the roleplaying details for a new adventurer.

✦ **Gaining Levels:** As adventurers overcome challenges, they become more experienced and increase in power. This section walks through the process of leveling up an adventurer.

CREATURE STATISTICS

The statistics that describe a creature in the game include numeric details, such as the creature's hit points, and story-oriented details, such the creature's moral alignment. An adventurer's statistics are typically recorded on a character sheet, whereas a monster's statistics appear in a stat block. The statistics are presented differently, but they function the same in play, unless otherwise noted.

Level

A creature's level is a measure of the creature's overall power: the higher its level, the greater its might. A high-level adventurer can overcome amazing odds, and a high-level monster can be a tremendous obstacle.

An adventurer typically starts at level 1, gains levels by earning experience points, and reaches the pinnacle of his or her power at level 30. Monsters don't gain levels, and some—particularly deities—have levels higher than 30.

A monster's level determines the experience point reward that adventurers gain for defeating it (see Appendix 2).

Origin

A creature's origin describes its place in the DUNGEONS & DRAGONS cosmos. Each origin is associated with a plane of existence.

+ **aberrant:** Aberrant creatures are native to or corrupted by the Far Realm. *Examples:* beholders and mind flayers.

+ **elemental:** Elemental creatures are native to the Elemental Chaos. *Examples:* demons, efreets, elementals, and titans.

+ **fey:** Fey creatures are native to the Feywild. *Examples:* cyclopses, eladrin, elves, gnomes, hags, and treants.

+ **immortal:** Immortal creatures are native to the Astral Sea. Unless they are killed, they live forever. *Examples:* angels and devils.

+ **natural:** Natural creatures are native to the natural world. *Examples:* dragons, dwarves, goblins, humans, orcs, and trolls.

+ **shadow:** Shadow creatures are native to the Shadowfell. *Examples:* nightmares and wraiths.

Most adventurers have the natural origin, unless otherwise noted. A monster's origin is noted in its stat block.

Type

Each creature has a type that broadly describes its appearance and behavior.

+ **animate:** Animate creatures are given life through magic. They don't need to breathe, eat, or sleep. *Examples:* golems, skeletons, and zombies.

+ **beast:** Beasts are either ordinary animals or creatures akin to them. They behave instinctively. *Examples:* bears, drakes, and owlbears.

+ **humanoid:** Humanoid creatures either are human or resemble humans in form, behavior, facial features, or all three. Most humanoids are bipedal. *Examples:* elves, gnolls, hobgoblins, and humans.

+ **magical beast:** Magical beasts resemble beasts but often behave like people, possess magical abilities, or both. *Examples:* dragons, manticores, and umber hulks.

Adventurers are humanoid, unless otherwise noted. A monster's type is noted in its stat block.

Race

Race is a category that usually applies only to humanoids. Each adventurer has a race that his or her player selects at character creation (explained later in this chapter). Members of a race have various characteristics in common. A character's race confers certain traits to the character and helps determine the character's starting languages.

The races that players choose from are often referred to as character races, and the adventurer members of a race typically have racial traits that other members of the race lack. Player books such as *Heroes of the Fallen Lands* and *Heroes of the Forgotten Kingdoms* specify the racial traits possessed by the adventurer members of character races.

Class

Class defines more about an adventurer than anything else. Class helps determine various statistics, including defenses and hit points, and it provides an adventurer with most of his or her powers.

Only rare nonplayer characters and monsters have classes. If a nonplayer character or a monster does have a class, the creature has only the class features, powers, and such that are included in the stat block. In other words, the creature functions as a full member of the class only if the creature's stat block says it does.

Creature Keywords

Some creatures have keywords that further define them. Such a keyword designates either a group to which the creature belongs (such as demon, devil, dragon, plant, or undead) or some other defining characteristic of the creature (such as aquatic, blind, or mount). This book's glossary contains definitions of creature keywords.

Size

Each creature falls into one of six size categories: Tiny, Small, Medium, Large, Huge, or Gargantuan. Each category corresponds to how much space a creature takes up in battle. See "Creature Size and Space," page 199, for how a creature's size can affect combat.

Role

Each adventurer and monster has a label that designates its primary role in battle. An adventurer's role is controller, defender, leader, or striker. A monster's role is artillery, brute, controller, lurker, skirmisher, or soldier. A monster might have a second role—elite, solo, or minion—as well as the leader subrole.

Whatever roles a creature might have, they do not constrain the creature's behavior. Roles are primarily a planning tool. An ideal group of adventurers comprises a variety of roles, as does an ideal group of monsters. Players therefore use roles to help build balanced adventuring groups, and DMs use them to help build balanced combat encounters.

Adventurer roles are defined in "Creating an Adventurer," later in this chapter. Monster roles are defined in Appendix 1.

Ability Scores

Six abilities provide a quick description of creatures' physical and mental characteristics: Strength, Constitution, Dexterity, Intelligence, Wisdom, and Charisma. Is a character muscle-bound and insightful? Brilliant and charming? Nimble and hardy? Ability scores define these qualities—a creature's strengths as well as weaknesses. Strength, Constitution, and Dexterity are sometimes called physical abilities, and Intelligence, Wisdom, and Charisma are sometimes called mental abilities.

Each of a creature's abilities has a score, a number that measures the might of that ability. A character who has Strength 16 is much stronger than a character who has Strength 6. A score of 10 or 11 is the normal human average, but adventurers and many monsters are a cut above average in most abilities. As adventurers advance in level (see "Gaining Levels," page 85), their ability scores improve.

Ability Modifiers

An ability score's main purpose is to determine an ability modifier, which is a bonus or a penalty that is added to any attack roll, damage roll, ability check, skill check, or defense that is based on that ability.

The Ability Modifiers table notes the ability modifiers for the most common ability scores. To determine an ability modifier without consulting the table, subtract 10 from the ability score and then divide the result by 2 (round down).

ABILITY MODIFIERS

Ability Score	Ability Modifier	Ability Score	Ability Modifier
1	-5	18-19	+4
2-3	-4	20-21	+5
4-5	-3	22-23	+6
6-7	-2	24-25	+7
8-9	-1	26-27	+8
10-11	+0	28-29	+9
12-13	+1	30-31	+10
14-15	+2	32-33	+11
16-17	+3	34-35	+12
		and so on . . .	

A power specifies which ability modifier, if any, to use with the power. For instance, when a character uses a melee attack power that says "Strength vs. Fortitude" in its "Attack" entry, add his or her Strength modifier (along with one-half his or her level and any other modifiers) to the attack roll.

When using a published monster, a Dungeon Master rarely uses the monster's ability modifiers; the relevant ability modifiers are already included in the monster's game statistics. However, the DM has to refer to them when the monster makes untrained skill checks and ability checks. Each of a monster's ability scores is followed by the adjusted ability modifier in parentheses (the number includes one-half the monster's level).

Strength (Str)

Strength measures physical power. This ability score is important for many adventurers who fight hand-to-hand.

✦ The default melee basic attack is based on Strength.

✦ Strength is the key ability for Athletics skill checks.

✦ An adventurer's Strength modifier contributes to Fortitude, unless his or her Constitution modifier is higher.

Constitution (Con)

Constitution represents health, stamina, and vital force. All adventurers benefit from a high Constitution score.

✦ A 1st-level adventurer's Constitution score is added to his or her hit points.

✦ The number of healing surges that an adventurer can use each day is influenced by his or her Constitution modifier.

✦ Constitution is the key ability for Endurance skill checks.

✦ An adventurer's Constitution modifier contributes to Fortitude, unless his or her Strength modifier is higher.

Dexterity (Dex)

Dexterity measures hand-eye coordination, agility, reflexes, and balance.

✦ The default ranged basic attack is based on Dexterity.

✦ Dexterity is the key ability for Acrobatics, Stealth, and Thievery skill checks.

✦ An adventurer's Dexterity modifier contributes to Reflex, unless his or her Intelligence modifier is higher.

✦ If an adventurer is wearing light armor or no armor, the adventurer's Dexterity modifier contributes to Armor Class, unless his or her Intelligence modifier is higher.

Intelligence (Int)

Intelligence describes how well a character learns and reasons.

✦ Intelligence is the key ability for Arcana, History, and Religion skill checks.

✦ An adventurer's Intelligence modifier contributes to Reflex, unless his or her Dexterity modifier is higher.

✦ If an adventurer is wearing light armor or no armor, the adventurer's Intelligence modifier contributes to Armor Class, unless his or her Dexterity modifier is higher.

Wisdom (Wis)

Wisdom measures common sense, perception, self-discipline, and empathy.

✦ Wisdom is the key ability for Dungeoneering, Heal, Insight, Nature, and Perception skill checks.

✦ An adventurer's Wisdom modifier contributes to Will, unless his or her Charisma modifier is higher.

Charisma (Cha)

Charisma measures force of personality, persuasiveness, and leadership.

✦ Charisma is the key ability for Bluff, Diplomacy, Intimidate, and Streetwise skill checks.

✦ An adventurer's Charisma modifier contributes to Will, unless his or her Wisdom modifier is higher.

Hit Points

Hit points (often shortened to "hp") measure a creature's ability to withstand punishment and turn deadly strikes into glancing blows. A creature is said to be bloodied when it drops to half its maximum hit points or fewer (various effects in the game rely on a creature being bloodied).

An adventurer's hit points are determined at character creation and increase each time the character levels up. A monster's hit points are specified in its stat block. See Chapter 6 for how hit points work.

Defenses

A creature's ability to avoid injury and other ill effects is measured by four defenses: Armor Class, Fortitude, Reflex, and Will. Defense scores rate how hard it is for attacks to hit a creature—they serve as the target numbers for attack rolls. An adventurer's defenses are set at character creation and increase with level. A monster's defenses are specified in its stat block.

Armor Class (AC) measures how hard it is to land a significant blow on a creature with an attack using a weapon or a magical effect that works like a weapon. Some creatures have a high AC because they are extremely quick or intelligent and able to dodge well, while other creatures have a high AC because they wear heavy armor that is difficult to penetrate.

Fortitude measures the inherent toughness, mass, and resilience of a creature. It is often the defense against attacks that include effects such as disease, poison, and forced movement.

Reflex measures a creature's ability to predict attacks or to deflect or dodge an attack. It's useful against attacks that affect an area, such as a dragon's *breath weapon* or a *fireball* spell.

Will is a creature's defense against effects that disorient, confuse, or overpower the mind. It measures self-control, strength of will, and devotion.

Initiative

In every battle, the participants act in an order determined by Dexterity checks that they make at the start of the battle. Making those checks is called rolling initiative (explained in Chapter 6). Each creature has an initiative modifier, which is the number that the creature adds when it rolls initiative.

An adventurer's initiative modifier is determined at character creation and increases with level. A monster's initiative modifier is specified in its stat block.

Powers

The heart of a creature's capabilities—particularly in combat—are its powers. Every creature has the five default attack powers presented in Chapter 6: *bull rush*, *grab*, *melee basic attack*, *opportunity attack*, and *ranged basic attack*.

An adventurer typically has a single power from his or her race and a collection of powers from his or her class. An adventurer might have additional powers from feats and magic items. A monster's powers are specified in its stat block.

Skills

Skills represent a creature's competence in a variety of fields, including tests of physical might, historical knowledge, and making the implausible believable. Each skill is tied to a particular ability (the Athletics skill is tied to Strength, for instance), and a creature has a basic level of competence in a skill based on the ability modifier associated with it. A creature goes beyond basic competence by obtaining training in a skill, which grants the creature a +5 bonus to checks using that skill. See Chapter 4 for how skills work.

The skills an adventurer has training in are selected at character creation, and the adventurer might gain further skill training through feats. If a monster has training in a skill, the skill is noted in the monster's stat block with the appropriate modifier.

Feats

A feat is a talent, a knack, or a natural aptitude. It embodies the training, the experience, and the abilities that a character has acquired beyond what his or her class provides. A feat is a flourish added to a character, a bit of customization that helps make him or her unique.

Feats primarily belong to adventurers. Monsters don't have feats, but a DM-controlled character might.

Benefit   Each feat confers a benefit to a character who has the feat. The benefit lasts only while the character has the feat. This rule means a character loses the benefit of a feat the instant he or she discards the feat, which would most likely happen as part of retraining (page 87).

Gaining Feats

An adventurer starts with at least one feat of the player's choice at 1st level and might also get one or two bonus feats from his or her race or class. Adventurers gain more feats as they advance in level (see "Gaining Levels," page 85).

A feat can be taken no more than once by a character, unless a feat's description states otherwise. If a feat has prerequisites specified, a character must meet those prerequisites to take the feat. Prerequisites take many different forms, including belonging to a particular race or class or having a certain weapon proficiency or class feature.

Some feats have minimum levels or ability scores as prerequisites. These feats represent specialized abilities that are too difficult for the average person to master. A character's level or ability score must be equal to or greater than the specified number in order for him or her to take the feat.

Speed

A creature's speed represents the number of 5-foot squares it can move when taking a move action to walk. Some creatures have speeds for movement modes other than walking: burrowing, climbing, flying, and swimming. See Chapter 6 for rules on using a creature's speed.

An adventurer's speed is initially determined by his or her race. It might be modified by a class feature, a feat, or something else. Wearing heavy armor usually reduces an adventurer's speed, by an amount specified in the description of that armor. A monster's speed is specified in its stat block and accounts for the monster's armor, if any armor is mentioned.

Action Points

Action points allow creatures to take more actions than normal, to use a special ability that requires an action point, or both. See Chapter 6 for how to spend and earn action points.

Each adventurer starts with 1 action point. Most monsters lack action points. Elite and solo monsters are the exception; they each have 1 or more action points, as noted in their stat blocks.

Senses

Most creatures have normal senses; they can see, hear, smell, taste, and feel things at least as well as a typical human can. Some creatures have special senses, which allow them to perceive things that others cannot. For instance, elves have low-light vision, which allows them to see in low light as if it were daylight. See Chapter 5 for how the most common special senses work.

A creature has normal senses, unless otherwise noted. An adventurer might gain a special sense, such as low-light vision or darkvision, from his or her race and might gain one or more from a feat, a class feature, or something else. If a monster has any special senses, they are specified in its stat block.

Resistance, Immunity, and Vulnerability

Certain creatures are resistant or vulnerable to particular types of damage, and some creatures are immune to specific effects. Resistance, immunity, and vulnerability can be permanent or temporary. See Chapter 6 for how the three work.

Adventurers typically gain resistance, immunity, or vulnerability from powers and feats, although certain character races have inherent resistances. If a monster has resistances, immunities, or vulnerabilities, they are noted in its stat block.

Special Traits

Some creatures have special traits, such as a magical aura, regeneration, or the ability to ignore difficult terrain.

An adventurer's race and class are the most likely sources for his or her special traits. A monster's special traits, if any, are noted in its stat block.

Equipment

Gear can be a defining aspect of a creature. Adventurers typically wear armor and travel outfits, and they carry weapons, adventuring gear (rope, torches, and the like), and various belongings of personal importance (a family signet ring, for instance). Many monsters have no equipment at all, and those that do have equipment usually have only their signature items noted in their stat blocks (the stat block of a goblin archer might note only a shortbow, for example).

Each adventurer starts with 100 gold pieces worth of gear, and adventurers gain more equipment—especially magic items—as they go on adventures and complete quests.

See Chapter 7 and Appendix 2 for more information on equipment.

Languages

Ten languages form the basis of every dialect spoken throughout the Dungeons & Dragons world and the planes beyond. These languages are transcribed in different scripts, most of which are alphabets, including the flowing characters of the Rellanic alphabet and the runes of the Davek alphabet. The Supernal script is a system of hieroglyphics.

Languages Known
Depending on an adventurer's race, he or she starts off knowing two or three languages and the script associated with each. Adventurers can learn additional languages by taking certain feats. The languages that a monster knows are noted in its stat block.

Unless the DM says otherwise, a character can't start off knowing the Abyssal or Supernal languages.

Language	Spoken by . . .	Script
Common	Humans, halflings, tieflings	Common
Deep Speech	Mind flayers, githyanki, kuo-toas	Rellanic
Draconic	Dragons, dragonborn, kobolds	Iokharic
Dwarven	Dwarves, galeb duhrs	Davek
Elven	Elves, eladrin, fomorians	Rellanic
Giant	Giants, orcs, ogres	Davek
Goblin	Goblins, hobgoblins, bugbears	Common
Primordial	Efreets, archons, elementals	Barazhad
Supernal	Angels, devils, gods	Supernal
Abyssal	Demons, gnolls, sahuagin	Barazhad

Languages in the World
The gods have their own language, Supernal, which they share with their angelic servants. When a god or an angel speaks Supernal, it can choose to speak so that any creatures that understand a language can understand this divine speech, as if the speaker used their own languages. Immortals that speak Supernal can understand speech and writing in any language.

When the gods created the races of the world, each race heard the Supernal language in a different way, based on fundamental characteristics of their nature. From those distinct ways of hearing, the foundational languages of the world arose: Common for humans and halflings, Elven for elves and eladrin, Goblin for the goblin races, Dwarven for the dwarves, and Draconic for dragons.

The primordials had their own language, Primordial, which has none of the special qualities of Supernal. The titans and giants adopted a debased version of this language for their own tongue, Giant. Abyssal is a form of Primordial warped and twisted by the evil at the heart of the Abyss.

These foundational languages spread to other creatures of the world and the planes, with dialect variation but no more significant alteration.

Scripts
Scripts are essentially independent of language. Just as different real-world languages use the same script to transcribe their different words, Common could be written in Davek or Rellanic as easily as in the Common script. Adventurers might run across old texts written by dwarves in Davek runes using Common words. Such a text would require familiarity with two languages to decipher.

Supernal and Primordial have their own scripts, and the main civilized races developed different scripts to transcribe the foundational languages: Common, Davek runes for Dwarven, the Rellanic script for Elven, and Iokharic lettering for Draconic. Goblin is the only foundational language that lacks its own script, owing to the brutal and barbaric nature of goblins. The Giant language uses the Davek runes of the dwarves, dating from the dwarves' long servitude to the giants.

Deep Speech is a language related to the alien communication of the Far Realm, used by creatures influenced by the corrupting energy of that realm. The language uses the Rellanic script; the drow were the first to transcribe Deep Speech, since they share Underdark haunts with aberrant creatures.

Davek, Dwarven Script

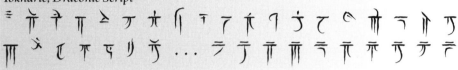

Rellanic, Elven Script

Iokharic, Draconic Script

Words of Power

The Supernal and Abyssal languages are both used to communicate, but they also include words of power—words whose syllables contain the raw magic of creation (in the case of Supernal) or primordial evil (Abyssal).

Adventurers don't normally know these languages to begin with. They might eventually learn the basics of communicating in these tongues, but without mastering the words of power. Similarly, mortals who learn Supernal don't gain the ability to have their words universally understood, but they do learn to read the Supernal script and to understand immortals speaking in that language, even if the immortals have not chosen to make themselves understood to all listeners.

Texts containing words of power in either language could unleash mighty effects, and these tomes or scrolls might be magic items in their own right.

WILLIAM O'CONNOR

Alignment

A creature's alignment describes its moral stance. Some adventurers, and many monsters, are unaligned, which means they have no overriding moral stance. Choosing an alignment for a character is indicating the character's dedication to a set of moral principles: good, lawful good, evil, or chaotic evil. In a cosmic sense, it's the team he or she believes in and fights for most strongly.

Alignments are tied to universal forces bigger than deities or any other allegiance that a creature might have. A lawful good cleric is on the same team as the god Bahamut, who is also lawful good, even if that cleric isn't devoted to Bahamut. Most people in the world, and plenty of adventurers, haven't signed up to play on any team; they're unaligned. Picking and adhering to an alignment represents a distinct choice.

If you're a player choosing an alignment for an adventurer, good and lawful good are the best choices. Unless the DM is running a campaign in which all the adventurers are evil or chaotic evil, playing an evil or chaotic evil character usually disrupts an adventuring group.

Unaligned
Just let me go about my business.

Unaligned creatures don't actively seek to harm others or wish them ill. But such creatures also don't go out of their way to put themselves at risk without some hope for reward. They support law and order when doing so benefits them. They value their own freedom, without worrying too much about protecting the freedom of others.

A few unaligned people, and most unaligned deities, aren't undecided about alignment. Rather, they've chosen not to choose, either because they see the benefits of both good and evil or because they see themselves as above the concerns of morality. The Raven Queen and her devotees fall into the latter camp, believing that moral choices are irrelevant to their mission, since death comes to all creatures regardless of alignment.

The Good Alignment
Protecting the weak from those who would dominate or kill them is simply the right thing to do.

Good creatures believe it is right to aid and protect those in need. Such creatures are not required to sacrifice themselves to help others, but might be asked to place others' needs above their own, even if doing so means putting themselves in harm's way. In many ways, that's the essence of being a heroic adventurer: The people of the town can't defend themselves from the marauding goblins, so the good adventurer descends into the dungeon—at significant personal risk—to put an end to the goblin raids.

Members of this alignment follow rules and respect authority but are keenly aware that power tends to corrupt those who wield it, too often leading them to exploit their power for selfish or evil ends. When that happens, good creatures feel no obligation to follow the law blindly. It's better for authority to rest with the members of a community than in the hands of a power-hungry individual or group. When law becomes exploitation, it crosses into evil territory, and good creatures feel compelled to fight it.

Good and evil represent fundamentally different viewpoints, cosmically opposed and unable to coexist in peace. In contrast, good and lawful good creatures get along fine, even if a good creature thinks a lawful good companion might be a little too focused on following the law, rather than just doing the right thing.

The Lawful Good Alignment
An ordered society protects us from evil.

Lawful good creatures respect the authority of laws and leaders and believe that codes of conduct are the best way of achieving one's ideals. Virtuous authority promotes the well-being of its subjects and prevents them from harming one another. Lawful good creatures believe just as strongly as good ones do in the value of life, and they put even more emphasis on the need for the powerful to protect the weak and lift up the downtrodden. The exemplars of the lawful good alignment are shining champions of what's right, honorable, and true, risking or even sacrificing their lives to stop the spread of evil in the world.

When leaders exploit their authority for personal gain, when laws grant privileged status to some citizens and reduce others to slavery or untouchable status, law has given in to evil and just authority becomes tyranny. Lawful good creatures are not only capable of challenging such injustice but are morally bound to do so. However, such creatures would prefer to work within the system to right such problems, rather than resorting to lawless methods.

For the purpose of game effects, a lawful good creature is also considered to be good.

The Evil Alignment
It is my right to claim what others possess.

Evil creatures don't necessarily go out of their way to hurt people, but they're perfectly willing to take advantage of the weakness of others to acquire what they want.

Evil creatures use rules and order to maximize personal gain. They don't care whether laws hurt other people. They support institutional structures that give them power, even if that power comes at the expense of others' freedom. Slavery and rigid caste structures are not only acceptable but desirable to evil creatures, as long as they are in a position to benefit from them.

The Chaotic Evil Alignment

I don't care what I have to do to get what I want.

Chaotic evil creatures have a complete disregard for others. They kill, steal, and betray others to gain power. Their word is meaningless and their actions destructive. Their worldviews can be so warped that they destroy anything and anyone that doesn't directly contribute to their interests.

By the standards of good and lawful good people, chaotic evil is as abhorrent as evil, perhaps even more so. Chaotic evil monsters such as demons and orcs are at least as much of a threat to civilization and general well-being as evil monsters are. An evil creature and a chaotic evil creature are both opposed to good, but they don't have much respect for each other either and rarely cooperate toward common goals.

For the purpose of game effects, a chaotic evil creature is also considered evil.

CREATING AN ADVENTURER

The first step in playing an adventurer is to imagine a character to create. An adventurer is a player's representative in the game, his or her avatar in the DUNGEONS & DRAGONS world. To begin, the player chooses a race such as human or elf, a class such as fighter or wizard, and other game elements appropriate to the adventurer, including skills, powers, and feats. Character creation also involves inventing details about the adventurer's personality, appearance, and background.

WHAT YOU NEED

Your adventurer is a fantastic figure who exists in the mind's eye and uses the game's rules to describe what he or she can do. On paper, he or she is a combination of game statistics and roleplaying hooks. Your adventurer's statistics help determine what he or she can do; roleplaying hooks define who he or she is.

Here's what you need to create an adventurer.

Player Book: The player books *Heroes of the Fallen Lands* and *Heroes of the Forgotten Kingdoms* contain the most common races and classes of the DUNGEONS & DRAGONS world. To create a member of one of those races or classes, you need the book containing the race or the class you want to play. You can also find races and classes in other sources, such as another player book or *DUNGEONS & DRAGONS Insider*.

Do you like the dwarves or the elves of fantasy fiction? Try making a character of one of those races. Do you want your character to be the toughest adventurer in the group? Consider making a fighter. Do you want the character to wield arcane magic? Consider a wizard. If you don't know where to begin, you can look at the illustrations in a player book and see what interests you.

Character Sheet: To keep track of the important information about your character, you can use a photocopy of the character sheet in your player book or download the character sheet available at www.DungeonsandDragons.com.

Creation Steps

Before diving into the details of character creation, it's a good idea to imagine the character and think about the kind of adventurer he or she should be. That character concept helps with choosing details such as class and race.

Character creation includes the following steps. The description of a class in a player book walks the reader through making a character and present the steps in a different order. (In general, steps are interchangeable; that is, you can choose feats and trained skills before choosing powers if you so desire.)

Choose Class and Race. Class represents the character's training or profession, and it is the most important part of his or her capabilities. The character's race offers several racial advantages. See "Class and Race," below.

Determine Ability Scores. Ability scores describe a character's fundamental strengths of body and mind. A character's race modifies his or her ability scores, and different classes rely on different ability scores when using their powers and class features. There are several ways to determine ability scores. See "Generating Ability Scores," page 77.

Choose Powers. The player books contain information for how many powers a character chooses at 1st level. Class choices might define some of the character's power choices. See Chapter 3 for how powers work.

Choose Trained Skills. Skills measure a character's ability to perform tasks such as jumping across chasms, hiding from observers, and identifying monsters. A character's class description states how many trained skills to pick at 1st level. Some races grant an additional skill choice. After choosing trained skills, note the character's modifier for every skill, including the +5 bonus for a trained skill. See Chapter 4 for details on skills.

Choose Feats. Feats represent natural advantages or special training. A character chooses at least one feat at 1st level and might also get one or two bonus feats from his or her race or class.

Choose Equipment. Each adventurer begins with 100 gold pieces at 1st level, enough to purchase basic gear. As a character adventures, he or she finds magic items, gains the ability to make them, or both. See Chapter 7 for more about equipment.

Fill in Other Numbers. Calculate the character's hit points, defenses (Armor Class, Fortitude, Reflex, and Will), attack roll modifiers, damage roll modifiers, and initiative modifier. These numbers should be recorded on the character sheet. See "Filling in the Numbers," page 79.

Other Character Details. Flesh out the character with details of alignment, god worshiped, background, personality, appearance, and languages. See "Other Character Details," page 81.

When making these choices, it's a good idea to look at what the character gains at higher levels from his or her class. The options at higher levels might influence choices made now. Even if a choice now turns out to be regrettable, it's possible to change it later using the retraining rules.

Class and Race

The first decision to make in character creation is picking the character's class and race. Many different types of heroes inhabit the world: sneaky rogues, clever wizards, burly fighters, and more. Race defines a character's basic appearance and natural talents, and class is the character's vocation.

The choice of class might also say something about the character's personality. A wizard might be quick-witted but a tad absentminded, for example, whereas a cleric might be serious in his or her religious devotions but cheerful in social interactions. The player books contain more details about classes.

Role An adventurer's class determines his or her role—the main job the character does when the party is in combat. Each class specializes in one of four roles: controller, defender, leader, or striker. Most classes have at least one secondary role, which is a role that a member of a class can fill in a pinch.

Roles mostly serve as handy tools for building adventuring groups. It's a good idea to cover each role with at least one character. If all the roles aren't covered, that's fine; it just means that the group needs to compensate for the missing function.

+ **Controllers** engage large numbers of enemies at the same time. They favor offense over defense, using powers that deal damage to multiple foes at once, as well as subtler powers that weaken, confuse, or delay their foes. The wizard is a classic example of a controller.

+ **Defenders** have the highest defenses in the game and good close-up offense. They are the party's frontline combatants; wherever they're standing, that's where the action is. Defenders have abilities and powers that make it difficult for enemies to move past them or to ignore them in battle. The fighter is a classic example of a defender.

+ **Leaders** inspire, heal, and aid the other characters in an adventuring group. Leaders have good defenses, but their strength lies in powers that protect their companions and target specific foes for the group to concentrate on. The cleric is a classic example of a leader.

  Members of this role encourage and motivate, but that doesn't mean a leader is necessarily a group's spokesperson or commander. The party leader—if the group has one—might as easily be a charismatic individual of another role. Leaders (the role) fulfill their function through their powers and class features; party leaders are born through roleplaying.

+ **Strikers** specialize in dealing high amounts of damage to a single target. They have the most concentrated offense of any character in the game.

Strikers rely on superior mobility, trickery, or magic to move around tough foes and single out the enemy they want to attack. The rogue is a classic example of a striker.

Race   A variety of fantastic races populate the world of DUNGEONS & DRAGONS—people such as dwarves, elves, and halflings—but humans outnumber them all. In any city or large town, members of several races intermingle. Some of them are residents, and others are travelers or wandering mercenaries looking for their next challenge.

Each character race has innate strengths that make it more suited to particular classes. However, any combination is possible. There's nothing wrong with playing against type; dwarves aren't usually rogues, but it's possible to create an effective dwarf rogue by choosing feats and powers carefully. The player books contain more information about character races.

Many different intelligent creatures populate the world, creatures such as dragons, mind flayers, and demons. These aren't races to play; they are monsters to encounter. A player's character is an adventurer of one of the civilized races of the world.

Generating Ability Scores

Players can use one of three methods to generate an adventurer's ability scores. Each method involves taking the generated numbers and assigning them to ability scores as the player chooses. Remember, class determines which ability scores are important to a character, and race modifies certain ability scores. An adventurer's age has no effect on these numbers—adventurers are considered to be in their prime.

Ability scores increase as a character gains levels (see the Character Advancement table, page 85). When assigning the initial scores, remember that they will improve with time.

Method 1: Standard Arrays   The preferred method for generating ability scores is using one of the standard arrays given below. Choose one of the three sets of scores and assign each number to one of the six abilities. Then apply racial ability bonuses.

Balanced Scores: 16, 14, 14, 11, 10, 10. This array represents a character who is fairly strong in one area and not weak in anything.

Specialist Scores: 18, 14, 11, 10, 10, 8. This array represents a character who is great in one area but also has a significant weakness.

Dual Specialist Scores: 16, 16, 12, 11, 11, 8. This array is a middle ground between the other two, offsetting two good scores with one weakness.

Method 2: Customizing Scores

This method is a little more complicated than the standard array, but it gives comparable results. This method allows building a character who excels in one ability score, but at the cost of having average scores in the other five. It's also possible to create a character who has nearly identical scores in every ability.

Start with these six scores: 8, 10, 10, 10, 10, 10. Then spend 22 points to improve them. The cost of raising a score from one number to a higher number is shown on the Ability Score Costs table. Apply racial ability bonuses after spending the points.

ABILITY SCORE COSTS

Score	Cost	Score	Cost
9	– (1)*	14	5
10	0 (2)*	15	7
11	1	16	9
12	2	17	12
13	3	18	16

* If a score is 8, it costs 1 point to make it 9 or 2 points to make it 10. That score must be raised to 10 before it can be improved further.

Here are some sample ability arrays that can be generated using this method.

14	14	13	13	13	11
14	14	14	12	12	11
14	14	14	14	12	8
15	14	13	12	12	11
15	15	13	12	11	10
16	14	14	11	10	10
16	16	12	10	10	10
17	15	12	11	10	8
17	14	12	11	10	10
18	14	11	10	10	8
18	12	12	10	10	10

Method 3: Rolling Scores

Some players like the idea of generating ability scores randomly. The result of this method can be really good, or it can be really bad. On average, the numbers work out to be a little worse than using the standard array. A player who rolls well can come out way ahead, but bad rolls might generate a character who's virtually unplayable. Use this method with caution.

Roll four 6-sided dice (4d6) and add up the highest three numbers. Do that six times, and then assign the numbers to the character's six ability scores. Then apply racial ability bonuses.

If the total of the character's ability modifiers is lower than +4 or higher than +8 before racial ability bonuses, the DM might rule that the character is too weak or too strong compared to the other characters in the group and decide to adjust the ability scores to fit better in the campaign.

Filling in the Numbers

After picking all the other aspects of the adventurer, it's time to fill in some numbers on the character sheet.

Hit Points and Healing Surges

An adventurer's maximum hit points are determined by his or her class and level. Here's where Constitution is useful to every adventurer; the hit point total includes his or her Constitution score.

The character's bloodied value equals one-half of his or her maximum hit points, and the character's healing surge value equals one-quarter of his or her maximum hit points.

The character's class determines the number of healing surges that he or she can use each day. The character's Constitution modifier contributes to this total.

See Chapter 6 for more about hit points and healing.

Defenses

Determine the character's defense scores as follows:

+ **Base Defense:** Each defense starts at 10 + one-half the character's level.
+ **Armor Class:** Add the armor bonus of the character's armor, if any. If the character uses a shield, add its shield bonus. If the character is wearing light armor or no armor, also add the character's Dexterity modifier or Intelligence modifier, whichever is higher.
+ **Fortitude:** Add the character's Strength modifier or Constitution modifier, whichever is higher.
+ **Reflex:** Add the character's Dexterity modifier or Intelligence modifier, whichever is higher. If the character uses a shield, add its shield bonus.
+ **Will:** Add the character's Wisdom modifier or Charisma modifier, whichever is higher.

Also add any of the following modifiers that apply:

+ A bonus from the character's class
+ Racial or feat bonuses
+ An enhancement bonus (usually from magic armor or from a neck slot magic item)
+ Any other bonuses or penalties

Base Attack Roll Modifiers

Because of how often your character will use his or her attack powers, it's helpful to calculate their base attack roll modifiers in advance. The base attack roll modifier of a character's power includes the following numbers:

+ One-half the character's level
+ The ability modifier specified by the power

Also add any of the following modifiers that apply:

+ Racial or feat bonuses
+ An enhancement bonus (usually from a magic weapon or implement)
+ A proficiency bonus (if the power is a weapon power and the character wields a weapon that he or she has proficiency with)
+ Any other bonuses or penalties

Base Damage Roll Modifiers

In addition to calculating the base attack roll modifiers for your character's powers, it's helpful to calculate their base damage roll modifiers in advance. The base damage roll modifier of a character's power includes the following numbers:

+ The ability modifier specified by the power. The modifier is usually the same one used for the power's attack roll.

Also add any of the following modifiers that apply:

+ Racial or feat bonuses
+ An enhancement bonus (usually from a magic weapon or implement)
+ Any other bonuses or penalties

Initiative Modifier

The character's initiative modifier includes the following numbers:

+ One-half the character's level
+ The character's Dexterity modifier
+ Racial or feat bonuses
+ Any other bonuses or penalties

ADDING CHARACTER TO CHARACTERS

A well-crafted adventurer personality expands the game experience. Here are a few tips to help you with roleplaying.

A simple roleplaying flourish is to adapt your own mannerisms to your adventurer. For example, if you are naturally inclined to spin dice or shuffle cards while the game takes place, you might consider incorporating similar habits of behavior into your character.

Even in combat, a character's personality can shine. Sometimes the role you play is defender or leader; the character you're playing is engaged in a fight and has a job to do so that the adventurers come out victorious. In that fight, you can interject bits of personality and dialogue that make your adventurer more than just statistics on a character sheet.

Finally, consider features that distinguish your character from others. Jewelry, clothing, tattoos and birthmarks, hairstyles and colors, and posture—one unusual feature from among those choices can make your adventurer stand out in the other players' minds.

Other Character Details

The DUNGEONS & DRAGONS game is, first and foremost, a roleplaying game, which means that it's all about taking on the role of a character in the game. Some people take to this playacting naturally and easily; others find it more of a challenge. This section is here to help players flesh out their characters, whether they're comfortable and familiar with roleplaying or new to the concept.

An adventurer is more than a combination of race, class, and feats. He or she is also one of the protagonists in a living, evolving story line. Like the hero of any fantasy novel or film, he or she has ambitions and fears, likes and dislikes, motivations and mannerisms, moments of glory and of failure. The best DUNGEONS & DRAGONS characters blend the ongoing story of their adventuring careers with memorable characteristics or traits. Jaden the 4th-level

WILLIAM O'CONNOR

human fighter is a perfectly playable character even without any embellishment, but the personality of Jaden the Grim—brooding, fatalistic, and honest—suggests a particular approach to negotiating with nonplayer characters or discussing issues with the other characters.

Personality
The DUNGEONS & DRAGONS game is one of heroic extremes, populated by legendary heroes and unrepentant villains. An adventurer needs only a few personality traits to use as roleplaying touchstones, key traits that the player can focus on and that are fun to play. A complex background and extensive motivations aren't necessary, although players can flesh out their characters' personalities as much as they like.

A typical DUNGEONS & DRAGONS adventure offers many opportunities for a character's personality to come to the forefront. Those roleplaying opportunities usually arise in three kinds of situations: social interactions, decision points, and dire straits. The following sections pose questions to help a player choose personality traits for his or her adventurer, which can be recorded on the character sheet. Select one personality trait for each kind of situation.

The questions posed here are directed to the adventurer to help a player get "inside the skin" of the character. If the player already has a personality in mind, skip this section; the information here is primarily for inspiration.

Social Interactions
When an adventurer communicates with a DM-controlled character outside combat and tries to influence that individual, that's a social interaction. The adventurer might try to persuade a guardian monster to let him or her pass, negotiate with a merchant lord to increase the pay offered for a dangerous mission, or question a surly centaur about the goblins that ambush travelers in the forest. The

How do others perceive you in social interactions?

Cheerful	Talkative	Reserved
Charming	Witty	Relaxed

How optimistic are you?

Enthusiastic	Hopeful	Fatalistic
Grim	Self-assured	Brooding

How trusting are you?

Gullible	Open-minded	Skeptical
Suspicious	Naive	Trusting

How assertive are you at a decision point?

Humble	Adaptable	Commanding
Timid	Easygoing	Impatient

How conscientious are you about following rules?

Scrupulous	Pragmatic	Dutiful
Honest	Flexible	Wild

How empathetic are you?

Kind	Stern	Thoughtful
Protective	Hard-hearted	Oblivious

DM plays the part of any other characters, while the players decide what their adventurers say, even speaking in character if they wish.

Decision Points A character's personality can influence the decisions he or she makes when facing tough choices in an adventure. Does she try to sneak past the dragon's cave, approach openly to parley, or storm in with blade drawn? Which of the six stone doors in the entry hall does he open first? Does he save the captives from the trap, or pursue the slavers? When the group tries to decide what to do next, how does the adventurer approach such conversations?

Dire Straits Some of the most memorable demonstrations of an adventurer's personality appear in dire straits. He or she responds to a villain's threat with a trademark one-liner, shouts a famous battle cry, leaps into harm's way to protect others, or turns and flees in the face of overwhelming odds. Every battle, hazard, or other dire situation offers opportunities for roleplaying, especially if things go awry. When the adventurer lands in a dire situation, how does he or she usually react? Does he or she adhere to a code, or follow the dictates of the heart? Does the adventurer look out for others or just for him- or herself?

How courageous are you in dire straits?

Brave	Competitive	Steady
Cautious	Reckless	Fierce

How do you feel when faced by setbacks?

Stoic	Driven	Happy-go-lucky
Vengeful	Bold	Impassioned

How are your nerves?

Calm	Skittish	Restless
Impulsive	Patient	Unshakable

Mannerisms

The easiest way to bring a character to life at the gaming table is to adopt distinctive mannerisms—particular patterns of speech or other behaviors that the player can take on to convey how his or her character looks, sounds, and acts. One character might carry a deck of cards that he shuffles when he's bored or nervous; another crouches to the ground and creates little sculptures out of rubble while she's waiting for her companions to decide where to go next. In contrast, another character might vociferously participate in those deliberations, frequently resorting to exclamations such as "By Kord's right arm!" to emphasize his opinion.

Speech patterns can be even more distinctive. A dwarf who never enters battle without shouting, "The dwarves are upon you!" injects a dose of fun roleplaying just as the die rolling is getting most intense. A wizard who never speaks except in haiku might be carrying the idea of distinctive speech to an extreme, but if the player can pull it off (perhaps writing a page full of standbys to cover common situations before the game begins), everyone at the table will remember that character for years.

Another good way to think about speech and other mannerisms is to create specific prompts that the adventurer says or does when using certain powers. For example, a cleric might yell, "Feel the might of Bahamut!" every time she uses a particular attack power and murmur, "Bahamut's healing breath wash over you" when she heals someone.

Character Appearance
Is an adventurer tall, short, or in between? Solid and muscular, or lean and wiry? Male or female? Old or young? These decisions have no impact on game statistics, but they might affect the way that others think about the adventurer.

Each race description gives the average height and weight for a character of that race. A player can decide that his or her adventurer is above or below average.

As well, choose what color skin, hair, and eyes he or she has. Most races approximate the human range of coloration, but some have unusual coloration, such as the stony gray skin of dwarves or the violet eyes of some elves.

Finally, consider features that distinguish this character from others. Some of these might be inborn, such as an unusual eye color or skin color, while others might be habits of fashion or the scars of past injuries.

Background
An adventurer's background often stays there—in the background. What's most important about a character is what he or she does over the course of various adventures, not what happened in the past. Even so, thinking about a character's birthplace, family, and upbringing can help with deciding how to play that character.

These questions—directed at the adventurer—can help a player start thinking about the adventurer's background.

✦ Why did you decide to be an adventurer? How old were you then, and how old are you now?

✦ How did you acquire your class? If you're a fighter, for example, you might have been in a militia, come from a family of soldiers, trained in a martial school, or be a self-taught warrior.

✦ How did you acquire your starting equipment? Did you assemble it piece by piece over time? Was it a gift from a parent or a mentor? Do any of your personal items have special significance?

✦ What's the worst event of your life?

✦ What's the best thing that's ever happened to you?

✦ Do you stay in contact with your family? What do your relatives think of you and your chosen career?

✦ Which cultures did you interact with as a child? Did those interactions influence your language choices?

GAINING LEVELS

As a character goes on adventures and gains experience points (XP), he or she advances in level. Gaining a level (also called leveling up) is one of the biggest rewards an adventurer receives in the game. Each character improves in several ways every time he or she gains a level.

Each time a character defeats monsters, overcomes a noncombat encounter, or completes a quest, the Dungeon Master awards experience points. When the character earns enough experience points, he or she reaches a new level. The Character Advancement table shows the total XP that a character needs to reach

each level. The table also notes when a character's ability scores increase, and it gives the minimum number of feats a character has at a certain level (some characters might have additional bonus feats because of their race or some other attribute).

CHARACTER ADVANCEMENT

Total XP	Level	Ability Scores	Feats	Total XP	Level	Ability Scores	Feats
0	1	See race	1	69,000	16	–	10
1,000	2	–	2	83,000	17	–	10
2,250	3	–	2	99,000	18	+1 to two	11
3,750	4	+1 to two	3	119,000	19	–	11
5,500	5	–	3	143,000	20	–	12
7,500	6	–	4	175,000	21	+1 to all	13
10,000	7	–	4	210,000	22	–	14
13,000	8	+1 to two	5	255,000	23	–	14
16,500	9	–	5	310,000	24	+1 to two	15
20,500	10	–	6	375,000	25	–	15
26,000	11	+1 to all	7	450,000	26	–	16
32,000	12	–	8	550,000	27	–	16
39,000	13	–	8	675,000	28	+1 to two	17
47,000	14	+1 to two	9	825,000	29	–	17
57,000	15	–	9	1,000,000	30	–	18

ERIC BELISLE

Step by Step

This section gives a step-by-step overview of how to level up a character. The player books detail what benefits a character gains at each level. For instance, if you're playing a slayer (a type of fighter), consult *Heroes of the Fallen Lands* to find out what benefits that class gains at each level.

At most levels, a character gains access to new capabilities: powers, class features, and feats. The game assumes that the character learns these capabilities in his or her spare time, studying tomes of lore or practicing a complex series of maneuvers. In game terms, though, as soon as characters gain a level, they can use their new capabilities.

1. Ability Scores
At 4th, 8th, 14th, 18th, 24th, and 28th levels, two ability scores of the player's choice increase by 1. At 11th and 21st levels, every ability score increases by 1.

Whenever an ability score increases to an even number, the related ability modifier goes up, and that change affects powers, skills, and defenses that rely on that ability score. Make a note of that fact, but don't change any numbers just yet.

2. Level Modifier
If the character's new level is an even number, everything that is based on one-half his or her level becomes better: defenses, attack rolls, skill checks, and ability checks.

In combination with any increased ability modifiers, the level modifier provides the information needed to increase those numbers. Record the increases on the character sheet.

3. Paragon and Epic Tiers
A character who has just reached 11th or 21st level has entered a new tier of play and gains special capabilities associated with that tier. If the player book requires choosing a paragon path or an epic destiny, make that choice. Make a note of any new capability the character gains, whether it's a power, a feature, or something else.

4. Hit Points
A character's class determines the number of hit points the character gains at each level. Add the number to that character's total.

If the character's Constitution score increased, his or her hit points also increase by 1. Also, if the Constitution score increased to an even number, the character's number of healing surges increases by 1.

5. Class Features
Consult the player book to see if a character gains a class feature at the new level. Also, check if any of the character's class features has improved with the new level. For instance, the rogue's Sneak Attack class feature deals more damage at certain levels.

6. Feats
Each character starts with a feat of the player's choice at 1st level and gains a feat at every even-numbered level after that, plus one feat at 11th and 21st levels. Descriptions of feats are in the player books.

Use the Total Feats column on the Character Advancement table to make sure the character has the right number of feats at each level.

7. Powers At levels specified in the player book, a character gains access to new powers. Whenever a choice of powers exists, the player must choose a power that the character doesn't already have.

Retraining

Sometimes a player makes decisions when creating or advancing a character that he or she later regrets. Perhaps a chosen power isn't working with the character concept, or a feat never comes into play as anticipated. Fortunately, no one is stuck with bad character decisions. There's an opportunity to change a decision whenever the character levels up.

Every time a character gains a level, he or she can retrain. This involves changing one feat, power, or trained skill. Only one change is allowed per level. If the player book says to replace one of the character's powers with a different power of a higher level, replacing the power doesn't count as retraining. The character can still retrain a feat, some other power, or a trained skill.

Replacing a Feat Retraining can replace one feat with another. The character must meet the prerequisites of the new feat. A feat can't be replaced if it's a prerequisite for any of the character's other attributes (such as another feat or a paragon path) or if the feat is a feature of his or her class, paragon path, or epic destiny.

Replacing a Power Retraining can replace a power with another power of the same type: at-will attack power, encounter attack power, daily attack power, or utility power. The new power must have a level, be of the same level as or lower in level than the old power, and come from the same class—a 5th-level cleric daily attack power for another 5th-level cleric daily attack power, for instance, or a 22nd-level utility power for a different 22nd-level utility power.

Retraining doesn't allow replacing a power that has no level, such as a cleric's *healing word*; a power designated as a feature; or a power gained from a paragon path or an epic destiny. If a power has no level but you chose it from a list of powers, you can replace it with a different power from that list.

Replacing a Trained Skill Retraining can replace one trained skill with another from the character's list of class skills. A skill can't be replaced if it's a prerequisite for a feat, a power, or any other attribute of the character, or if it's predetermined by class (such as Arcana for wizards and Religion for clerics).

If the character's class requires the choice of one of two skills (such as either Dungeoneering or Nature), retraining can alter the choice, but the character is limited to replacing one skill with the other.

CHAPTER 3

UNDERSTANDING POWERS

Characters and monsters have powers: special capabilities with instantaneous or lingering effects. Powers can harm enemies or help allies, and some powers do both. They can be magical or nonmagical. Examples include a wizard's spells, a cleric's healing prayers, a fighter's battle stances, and a dragon's breath.

Characters and monsters have powers: some are magical, some are not.

Character classes grant powers, as do some races. Adventurers might also gain additional powers through magic items. A monster's stat block describes its powers. Traps and hazards usually have powers as well.

This chapter contains everything you need to know about powers.

✦ **Power Types:** Descriptions of the two types of powers (attack and utility), as well as how to swap powers.

✦ **Usage Types:** Discussion of the three usage types (at-will, encounter, and daily), including how rechargeable powers work.

✦ **Power Formats:** A breakdown of how to read a power description, with an explanation of each entry, such as "Trigger," "Target," and "Attack."

✦ **Attack and Utility Types:** Rules for how the five attack and utility types work: melee, ranged, close, area, and personal.

✦ **Choosing Targets:** General rules for determining the targets of powers and finding out whether a creature is within line of effect or within an area of effect.

✦ **Areas of Effect:** Explanations of the three types of areas of effect: blast, burst, and wall.

✦ **Keywords:** How keywords work, including an explanation of each keyword within these five categories: power sources, schools of magic, accessories, damage types, and effect types.

POWER TYPES

There are two types of powers.

✦ **Attack Powers:** These powers are used to damage or hinder others. Some attack powers have beneficial effects as well.

JULIE DILLON

✦ **Utility Powers:** These powers have a variety of uses, including granting bonuses. Some are useful only outside combat, and others are useful only in combat. Some utility powers can be used in any situation.

As adventurers gain levels, they acquire a mix of attack powers and utility powers. Monsters and traps have attack powers, but they do not always have utility powers.

A power's type is usually relevant only when a character uses a feat or some other game feature that works with powers of one type or the other. If a power's type isn't stated, the power is an attack power if it includes an attack roll or if it deals damage. Otherwise, it is a utility power. If a power is not available to an adventurer, its type is rarely stated.

A conscious creature affected by a power knows what a power has done to it, regardless of the power's type.

SWAPPING POWERS

Some game features, particularly feats, give you the option of swapping one of your adventurer's powers for a different power. This option provides a way to customize your adventurer and to experiment with different abilities.

You might be given the option of swapping a class power for a power that is not from your character's class. You cannot make the swap if doing so would eliminate your character's last class power of a particular type: utility power, at-will attack power, encounter attack power, or daily attack power. For instance, if your wizard has only one wizard utility power, you cannot swap that power for a nonwizard power. Unless instructed otherwise, you cannot replace powers that your character gained from a paragon path or an epic destiny.

USAGE TYPES

Whether a power is an attack or a utility power, it has a usage type: at-will, encounter, or daily. The usage type indicates how often a power can be used. A creature can use a power only if it is able to take the action that the power requires, regardless of the power's usage type (see "Action Types," page 194).

At-Will Powers

At-will powers are not expended when they're used, so a creature can use them again and again. They represent easy weapon swings or simple magical effects that require little effort to pull off.

Encounter Powers

An encounter power can be used once per encounter. When a creature uses an encounter power, the power is expended, and the creature needs to take a short rest (page 172) before it can use that power again.

Encounter powers produce effects that are more powerful and dramatic than those of at-will powers. A nonmagical encounter power represents a maneuver or a stunt that a creature can pull off only once before recuperating. A magical encounter power requires enough magical energy that the user must replenish his or her magic reserves during a short rest before using the power again.

Rechargeable Powers

Some monsters, traps, and other game elements have encounter powers that recharge in certain circumstances, not just after a rest. Such powers are often referred to as rechargeable powers or recharge powers.

Recharge ⚀ ⚁ ⚂ ⚃ ⚄: The power has a random chance of recharging during each round of combat. At the start of each of the monster's or trap's turns, the DM rolls a d6. If the roll is one of the die results shown in the power description, the monster or trap regains the use of that power. The power also recharges after a short rest.

Recharge if/when . . . : The power recharges in a specific circumstance, such as when a monster is first bloodied during an encounter. The power also recharges after a short rest.

Daily Powers

A daily power can be used only once per day. When a creature uses a daily power, the power is expended, and the creature must take an extended rest (page 172) before it can use that power again. A daily attack power usually includes an effect that takes place whether or not its attacks hit, or it might not be expended when its attacks miss.

A daily power represents the most powerful effect that a creature can produce, and using one takes a significant toll on one's physical and mental resources. When a creature uses a nonmagical daily power, the creature is reaching into deep reserves of energy to pull off an amazing deed. When using a magical daily power, the creature might be reciting an arcane formula of such complexity that its mind can hold it for only so long; once recited, the formula is wiped from memory and can be regained only as part of an extended rest. Alternatively, the magic of a power might be so perilously strong that a creature's mind and body can harness it safely only once per day.

POWER FORMATS

Powers are incredibly diverse, yet the way in which they are described follows a structured format. The format has several variations, the main two being the format for player powers and that for monster powers.

Whatever format is used, a power description follows three basic principles.

Entries: A power's information is organized into named entries. The entries' names are a guide to what happens in the entries: "Attack," "Hit," "Miss," and so forth.

Sequence: The order of entries in a power description is a general guide to the sequence in which the power's effects occur. For instance, an "Effect" entry might appear before an "Attack" entry to show that something happens before the attack.

Indentation: When a power entry is indented, that entry is a subentry and is contingent on the entry above it. For instance, an indented "Secondary Attack" subentry right below the primary attack's "Hit" entry is a reminder that the secondary attack occurs only if the primary attack hits. Often, the text of an entry states when to proceed to a subentry. For instance, the "Hit" entry that leads to a "Secondary Attack" subentry most likely instructs the player to make the secondary attack.

POWER EFFECTS

Powers create a huge variety of effects: damage, healing, penalties, bonuses, conjured objects, zones of magical energy, and so on. The first step in understanding a power's effects is to read the definitions of the power's keywords (page 110).

The next step is making sure you're familiar with the other rules used in the power. Here are page references for the rules used most commonly in powers.

+ Bonuses and penalties: page 27
+ Damage, including the meaning of "[W]": page 222
+ Forced movement, including the rules for pulling, pushing, and sliding: page 211
+ Healing: page 256
+ Durations: page 226
+ Saving throws, including the meaning of "save ends": page 227
+ Ongoing damage: page 224
+ Conditions: page 229

Entries in a Power Description

A power description contains various entries. Some entries appear in every power description, while others appear only when needed by a particular power. This section presents the entries in the typical order of an adventurer power and provides explanations for each one.

The descriptions of non-adventurer powers, such as those of traps, monsters, and magic items, contain many of the same entries as adventurer powers, but the entries sometimes appear in a different order or format. Some non-adventurer power descriptions also lack common adventurer power entries, such as flavor text.

Name, Type, and Level

The first line of an adventurer power description is a colored bar that contains the power's name, its type (attack or utility), the game element that provides it (a class, a race, or something else), and the power's level, if any. The color of the bar indicates how often the adventurer can use the power: Green means the power is an at-will power, red means it's an encounter power, and black means it's a daily power.

In non-adventurer powers, the type and level are rarely stated. When such a power lacks a level, the power is considered to be of the same level as the game element in which the power appears. For instance, any powers in a level 15 suit of magic armor would also be level 15.

Flavor Text

The next entry in an adventurer power description, in italic text, briefly explains what the power does, from the perspective of the character. This material helps narrate what the power is doing in the game world. Players are free to invent their own descriptions of powers, sprinkling them with details specific to their adventurers or the campaign setting.

Non-adventurer powers usually lack flavor text, though similar text might appear elsewhere in or near a stat block, describing the trap, the magic item, the monster, and so forth.

Usage The first word on the next line of an adventurer power description states how often a character can use the power; that is, whether it is an at-will, an encounter, or a daily power.

In non-adventurer powers, this information usually appears near the beginning of the power description. In a monster power, it follows a power's name and any of its keywords. In a magic item power, it is one of the first pieces of information.

Keywords The power's keywords appear next in adventurer power descriptions. The keywords state the power source, any damage types associated with the power, accessories that can be used with it—weapons or implements—and other associated effects. See "Keywords," later in this chapter, for keyword definitions.

Non-adventurer powers also have keywords, but they often lack those associated with power sources.

Action Type The next line in an adventurer power description begins with the type of action required to use the power: standard action, move action, minor action, free action, immediate reaction, immediate interrupt, or opportunity action. Some powers require no action to use. See "Action Types," page 194, for more information.

All adventurer and non-adventurer powers have an action type, except for those that require no action to use. The action type of a non-adventurer power usually appears as part of the power description, as is the case in magic items, or as a header in a power subsection, such as in many monster stat blocks.

Attack/Utility Type and Range In an adventurer power description, the attack/utility type and range appear on the same line as the power's action type. If the power creates an area of effect, such as a burst or a blast, that fact is specified here as well. The attack/utility types are melee, ranged, area, close, and personal. See "Attack and Utility Types," later in this chapter, for how each type works.

In most non-adventurer power descriptions, the attack/utility type and range appear near the beginning of a power description or as part of another entry, such as "Attack."

Trigger Powers that are immediate actions (interrupts or reactions) or opportunity actions have a trigger, which defines the moment the creature is allowed to use the power. Some powers that are free actions, or that require no action to use, have triggers as well. See "Triggered Actions," page 195.

Prerequisite If a power description has this entry, an adventurer must meet the noted prerequisite to select the power. Non-adventurer powers rarely have prerequisites.

Requirement
If a power description has this entry, the requirement must be met every time the power is used. Some requirements are things that must have happened recently, such as a creature attacking someone earlier in a turn. Other requirements are things a creature must do to use the power, such as wielding a certain weapon.

Target
If a power directly affects one or more creatures other than the user, its description has a "Target" entry that specifies whom or what the power can affect. If a power directly affects only its user or the environment, the power description lacks this entry. Non-adventurer powers often lack a "Target" entry and include the information as part of another entry, often "Attack."

If the power description includes a secondary or a tertiary target, the "Target" entry is called "Primary Target" to distinguish this target definition from the power's other target definitions. See "Secondary Attacks" and "Secondary Powers" below.

See "Choosing Targets," later in this chapter, for the rules on target selection.

Attack
In most power descriptions, this entry specifies the ability modifier used to make an attack roll with the power and which of the target's defenses the power attacks. The entry also notes any special modifiers that apply to the attack roll, such as a bonus if the target is bloodied. If a creature uses a power against multiple targets at once, it makes a separate attack roll against each target. See "Attack Rolls," page 215, for more information on making an attack.

Some "Attack" entries list multiple abilities, which a player can choose from to determine his or her adventurer's attack roll modifier. A player usually picks the adventurer's highest ability score from among the choices. Some powers simply instruct a player to use his or her adventurer's highest ability score to determine the attack roll modifier.

The "Attack" entry in many non-adventurer power descriptions, such as for monster attack powers, provides a predetermined attack roll modifier rather than an ability modifier. It also sometimes includes additional pieces of information, such as a power's attack/utility type, its range, and its targets.

Hit
This entry specifies what happens when a target is hit by the power's attack. If the power hits multiple targets, this entry applies to each of those targets individually.

Miss
This entry specifies what happens when a target is missed by the power's attack. If the power misses multiple targets, this entry applies to each of those targets individually.

"Half damage" in this entry means a missed target takes damage as if hit by the attack, but that damage is halved. Roll the damage specified in the power's "Hit" entry, add the appropriate modifiers, and deal half of the result (rounded down) to each target missed by the power's attack.

Unless otherwise noted, the "half damage" notation does not apply to ongoing damage or to any other damaging effects in the "Hit" entry.

Effect
Whatever is described in an "Effect" entry simply happens, regardless of its position in the sequence of entries. If the entry is part of an attack power description, the effect happens whether or not the attack hits.

Unless otherwise stated, an "Effect" entry is not repeated, even if the power attacks multiple targets.

Example: A fighter has a power that targets one or two creatures within his weapon's reach. Each attack deals 1[W] + Strength modifier damage, and the power also has an effect that lets the fighter push a single enemy adjacent to him up to 2 squares. The fighter first resolves each attack separately, making a single attack roll and damage roll against each creature. Even if he hits both creatures, though, and both are adjacent to him after being hit, the effect occurs only once. In other words, he can push only one enemy adjacent to him; he cannot push two adjacent enemies.

Secondary Attacks
Some powers include secondary, or even tertiary, attacks. A "Hit," a "Miss," or an "Effect" entry tells the user when to make such an attack. Unless otherwise noted, the attack type and range of a secondary attack are the same as those of the power's primary attack, and the secondary attack doesn't require a separate action from the action used for the primary attack.

If a secondary attack has keywords that differ from those of the primary attack, its keywords are noted in parentheses. Otherwise, the secondary attack has the same keywords.

Some secondary attacks have the same targets as their primary attacks, whereas others have targets of their own, noted in "Secondary Target" entries. The *chain lightning* spell presented here is an example of a power that has secondary and tertiary attacks.

Chain Lightning	**Wizard Attack 23**

From your fingertips springs a tremendous stroke of blinding purple-white lightning that leaps from one enemy to another.

Encounter ✦ Arcane, Evocation, Implement, Lightning
Standard Action   **Ranged** 20
Primary Target: One creature
Primary Attack: Intelligence vs. Reflex
Hit: 4d6 + Intelligence modifier lightning damage.
Miss: Half damage.
Effect: Make the secondary attack.
Secondary Attack
  Secondary Target: One or two creatures within 5 squares of the primary target
  Attack: Intelligence vs. Reflex
  Hit: 2d6 + Intelligence modifier lightning damage.
  Miss: Half damage.
  Effect: Make the tertiary attack.

Tertiary Attack
    Tertiary Target: Each enemy within 20 squares of you that was not a primary or a
      secondary target
    Attack: Intelligence vs. Reflex
    Hit: 1d6 + Intelligence modifier lightning damage.
    Miss: Half damage.

Secondary Powers

Some powers encompass what are called secondary powers. A creature must use the encompassing power to gain access to the secondary power. A secondary power requires a separate action from the action used to perform the encompassing power.

A secondary power's entry specifies its action type, attack/utility type, range, and effects. If a secondary power has keywords that differ from those of the encompassing power, its keywords are noted in parentheses. Otherwise, the secondary power has the same keywords.

Some secondary powers have the same targets as their encompassing powers, whereas others have targets of their own, noted in "Secondary Target" entries. The *phantasmal killer* spell presented here is an example of a power that includes a secondary power.

Phantasmal Killer	Wizard Attack 9

Your enemy wails as its greatest fears manifest within its mind.

Daily ✦ Arcane, Fear, Illusion
Minor Action   **Ranged** 10
Target: One creature
Effect: The target becomes haunted by an illusion of its deepest fears (save ends). Until the illusion ends, the target can't make opportunity attacks and you can use the secondary power against it. Whenever the target is hit by or takes damage from any effect other than the secondary power, it can make another saving throw to end the illusion.
Secondary Power (Arcane, Illusion, Implement, Psychic)
    Standard Action   **Ranged** 20
    Attack: Intelligence vs. Will. The attack roll takes no penalty from concealment, if any.
    Hit: 3d10 + Intelligence modifier psychic damage.
    Miss: Half damage.

Sustain

If a creature uses a power that has a "Sustain" entry, it can keep an effect of that power active by taking a specific type of action before the end of each of its turns. The creature cannot take this sustaining action until its turn after it uses the power and can take the action no more than once per round. The entry specifies the action type that must be taken—most often minor, move, or standard. The entry then notes which of the power's effects continue when the power is sustained. If the "Sustain" entry has an instantaneous effect that occurs each time the power is sustained, that fact is noted in the entry too. See "Durations," page 226, for more about sustaining a power.

Class Feature Rider
Some power descriptions contain entries that are riders—additions or changes to powers tied to certain class features. If a power description contains a class feature rider, the class feature's name appears as the entry's name. The rider applies only if the character using the power has the class feature.

Many class feature riders are indented and are therefore contingent on another entry in a power. Unless otherwise noted, a class feature rider that is not indented should be treated like an "Effect" entry. In other words, the rider's effects simply happen for the character who has the class feature.

Aftereffect
An aftereffect automatically occurs after another effect ends. An "Aftereffect" entry follows the effect it applies to, which is typically in a "Hit" or an "Effect" entry. For instance, a power's "Hit" entry might state that the target is stunned (save ends), and then the power's "Aftereffect" entry might state that the target is dazed instead of stunned (save ends). Together those entries mean that the target is dazed as soon as it saves against the stunned condition.

If a target is subjected to an aftereffect as a result of a save, and that save occurs when the target is making multiple saving throws, the aftereffect takes effect only after the target has finished making all its saving throws. In other words, a target usually can't save against an aftereffect in the same turn in which it is subjected to an aftereffect. See "Saving Throws," page 227, for how saving throws work.

Failed Saving Throw
Sometimes an effect changes when a target fails a saving throw against it. The new effect, specified in a "Failed Saving Throw" entry, occurs only after the target has finished making all its saving throws at the end of its turn. The effect does not change if the target fails a saving throw against it at a time other than the end of its turn. For instance, Lyriel is subjected to an effect that worsens the first time she fails a saving throw against it. Her cleric companion Valenae then takes her turn and grants Lyriel a saving throw against the effect. Lyriel fails the saving throw, but the effect doesn't worsen, because she failed the saving throw on Valenae's turn and not at the end of her own turn.

Level
The strength of some powers increases as their users gain levels. Such a power's description contains one or more entries that specify what part of the power changes, and in what ways, when its user reaches a certain level.

Example: A power description contains the following subentry beneath its "Hit" entry: "*Level 21:* 2d8 + Intelligence modifier fire damage." That means the "Hit" entry's damage changes to the specified amount when the user reaches 21st level.

Special
Any unusual information about the use of a power appears in this entry. For instance, some powers can be used as basic attacks, which is noted in a "Special" entry.

ATTACK AND UTILITY TYPES

Powers in the DUNGEONS & DRAGONS world take many forms. A fighter swings a greatsword at a foe; a ranger looses an arrow at a distant target; a dragon exhales a blast of fire; a wizard creates a burst of lightning; a rogue tumbles through the midst of combat. These examples illustrate the five attack and utility types: melee, ranged, close, area, and personal. These types differ primarily in two areas of the rules: targeting and range.

Melee Powers

The most common kind of melee power affects a nearby target. A typical melee attack involves using a weapon—such as a sword, a mace, a claw, or a fist—against a target within the weapon's reach. A typical melee utility power involves one creature granting some beneficial effect to another one by touching it.

Origin Square A melee power's origin square is the space of the power's user, unless otherwise noted. For example, a melee power of a Medium creature, such as a human, has an origin square that is literally 1 square—the human's space. A melee power of a Large creature, such as an ogre, has an origin square that is 2 squares by 2 squares.

KEY TERMS

The rules in this section rely on several key terms.

origin square: The square where an effect originates. Every power has an origin square. A power's attack or utility type (melee, ranged, close, area, or personal) determines the origin square's location.

range: The maximum distance that an effect can reach. Range is often expressed as a number of squares. For instance, a power might have a range of 5, which means the power can produce an effect up to 5 squares away.

line of effect: A clear line from one point in space to another point in an encounter that doesn't pass through or touch blocking terrain. Unless otherwise noted, there must be line of effect between the origin square of an effect and its intended target for that target to be affected. See "Line of Effect," later in this chapter.

line of sight: A clear line from one point in space to another point in an encounter that doesn't pass through or touch an object or an effect—such as a stone wall, a thick curtain, or a cloud of fog—that blocks the vision of the viewer. See "Line of Sight," later in this chapter.

area of effect: An area of a specific size where a particular effect takes place. An area of effect is usually a blast, a burst, or a wall. Area powers and close powers almost always involve an area of effect.

Targets
A melee power targets individuals, which are specified in the power description. For example, a melee power might target "one creature," "one enemy," or "one or two creatures."

Multiple Targets: If a melee power has multiple targets and includes attack rolls or damage rolls, those rolls are made separately against each target.

Line of Effect: There must be line of effect between the power's origin square and the target.

Line of Sight: Unless otherwise noted, the power's user doesn't have to be able to see the target of the power, though concealment (page 220) might apply.

Range
A melee power's range is specified in the power description. Here are the most common ranges that appear in such powers.

✦ **Melee [number]:** The power can be used against a target that is within the specified number of squares of the power's origin square. For example, a melee power that has a range of 1 can normally be used only against an adjacent target, whereas a melee power that has a range of 0 can be used only against a target sharing the attacker's space.

✦ **Melee weapon:** The power can be used against a target within the reach of the melee weapon that is used with the power. Unless otherwise noted, a melee weapon has a reach of 1 (a creature's limbs, fists, claws, and other appendages can be used as melee weapons). An adventurer sometimes increases a weapon's reach through powers, feats, or other attributes.

Example: A character uses a melee attack power that has a range of "weapon" and wields a dagger. The character can attack a target within 1 square of him or her. If the character uses the same power with a halberd (a weapon that normally has a reach of 2), the character can attack a target within 2 squares of him or her.

If a creature has a reach greater than 1, the creature uses its reach for the power's range, instead of the weapon's reach. If the same creature uses a weapon that has a reach greater than 1, the creature still uses its own reach but adds 1.

Example: A creature has a reach of 2 and uses an attack power that has a range of "weapon." If the creature wields a weapon that has a reach of 1 (such as a longsword), the power's range is 2. If the creature instead uses a weapon that has a reach greater than 1 (such as a halberd), the power's range is 3.

✦ **Melee touch:** The power can be used on a target within the reach of the power's user. A creature has a reach of 1 unless otherwise noted, so it can typically use a melee power only against a target that is within 1 square of it. Creatures larger than Medium often have a reach greater than 1 (see "Creature Size and Space," page 199). Adventurers sometimes increase their reach through powers, feats, or other attributes.

Ranged Powers

The most common kind of ranged power affects a distant target. A typical ranged attack power targets one creature within its range. Shooting a bow and casting the spell *magic missile* are examples of ranged attacks. A typical ranged utility power involves casting beneficial magic on a target that is across the battlefield.

Origin Square

A ranged power's origin square is the space of the power's user, unless otherwise noted. For example, the ranged power of a Medium creature, such as an elf, has an origin square that is literally 1 square—the elf's space. The ranged power of a Large creature, such as a beholder, has an origin square that is 2 squares by 2 squares.

Targets

A ranged power targets individuals, which are specified in the power description. For example, a ranged power might target "one creature," "one enemy," or "one or two creatures."

WILLIAM O'CONNOR

Multiple Targets: If a ranged power has multiple targets and includes attack rolls or damage rolls, those rolls are made separately against each target.

Line of Effect: A target must be within line of effect of the power's origin square.

Line of Sight: Unless otherwise noted, the power's user doesn't have to be able to see the target of the power, though concealment (page 220) might apply.

Range

A ranged power's range is specified in the power description. Here are the most common ranges that appear in such powers.

+ **Ranged [number]:** The power can be used against a target that is within the specified number of squares of the power's origin square. For instance, a ranged power that has a range of 10 can be used against a target that is up to 10 squares away.

+ **Ranged weapon:** The power can be used against a target within the range of the weapon that is used with the power. A ranged weapon has both a normal range and a long range. The user of the power takes a -2 penalty to attack rolls against targets beyond the normal range but within the long range. The weapon can't be used to target something beyond its long range.

    Example: A character using a shortbow (normal range 15, long range 30) takes a -2 penalty when attacking targets 16–30 squares away, and the character can't attack creatures farther away than 30 squares.

+ **Ranged sight:** The power can be used against a target that the power's user can see.

Provokes Opportunity Attacks

When a creature uses a ranged power, the creature provokes opportunity attacks (page 246). This rule arises from the fact that a ranged power requires the creature to focus its attention elsewhere, lowering its guard for a moment.

Close Powers

A close power creates an area of effect that emanates from the power's user (an exceptional close power might create an area of effect that emanates from a different location). Swinging a sword in an arc to hit every adjacent enemy with one blow, creating a blast of fire from one's hands, or causing divine energy to burst out in all directions are examples of close powers.

Origin Square

A close power's area of effect, whether a blast or a burst, uses the space of the power's user as its origin square, unless otherwise noted. Just as with melee and ranged powers, the origin square for a Medium creature using a close power is literally 1 square, while a larger creature has an origin square that encompasses several squares.

Area of Effect

The area of effect created by a close power has a particular size. Both the area of effect and the size are specified in the power description, using one of the following presentations.

+ **Close blast [number]:** The power creates a blast of the specified size adjacent to the origin square. The power's user decides where to place the blast.
+ **Close burst [number]:** The power creates a burst of the specified size centered on the origin square. This rule means the larger the creator, the larger the origin square, and the larger the burst.

See "Areas of Effect," page 108, for more about blasts and bursts.

Range: A close power's range rarely matters. If it is ever relevant, the number given for the size also functions as the range. For instance, a close blast 5 might conjure a spectral guardian that must be within range of the conjurer at the end of the conjurer's turn, which means the guardian must be within 5 squares of the conjurer at that time.

Targets

A close power targets specific individuals within the power's area of effect. For example, the power might target "each creature in the burst," "each enemy in the blast," or "one ally in the burst."

EVA WIDERMANN

Multiple Targets: If a close power has multiple targets and includes attack rolls or damage rolls, the attack rolls are made separately against each target, but a single damage roll is made against all the targets.

Line of Effect: A target must be within line of effect of the power's origin square.

Line of Sight: Unless otherwise noted, the power's user doesn't have to be able to see the target of the power, and concealment (page 220) between the origin square and a target doesn't apply.

Area Powers

An area power creates an area of effect that can appear in a distant square. A ball of fire that streaks across the battlefield and explodes is an example of an area attack power. A magical wall of fog that springs from the ground to obscure a dungeon corridor is an example of an area utility power.

Origin Square
An area power's origin square is a single square that can be some distance away from the power's user, unless otherwise noted. Each area power specifies how far away the origin square can be. The power's user must have line of effect to the origin square.

Area of Effect
The area of effect created by an area power has a particular size and can be up to a certain distance away from the power's user. The area of effect, size, and range are all specified in the power description, using one of the following presentations.

✦ **Area burst [number] within [number] squares:** The power's user decides where to place the origin square, which must be within the range specified by the second number. Centered on the origin square, the power creates a burst of the size that is specified by the first number. For instance, an area burst 2 within 10 squares creates a burst 2, the origin square of which is up to 10 squares away from the power's user.

✦ **Area wall [number] within [number] squares:** The power's user decides where to place the origin square, which must be within the range specified by the second number. The power creates a wall in a number of squares, including the origin square, specified by the first number. Every square of the wall must be within range of the power's user, but only the origin square has to be within line of effect of the user. The user decides where to place the wall's squares. For instance, a wall 8 within 10 squares creates a wall that contains 8 contiguous squares, all of which are within 10 squares of the power's user.

See "Areas of Effect," page 108, for more about bursts and walls.

Targets

An area power targets specific individuals within the power's area of effect. For example, the power might target "each creature in the burst," "each enemy in the burst," or "each creature in the wall."

Multiple Targets: If an area power has multiple targets and includes attack rolls or damage rolls, the attack rolls are made separately against each target, but a single damage roll is made against all the targets.

Line of Effect: A target must be within line of effect of the power's origin square. The target does not need to be within line of effect of the power's user, though.

Line of Sight: Unless otherwise noted, the power's user doesn't have to be able to see the origin square or the target of the power, and concealment (page 220) between the origin square and a target doesn't apply.

Provokes Opportunity Attacks

When a creature uses an area power, the creature provokes opportunity attacks (page 246). This rule arises from the fact that an area power requires the creature to focus its attention elsewhere, lowering its guard for a moment.

AMMUNITION

If a creature uses a projectile weapon to use an attack power against multiple targets, the creature needs one piece of ammunition for each target. Similarly, if the creature uses thrown weapons, it needs one for each target. The DM might choose to ignore this rule, allowing limitless ammunition.

Personal Powers

A personal power typically affects its user only. Examples include creating magic armor on oneself or giving oneself the ability to fly.

CHOOSING TARGETS

Powers often involve the selection of targets. When choosing targets, the power's user must make sure that each target meets several criteria.

✦ The target must meet the power's target definition.

✦ The target must be within the range or area of effect of the power.

✦ The target must be within line of effect of the power's origin square.

Target Definitions

Each power defines whom or what it can target. The simplest target definition is "one creature," which means a single creature of any type. Many powers have more elaborate target definitions. For instance, a power might define what sort of creature can be targeted (such as an ally), what state that creature must be in (such as bloodied), what circumstances must be present (such as the target being visible), and so on.

Creatures, Enemies, and Allies
The most common targets are creatures, enemies, and allies.

✦ **Creature** means a creature of any sort, whether it is an enemy or an ally of the power's user. A power that targets "each creature" treats creatures indiscriminately; it makes no distinction between friend and foe.

✦ **Enemy** means an opponent of the power's user.

✦ **Ally** means a companion of the power's user. When a power defines a target as an ally, the ally is free to ignore the power's effects. For instance, a power that allows a creature to move its allies on the battlefield can be ignored by those allies. In contrast, a creature targeted by an ally's power cannot ignore its effects if the power targets a "creature" or "creatures," instead of an "ally" or "allies."

Number of Targets
Each power specifies how many targets it can affect: "one creature," "one or two enemies," "each creature in the burst," and so on.

When a number of targets is specified in a power, the user of the power chooses the targets. For instance, a power that targets "one or two creatures" can target up to two creatures of the user's choice. In contrast, a power that targets "two creatures" can target no fewer than two creatures of the user's choice. The power can't target a lone creature.

Certain powers allow their users to place areas of effect but not to choose targets. For instance, an area power that targets "each creature in the burst" requires the user to target each creature in the burst, whether or not the user wants to.

Line of Sight
Typically the user of a power doesn't have to be able to see the power's targets. A few powers do require a user to be able to see a creature to target it, however. For instance, a power might specify that it targets "one creature you can see." In other words, the creature must be within the user's line of sight.

To determine whether a power's user can see a target, pick a corner of the user's space and trace an imaginary line from that corner to any part of the target's space. The user can see the target if at least one line doesn't pass through or touch an object or an effect—such as a stone wall, a thick curtain, or a cloud of fog—that blocks the user's vision.

Even if a power's user can see a target, objects and effects can still partially block its view. If the user can see a target but at least one line passes through an obstruction, the target has cover (page 219) or concealment (page 220).

Targeting Objects
At the DM's discretion, a power that targets one or more creatures can target one or more objects, as long as the number of targets does not exceed the number specified by the power.

For example, a player might want her wizard to attack a door with a thunder power that normally targets a single creature. If the DM says yes to her, she can use the spell against the door but can't use it against the door and another creature, because doing so would exceed the number of targets specified in the power. See "Attacking Objects," page 176, for objects' defenses, hit points, and so forth.

Range and Areas of Effect
In many powers—particularly melee powers and ranged powers—the range to a target is important. For instance, a ranged power that has a range of 10 can affect a target only if the target is within 10 squares of the power's user. In other powers—particularly close powers and area powers—a target's position in relation to an area of effect is important. For instance, a close power that creates a burst 2 can affect a target only if the target is within the burst.

To determine the range between a power's user and its target, count the distance between them as normal (see "Determining Distance," page 201), including 1 square that the target occupies. If the target's space is larger than 1 square, it is an eligible target as long as any square of its space is within the power's range.

A target is in an area of effect if at least 1 square of the target's space is in the area of effect.

Line of Effect
When there is a clear line from one point to another in an encounter, there is line of effect. Unless otherwise noted, there must be line of effect between the origin square of an effect and its intended target for that target to be affected. If every imaginary line traced from the origin square to the target passes through or touches blocking terrain, there is no line of effect between the two.

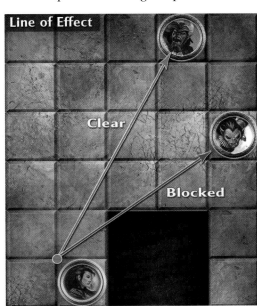

Line of Effect

Clear

Blocked

Fog, darkness, and similarly obscured squares block vision, but they don't block line of effect. If Albanon the wizard hurls a *fireball* into a pitch-black room, he doesn't have to see creatures in the room for the fire to hit them. In contrast, a character can see through a transparent wall of magical force but doesn't have line of effect through it. The character can see the snarling demon on the other side, but the wall blocks attacks.

AREAS OF EFFECT

An area of effect is a location of a specific size where a particular effect takes place. The effects of most area powers and close powers are contained within one of three kinds of areas of effect: a blast, a burst, or a wall.

Some melee powers and ranged powers create these areas of effect as well. For instance, a character might use a melee power that involves a weapon attack followed by a burst of divine radiance.

Large, Huge, and Gargantuan Targets: If a Large or larger target occupies multiple squares of an area of effect, the target still counts as a single target. For instance, if a Large ogre occupies 4 squares of the burst of Albanon's *fireball*, the wizard attacks the ogre once, not four times.

LEGITIMATE TARGETS

When a power has an effect that occurs upon hitting, missing, or otherwise affecting a target, the effect takes place only if the target in question is a meaningful threat. For instance, characters can gain no benefit from carrying a sack of rats in the hope of healing their allies by hitting the rats.

When a power's effect involves a character's allies, use common sense when determining how many allies can be affected. DUNGEONS & DRAGONS is a game about adventuring parties fighting groups of monsters, not the clash of armies. When read strictly, a cleric's power might be able to give a hundred "allies" a free basic attack, but that doesn't mean that cleric characters should assemble armies to march before them into a dungeon. In general, a power's effect should be limited to a small group of about eight people—the size of an adventuring group plus a couple of friendly nonplayer characters—not hired soldiers or lantern-bearers.

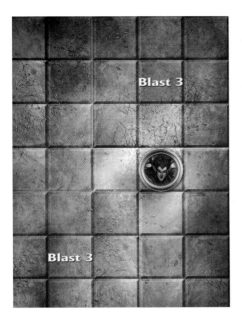

Blast

A blast fills an area adjacent to its origin square, which is almost always the space of its creator, and is a specified number of squares on a side. For instance, if Albanon uses a wizard power that is a close blast 3, the power's area of effect is a 3-square-by-3-square area adjacent to him. A blast is normally part of a close power (page 102).

The origin square of a blast is not in the blast, and a blast affects a target only if the target is in the blast's area and there is line of effect from the origin square to the target. For instance, if a red dragon breathes fire in a close blast 5, the fire fills a 5-square-by-5-square area adjacent to the dragon and does not burn it. Even if a creature is in the area of the fire, the creature isn't affected by the fire if it is behind an obstacle that blocks line of effect between the creature and the origin square.

Burst

A burst starts in an origin square and extends in all directions to a specified number of squares from the origin square. For instance, a burst 2 extends 2 squares in every direction from its origin square: for a Medium creature, a 5-square-by-5-square area. A burst is normally part of a close power (page 102) or an area power (page 104).

Unless a power description indicates otherwise, a close burst does

not affect its creator, even though the burst does include the origin square (normally the creator's space). In contrast, an area burst can affect its creator. For instance, Albanon might place a *shock sphere* (area burst 2 within 10) so close to himself that he is damaged by the explosion of lightning.

A burst affects a target only if the target is in the burst's area and there is line of effect from the burst's origin square to the target. Even if a creature is in the area of Albanon's *shock sphere*, the creature isn't affected by the lightning if it is behind an obstacle that blocks line of effect between the creature and the origin square.

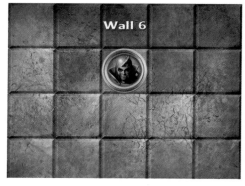

Wall

A wall fills a specified number of contiguous squares within range, starting from and including an origin square. For instance, a wall 8 fills eight contiguous squares. The squares can be lined up horizontally or stacked vertically. A wall is at least 1 square high. If a particular wall can be higher, the wall's maximum height is specified in the power's description.

A wall's creator can shape the wall within the following limitations.

✦ Each square of the wall must share a side—not just a corner—with at least one other square of the wall.

✦ A square of the wall can share no more than two sides with other squares in the wall, but this limitation does not apply when stacking squares on top of each other.

✦ A solid wall, such as a wall of ice, cannot be created in creatures' squares. In other words, the wall can be used neither to smash or displace a creature nor to cut a Large or larger creature in half.

For instance, a wall 8 could be shaped into a line of squares, a zigzag of squares, or a mix of the two. If the wall's maximum height is 4 squares, the wall could have only two squares as its base with the rest stacked on top of them.

KEYWORDS

A power's keywords summarize important aspects of the power. With a glance at a power's keywords, a reader can learn various things about the power: what its power source is, whether it has any damage types, and what special rules are required to use it.

Keywords help in describing a power's effects and can aid in classifying types of powers. For example, powers that have the thunder keyword are called thunder powers, and powers that create illusion effects have the illusion keyword. Various rules in the game, such as those for feats and class features, refer to powers by using keywords. For instance, a feat might grant a bonus to the damage rolls of a character's fire powers, which is another way of saying the character's powers that have the fire keyword.

Keywords help determine how, or if, a power works when a target has resistance, vulnerability, or immunity to a damage type or an effect type, or if the power interacts with the environment in some unusual way. For example, a magic circle that forbids teleportation could block a power that has the teleportation keyword.

When first using a power, a player should make sure he or she is familiar with the definitions of its keywords, if any. This section defines the most common keywords in the game and organizes them into five categories: power sources, schools of magic, accessories, damage types, and effect types.

Power Sources

Every class relies on a particular source of energy to fuel its powers. The source of a power is identified by its power source keyword. If a power has more than one power source keyword, the power counts as belonging to each of those power sources.

The most common power sources are arcane, divine, martial, and primal. Other power sources exist, including psionic and shadow. Most non-adventurer powers lack power source keywords.

Arcane: Drawing on magical energy that permeates the cosmos, the arcane power source can be used for a variety of effects, from fireballs to flight to invisibility. Wizards and warlocks are examples of arcane magic users. Each class is the representative of a different tradition of arcane study, and other traditions exist. Arcane powers are called *spells*.

Divine: Divine magic comes from the gods, who grant power to their devotees, such as clerics and paladins. Divine magic excels at healing, protection, and smiting enemies of the gods. Divine powers are called *prayers*.

Martial: Martial powers are not magic in the traditional sense, although some martial powers are well beyond the capabilities of ordinary mortals. Martial characters use their own strength and willpower to vanquish their enemies. Training and dedication replace arcane formulas and prayers to grant power to fighters, rangers, and rogues, among others. Martial powers are called *exploits*.

Primal: Primal magic draws on the spirits of nature that pervade the world. Some primal powers are more overtly magical than others, but they all evoke these primal spirits. Some characters channel primal spirits through their bodies to transform themselves and make their physical attacks more formidable. Others evoke primal spirits to create external effects, including terrain effects, localized storms, bursts of fire, or temporary manifestations of the spirits. Primal powers are called *evocations*.

Psionic: Characters who use the psionic power source harness the potential of their minds to create dramatic effects. Some psionic powers manipulate the minds of enemies or allies, while others create more tangible effects in the world. Psionic power is thought to be the world's response to the intrusion of the Far Realm, similar to a mortal body's reaction to disease. Psionic powers are called *disciplines*.

Shadow: Few creatures embrace shadow energy without a compelling reason and a measure of desperation. To claim and wield the power of shadow, a character must pledge a shard of his or her soul to the Shadowfell, the dark realm of the dead. This soul fragment is replaced with a dark reflection of the character's true self, which becomes the source of the character's new power. Shadow powers are called *hexes*.

Schools of Magic

After generations of study, practitioners of arcane magic have identified various types of magic and have grouped them into categories, which are called schools. Wizardry is particularly focused on the schools, and wizards often specialize in the practice of one or two of the schools. Each school of magic includes a variety of damage types and effects. Here are some of the most common schools.

✦ **Enchantment:** Enchantment powers alter creatures' emotions, thoughts, and actions, including beguiling onlookers, terrifying foes, and encouraging allies.

✦ **Evocation:** Evocation powers bring various magical effects into being, including explosions, rays of magical energy, and lingering environmental effects. This is the most widely practiced school of magic. Scholars have various theories about the connection, if any, between this school of magic and primal powers, which are sometimes called evocations. Both evocation powers and primal powers involve calling on magical energy in the cosmos.

Evocation powers draw on the vary fabric of existence, whereas primal powers call on the spirits found throughout the world.

✦ **Illusion:** Illusion powers deceive the mind or the senses, often creating elaborate apparitions. Illusion is also an effect type (see page 115).

✦ **Transmutation:** A transmutation power magically transforms its target in some way, changing the target's form, composition, or both. Damage caused by such a power is usually the result of the trauma brought about by the transformation. Transmutation powers sometimes cause such extensive changes that they are also polymorph powers (page 118), but the power might also keep a target's form intact. For instance, a transmutation power that slows a creature by turning its feet to stone is not subjecting the creature to a polymorph effect. The creature's original form remains, though the material of its body has been altered.

Accessories

The two accessory keywords—implement and weapon—indicate whether a power can be used with an implement or a weapon.

Implement
The implement keyword identifies a power that can be used with an implement: an item, such as a wand, that certain creatures can wield to channel powers. An adventurer must have proficiency with an implement to use it with his or her powers. An adventurer's class and feats determine his or her implement proficiencies. If an adventurer does have proficiency with an implement, he or she can use it with any of his or her implement powers. See "Implements," page 274.

Magic implements provide special benefits, such as bonuses to attack rolls and damage rolls, when used with implement powers. See "Magic Implements," page 283.

Weapon
The weapon keyword identifies a power that is used with a weapon, including an improvised weapon such as an unarmed strike (see "Improvised Weapons," page 272). The range and the damage of a weapon power is usually determined by the weapon used with it. The symbol [W] in a power's damage expression stands for the damage die of the weapon used with it (see "Damage," page 222).

If an adventurer uses a weapon power with a weapon that he or she has proficiency with, add the weapon's proficiency bonus to the attack rolls of that power. An adventurer's class and feats determine his or her weapon proficiencies.

Magic weapons provide special benefits, such as bonuses to attack rolls and damage rolls, when used with weapon powers. See "Magic Items," page 275.

Damage Types

Many attacks deal a specific type of damage, and each damage type has a keyword associated with it.

- ✦ **Acid:** Corrosive liquid or vapor.
- ✦ **Cold:** Ice crystals, arctic air, or frigid liquid.
- ✦ **Fire:** Explosive bursts, fiery rays, or simple ignition.
- ✦ **Force:** Invisible energy that can be used as if it were solid.
- ✦ **Lightning:** Electrical energy.
- ✦ **Necrotic:** Deathly energy that deadens flesh or wounds the soul.
- ✦ **Poison:** Toxins that harm or hinder.
- ✦ **Psychic:** Effects that assault the mind.
- ✦ **Radiant:** Searing white light or shimmering colors.
- ✦ **Thunder:** Shock waves and deafening sounds.

If a power has one of these keywords, it deals the associated type of damage. The exception is poison, which is a keyword for both a damage type and an effect type.

"Varies": If the notation "Varies" appears among a power's keywords, that means the power has variable damage types, which the user or the circumstances determine.

Resistance and Vulnerability: Creatures sometimes have resistance or vulnerability to certain damage types, and some effects grant temporary resistance or impose short-term vulnerability. See "Resistance" and "Vulnerability," pages 224-225.

Adding and Removing Damage Types: If a power gains or loses damage types, the power gains the keywords for any damage types that are added, and it loses the keywords for any damage types that are removed. The poison keyword, however, is removed from a power only if that power neither deals poison damage nor has any nondamaging effects.

Example: If Albanon casts a lightning power through a magic staff that changes the damage to fire, the power gains the fire keyword and loses the lightning keyword for that use, since the power is dealing fire damage instead of lightning damage. That use of the power can therefore benefit from game elements, such as feats, that affect fire powers, but not from those that affect lightning powers.

Effect Types

Effect type keywords signify the presence of particular effects in powers, and many of these keywords have special rules that govern how their powers are used. Whether or not an effect type keyword has special rules, other effects in the game refer to that keyword. For instance, the charm keyword has no special rules, but some creatures gain a bonus to saving throws against charm powers.

This section contains the definitions of the game's main effect type keywords.

Augmentable
A power that has the augmentable keyword has optional augmentations, which a character can use at the cost of power points. Only certain characters have power points, usually as a result of their class. Unless otherwise noted, using an augmentable power follows these rules.

Decide First: A creature must decide whether and how to augment an augmentable power when it chooses to use the power, before making any attack rolls or applying any of the power's effects.

Power Point Cost: An augmentation specifies its cost in power points. For example, "Augment 1" means a creature must spend 1 power point to use an augmentation. The creature must spend the required power points when it decides to use the augmentation.

One at a Time: A creature can use only one augmentation on a power at a time, so it can't, for example, spend 3 power points to use both a 1-point and a 2-point augmentation on a single power.

Replace Base Effects: When a power is augmented, changes to the power are noted in the description of the augmentation. If an augmentation includes a specific power entry, such as "Hit" or "Effect," that entry replaces the entry in the base power that has the same name. An augmented version of a power is otherwise identical to the base power.

Unaugmented: When a creature uses an augmentable power without augmenting it, the power is referred to as unaugmented for that use (some effects apply only when a power is unaugmented). A power that doesn't have the augmentable keyword is never considered unaugmented.

At-Will Attack Powers: When a power or some other effect lets a creature use an at-will attack power, the creature can choose to use one of its augmentable at-will attack powers, but must use it unaugmented.

When a racial trait lets an adventurer choose an extra at-will attack power and the adventurer chooses an augmentable at-will attack power, the power loses both the augmentable keyword and its augmentations.

Aura
An aura is a continuous effect that emanates from a creature. Unless otherwise noted, an aura uses the following rules.

Fills an Area: The aura fills the creature's space and each square that is both within a specified distance of the creature and within line of effect of it. For instance, an aura 1 affects each square adjacent to the creature. A creature is normally unaffected by its own aura.

Unaffected by the Environment: The aura is unaffected by environmental phenomena and terrain, although blocking terrain blocks an aura. For instance, an aura of fire is unaffected by an area of extreme cold.

Overlapping Auras: If auras overlap and impose penalties to the same roll or game statistic, a creature affected by the overlapping auras is subjected to the worst penalty; the penalties are not cumulative. For instance, if a creature is affected by three overlapping auras that each impose a -2 penalty to attack rolls, the creature takes a -2 penalty, not a -6 penalty.

Deactivating an Aura: A creature can take a minor action to deactivate or reactivate one of its auras. However, certain auras have set durations and cannot be reactivated after they end.

Death or Unconsciousness Ends: A creature's auras end immediately when it falls unconscious or dies.

Beast
Certain creatures have beast companions, and beast powers are used in conjunction with those companions. A creature can use a beast power only if its beast companion is conscious and present in an encounter.

Beast Form
Certain creatures have the ability to transform into a beast form. A creature can use a beast form power only while it is in that form.

Channel Divinity
A channel divinity power allows a creature to harness the magic of the gods. A creature can use no more than one channel divinity power per encounter.

Charm
A charm power controls a creature's actions in some way. This control is often represented by the creature being forced to move, being compelled to attack its ally, or being subjected to the dominated condition. Some charm powers even beguile targets into unconsciousness.

Conjuration
A conjuration power produces a conjuration, which is a creation of magical energy that resembles a creature, an object, or some other phenomenon. Even if a conjuration looks like a creature or displays some degree of sentience, it is not considered a creature. Unless otherwise noted, a conjuration uses the following rules.

Occupies No Squares: The conjuration occupies no squares. The conjuration does not need to be supported by a solid surface, so it can float in the air.

Unaffected by the Environment: Terrain and environmental phenomena have no effect on the conjuration. For instance, a conjuration that is an icy hand functions in an inferno without penalty.

Creator's Defenses: Normally, a conjuration cannot be attacked or physically affected. If a conjuration can be attacked or physically affected, it uses its creator's defenses. Unless an attack specifically targets conjurations, only the attack's damage (not including ongoing damage) affects the conjuration. For instance, an attack power that would cause a creature to take 20 cold damage and become immobilized would instead deal only the cold damage to a conjuration.

Attacking with a Conjuration: Normally, a conjuration cannot attack. If a conjuration can attack, its creator makes the attack, determining line of effect from the conjuration as if the creator were in the conjuration's space. If line of sight is relevant, determine it from the creator, not the conjuration.

Movable Conjurations: If the power used to create a conjuration allows it to be moved, it's a movable conjuration. At the end of the creator's turn, a movable conjuration ends if the creator doesn't have line of effect to at least 1 square of the conjuration or if the creator isn't within range (using the power's range) of at least 1 square of the conjuration.
A conjuration can't be moved through blocking terrain.

Death Ends: A conjuration ends immediately if its creator dies.

Disease
Some powers expose a creature to a disease. Unless instructed otherwise, the creature makes a saving throw at the end of the encounter to determine if it contracts the disease. If the saving throw fails, the creature is infected. See "Disease," page 184.

Fear   A fear power inspires fright. This fright is often represented by a creature being forced to move, taking a penalty to attack rolls or defenses, or granting combat advantage.

Full Discipline

A full discipline power contains what are effectively two mini-powers, an attack technique and a movement technique. Unless otherwise noted, using a full discipline power follows these rules.

One per Round: A creature can use only one full discipline power per round, unless it spends an action point. If the creature does spend an action point to take an extra action, the creature can switch to a different full discipline power.

Separate Actions: Each of the techniques in a full discipline power requires a separate action to use. The action types are specified in the power's description. A creature can use the techniques in whatever order it likes during a round, and it can use one of the techniques and not the other during a particular round.

The number of times a creature can use a technique during a round is determined by the power's type (at-will or encounter) and by the actions the creature has available in that round. For example, a creature can use the techniques of an at-will full discipline power as many times during a round as it likes, provided it has enough of the required actions. If a creature uses an encounter full discipline power, the creature can use both techniques, but can use each technique only once during that round.

Healing

A healing power restores hit points, usually either by restoring hit points immediately or by granting regeneration (page 260).

Illusion

An illusion power deceives the mind or the senses. Illusions often obstruct vision or redirect attacks. If an illusion power deals damage, the damage itself is not an illusion. Users of arcane magic, such as wizards, consider illusion to be one of the schools of magic.

Invigorating

If a creature has training in Endurance, it gains temporary hit points equal to its Constitution modifier when it hits with a power that has the invigorating keyword. No invigorating power grants temporary hit points more than once during a turn, even if the user hits more than once with that power.

Poison

A poison power delivers a nondamaging poisonous effect, deals poison damage (see "Damage Types," page 223), or both.

Polymorph

Polymorph powers change a creature's physical form in some way. For instance, a polymorph power might transform a creature into a mouse. Unless otherwise noted, a creature uses the following rules when it is affected by a polymorph power.

One Polymorph at a Time: If a creature is affected by more than one polymorph power, only the most recent one has any effect. The other powers' effects remain on the creature and their durations expire as normal, but those effects don't apply. However, when the most recent effect ends, the next most recent one that is still active applies to the creature.

Example: If a druid uses a polymorph power on herself and then a monster uses a polymorph power on her, the polymorph effect of the druid's power is suppressed until the monster's polymorph effect ends on her.

Changing Size: If a polymorph power reduces a creature's space, the creature does not provoke opportunity attacks for leaving squares as it shrinks.

If a polymorph effect would make a creature too large to fit in the available space, the effect fails against the creature, but it is stunned (save ends).

Example: If Keira is crawling through a narrow tunnel and a polymorph effect tries to make her too large for the tunnel, the effect fails, but she is stunned until she saves against that effect.

Death Ends: Polymorph effects end immediately on a creature that dies.

Rage
A rage power allows the user to enter a rage specified in the power. The rage lasts until the user enters a new rage or until the end of the encounter.

Rattling
If a creature has training in Intimidate and deals damage with a power that has the rattling keyword, the target takes a -2 penalty to attack rolls until the end of the user's next turn. A target that is immune to fear is not subject to this penalty.

Reliable
If a reliable power misses every target, the power is not expended. This rule means an encounter attack power or a daily attack power that has this keyword can be used again and again until it hits.

Runic
A runic power channels the magic of runes that are specified in the power. Unless otherwise noted, using a runic power follows these rules.

Choose First: When a creature is going to use a runic power, it first chooses one of the runes in the power and then uses the power, applying the chosen rune's effects at the time indicated in the power (after hitting with the power, for instance).

Rune State: The creature is then in the rune state associated with the chosen rune until it enters a new rune state or until the end of the encounter.

Sleep
Sleep powers knock creatures unconscious. Unless otherwise noted, this unconsciousness is not normal sleep, so a creature that is subjected to it cannot be simply awakened; the power specifies how the unconsciousness ends.

Spirit Certain creatures have spirit companions, and spirit powers are used in conjunction with those companions. A creature can use a spirit power only if its spirit companion is present in the encounter. If a spirit power includes "spirit" in its range, determine line of sight and line of effect from the spirit companion's space, which is the power's origin square.

Stance When a character uses a stance power, the character assumes a stance.

Duration: A stance lasts until the character assumes another stance or until the character falls unconscious or dies. A stance also ends at the end of the encounter, unless the stance can be assumed at will.

One per Turn: A character can assume no more than one stance per turn.

Summoning Powers that have the summoning keyword bring creatures magically from elsewhere—often from other planes—to serve the summoner. Normally, a summoning power includes all the information needed to summon and control a creature, as well as the creature's game statistics.

The following rules are a reference for summoning in general. As usual, if a particular power contains exceptions to these rules, the exception takes precedence.

Allied Creature: A summoned creature is an ally to its summoner and the summoner's allies.

Size, Speed, and Position: The power specifies the summoned creature's size and speed, and it determines where the creature appears.

Summoner's Defenses: The summoned creature's defenses equal the summoner's, not including any temporary bonuses or penalties.

Hit Points: The summoned creature's maximum hit points equal the summoner's bloodied value. When the summoned creature drops to 0 hit points, it is destroyed, and the summoner loses a healing surge. If the summoner has no healing surges left, the summoner instead takes damage equal to half his or her bloodied value.

The summoned creature lacks healing surges, but if an effect allows it to spend a healing surge, the summoner can spend a healing surge for it. The summoned creature, rather than the summoner, then gains the benefit of the healing surge.

Commanding the Creature: The summoned creature has no actions of its own; the summoner spends actions to command it mentally. The summoner can do so only if he or she has line of effect to the creature. When commanding the creature, the summoner shares its knowledge but not its senses.

The summoning power determines the special commands that the summoned creature can receive and gives an action type for each command. If a command is a minor action, it can be given only once per round.

If a summoned creature's description lacks a command for it to move, the summoner can take a minor action to command it to take one of the following actions, if it is physically capable of taking that action: crawl, escape, run, stand up, shift, squeeze, or walk.

Attacks and Checks: If a summoning power allows the summoned creature to attack, the summoner makes an attack through the creature, as specified in the power description. If the summoned creature can make a skill check or an ability check, the summoner makes the check. The attack or check uses the summoner's game statistics, unless the descriptions of the power or creature specify otherwise. Attacks and checks made through the creature do not include any temporary bonuses or penalties to the summoner's statistics.

Duration: The summoned creature lasts until the summoner takes a minor action to dismiss it or until the end of the encounter.

Teleportation
A teleportation power transports creatures or objects instantly from one location to another. Unless otherwise noted, use the normal teleportation rules (page 213) when a creature uses a teleportation power on a target, which might be itself, another creature, or an object.

Zone
Powers that have the zone keyword create zones, which are magical areas that last for a round or more. Unless otherwise noted, a zone uses the following rules.

Fills an Area: The zone fills each square in a specific area, which is usually a burst or a blast. The squares must be within line of effect of the origin square.

Unaffected by Attacks and the Environment: The zone cannot be attacked or physically affected, and terrain and environmental phenomena have no effect on it. For instance, a zone that deals fire damage is unaffected by a freezing environment.

Overlapping Zones: If zones overlap and impose penalties to the same roll or game statistic, a creature affected by the overlapping zones is subjected to the worst penalty; the penalties are not cumulative.

   Example: If a creature is affected by two overlapping zones that each impose a -2 penalty to all defenses, the creature takes a -2 penalty, not a -4 penalty.

Movable Zones: If the power used to create a zone allows it to be moved, it's a movable zone. At the end of the creator's turn, a movable zone ends if the creator doesn't have line of effect to at least 1 square of the zone or if the creator isn't within range (using the power's range) of at least 1 square of the zone.

   A zone can't be moved through blocking terrain.

Death Ends: A zone ends immediately if its creator dies.

CHAPTER 4

SKILLS

Has a wizard studied ancient tomes that describe the nature of magic and the structure of the universe? Does a rogue have a golden tongue that can pass off the most outrageous lies as truth? Does a fighter have a knack for getting information out of people? In the DUNGEONS & DRAGONS game, questions such as these are answered by the skills a character possesses.

Characters and monsters have a basic degree of competence in every skill. As a character advances in level, his or her degree of competence improves. A character's ability scores also affect his or her use of skills; a halfling rogue who has a high Dexterity is better at Acrobatics than a clumsy dwarf fighter who has a low Dexterity. When a creature uses a skill in the game, the outcome is determined by a skill check, a d20 roll that indicates whether—and sometimes how well—the creature accomplishes a skill-based task.

A studious nature, a golden tongue, a knack for extracting information—these are skills a character may possess.

This chapter presents everything players need to know about skills.

✦ **Skill Check Modifier:** How to calculate a character's skill check modifiers, including how skill training works.

✦ **Using Skills:** How to make a skill check, what the target number is, and how to make a check without rolling a die.

✦ **Knowledge Skills:** General rules for the skills that determine how much a character knows about the DUNGEONS & DRAGONS universe and the creatures that populate it.

✦ **Skill Descriptions:** Explanations of what creatures can do with the game's skills, from Acrobatics to Thievery.

✦ **Skill Challenges:** Information on how to set up a skill challenge, including how to determine difficulty and the consequences of success or failure.

SKILL CHECK MODIFIER

A creature has a skill check modifier for each skill.

A player should determine his or her adventurer's skill check modifier for each skill and record it on the character sheet.

JIM NELSON

A monster's skill check modifiers are listed in its stat block. If a skill check modifier is absent in a monster's stat block, then the monster uses its ability modifier related to that skill's key ability (see below).

A creature's skill check modifier for a skill always includes the following.

✦ One-half the creature's level
✦ The creature's ability modifier for the skill's key ability

Any of these other factors might also apply to a skill check modifier.

✦ A +5 bonus if the creature has training in the skill (see below)
✦ An armor check penalty if the adventurer is wearing certain kinds of armor and the skill's key ability is Strength, Dexterity, or Constitution
✦ Any racial or feat bonuses
✦ An item bonus from a magic item
✦ Any other bonuses or penalties that might apply

Skill Training

Having training in a skill means that a creature has some combination of formal instruction, practical experience, and natural aptitude using that skill. Skills a creature has training in are often called trained skills.

When a creature has training in a skill, it gains a +5 bonus to checks involving that skill. A creature can't gain training in a given skill more than once.

For adventurers, class descriptions specify how many skills a member of that class has training in and what skills the player can choose from at 1st level. For example, a player creating a 1st-level fighter (slayer) picks three skills from the slayer's list of class skills. Some feats, such as Skill Training, give an adventurer training in a skill even if it's not on the character's class skills list.

If a monster has any trained skills, those skills are listed in the bottom portion of its stat block. Perception is the only exception, and it appears in the top portion of the stat block whether the monster has training in it or not. For example, if a 2nd-level monster has 12 Strength and has training in Athletics, its stat block includes "Athletics +7" (5 for skill training + 1 for the monster's Strength modifier + 1 for one-half the monster's level), assuming it has no other modifiers to Athletics.

Key Ability

The Skills table below shows the skills available in the game and the key ability for each one. A skill's key ability determines the ability modifier used when calculating a creature's skill check modifier.

SKILLS

Skill	Key Ability		Skill	Key Ability
Acrobatics	Dexterity		Insight	Wisdom
Arcana	Intelligence		Intimidate	Charisma
Athletics	Strength		Nature	Wisdom
Bluff	Charisma		Perception	Wisdom
Diplomacy	Charisma		Religion	Intelligence
Dungeoneering	Wisdom		Stealth	Dexterity
Endurance	Constitution		Streetwise	Charisma
Heal	Wisdom		Thievery	Dexterity
History	Intelligence			

USING SKILLS

The Dungeon Master determines if a skill check is appropriate in a given situation and directs a player to make a check if circumstances call for one. A player often initiates a skill check by asking the DM if he or she can make one. Almost always, the DM says yes.

Making a skill check for a creature follows these steps.

1. Roll a d20.
2. Add the creature's skill check modifier for the skill.
3. Add any situational modifiers that apply, including any bonuses or penalties from powers affecting the creature.
4. Figure out the total, which is called the check result.
5. Compare the check result to the Difficulty Class (see below) to see if the check succeeds.

The elements of the check account for the creature's training, natural talent (ability modifier), overall experience (one-half the creature's level), other applicable factors (relevant bonuses), and sheer luck (a die roll).

Difficulty Class

When making skill checks, high results are best. A creature is always trying to meet or beat a certain number, referred to as the Difficulty Class (DC) of the check. A skill check's DC depends on what a creature is trying to accomplish with the skill check, and the number is set by the Dungeon Master.

Typically, a creature either succeeds or fails at a skill check, meaning that the check result meets or exceeds (beats) the DC or else falls below it. Some skill checks have degrees of success or failure that depend on the difference between the check result and the DC. Unless otherwise noted, when a creature fails a skill check, it can try again with a new check.

The skill entries in this chapter give sample DCs for common uses of the skills. Some DCs are fixed, whereas others scale with level. A fixed DC represents a task that gets easier as an adventurer gains levels. By the time an adventurer reaches the epic tier, certain tasks become trivial. In contrast, a DC that scales with level represents a task that remains at least a little challenging throughout an adventurer's career.

The Dungeon Master can use the suggested DC for a task or set one using the Difficulty Class by Level table. The table provides DCs at each level for three categories of difficulty: easy, moderate, and hard. When choosing a DC from the table, the Dungeon Master should use the level of the creature performing the check, unless otherwise noted.

DIFFICULTY CLASS BY LEVEL

Level	Easy	Moderate	Hard	Level	Easy	Moderate	Hard
1	8	12	19	16	16	22	31
2	9	13	20	17	16	23	31
3	9	13	21	18	17	23	32
4	10	14	21	19	17	24	33
5	10	15	22	20	18	25	34
6	11	15	23	21	19	26	35
7	11	16	23	22	20	27	36
8	12	16	24	23	20	27	37
9	12	17	25	24	21	28	37
10	13	18	26	25	21	29	38
11	13	19	27	26	22	29	39
12	14	20	28	27	22	30	39
13	14	20	29	28	23	30	40
14	15	21	29	29	23	31	41
15	15	22	30	30	24	32	42

The following definitions help the Dungeon Master determine which of the three DCs is appropriate for a particular check. The goal is to pick a DC that is an appropriate challenge for a particular scenario or encounter.

Easy: An easy DC is a reasonable challenge for creatures that do not have training in a particular skill. Such creatures have about a 65 percent chance of meeting an easy DC of their level. An easy DC is a minimal challenge for a creature that has training in the skill, and it is almost a guaranteed success for one that also has a high bonus with the skill. In group checks (page 128) or when every adventurer in a party is expected to attempt a given skill check, particularly when no one necessarily has training, an easy DC is the standard choice for the scenario.

Moderate: A moderate DC is a reasonable challenge for creatures that have training in a particular skill as well as for creatures that don't have training but do have a high score (18 or higher) in the skill's key ability. Such creatures have about a 65 percent chance of meeting a moderate DC of their level. In a skill challenge (page 157), a moderate DC is the standard choice for a skill check that a single creature is expected to make.

Hard: A hard DC is a reasonable challenge for creatures that have training in a particular skill and also have a high score (18 or higher) in the skill's key ability. Such creatures have about a 65 percent chance of meeting a hard DC of their level. A hard DC is the standard choice for a skill check that only an expert is expected to succeed at consistently.

Opposed Checks

Sometimes a creature makes a skill check that tests its ability against that of another creature using either the same skill or a different one. A creature's Stealth modifier, for instance, measures that creature's ability to hide against another creature's ability to spot it using the Perception skill. These skill contests are called opposed checks.

In an opposed check, two creatures make checks, and the higher result wins. If there's a tie, the creature with the higher skill check modifier wins. If it's still a tie, both sides roll again.

Checks without Rolls

In some situations, luck does not affect whether a skill check succeeds or fails. Two special types of checks reflect this fact: taking 10 and passive checks.

Taking 10 When creatures are not in a rush or not involved in an encounter or a skill challenge, they can choose to take 10 on a skill check. When a creature takes 10, its player doesn't roll a d20 for the skill check. Instead, the check result is determined as if the player had rolled a 10, meaning the result equals 10 + the creature's skill check modifier. For mundane tasks, taking 10 usually results in a success.

Passive Checks When creatures aren't actively using a skill, they're assumed to be taking 10 for any opposed checks using that skill. Doing so is called making a passive check. Passive checks are a convenient way to use creatures' skills without bogging the game down with die rolls.

For example, a group of adventurers is walking through an area without making Perception checks to look for danger, so each character is assumed to be using his or her passive Perception to notice hidden objects and creatures. If an adventurer's passive Perception beats a creature's Stealth check, the adventurer notices the creature without having to make a Perception check. If the adventurer's passive Perception and the creature's Stealth check are the same, the adventurer notices the creature if his or her Perception modifier is higher than the creature's Stealth modifier.

Passive checks are most commonly used for Perception checks and Insight checks, but the DM might also use a passive check for a skill such as Arcana or Dungeoneering to determine how much the characters know about a monster at the start of an encounter.

Aid Another

In some situations, creatures can work together to use a skill or an ability. A creature can help another make a skill check or an ability check by taking the aid another action. Given a choice, a group of adventurers should have the character who has the highest ability modifier or skill check modifier take the lead, while the other characters cooperate to provide assistance.

Aid Another

+ **Action:** Standard action. When a creature takes this action, it chooses a target adjacent to it.
+ **DC:** The assisting creature makes a skill check or an ability check against a DC equal to 10 + one-half its level.
+ **Success:** The target gains a +2 bonus to the next check using the same skill or ability before the end of the assisting creature's next turn.
+ **Failure:** The target takes a -1 penalty to the next check using the same skill or ability before the end of the assisting creature's next turn. This penalty represents the distraction or interference caused by the failed assistance.

A creature can affect a particular check only once using the aid another action. However, up to four creatures can use aid another to affect a single check.

In certain circumstances, the DM might decide that only fewer than four creatures—or even no creatures—can try to aid a check. For instance, it is unlikely that more than one creature can assist in picking a lock.

Group Checks

The Dungeon Master sometimes asks the adventurers to make a check as a group. Doing this is called making a group check, which is useful when a number of individuals are trying to accomplish something as a group. In such a situation, the characters who are skilled at a particular task help cover those who aren't.

To make a group check, everyone in the group makes a skill check or an ability check specified by the DM. A group check is almost always against an easy DC. If at least half the group succeeds, the whole group succeeds. Otherwise, the group fails.

Group checks might come up in a variety of situations: when the adventurers try to sneak past some sentries (using Stealth), try to scale a sheer cliff together (using Athletics), use disguises to pass as a group of orc soldiers (using Bluff), and so on. Such checks are particularly common in skill challenges, discussed later in this chapter.

KNOWLEDGE SKILLS

A character's skill in Arcana, Dungeoneering, History, Nature, and Religion helps determine what knowledge he or she possesses about particular topics. A character can use these skills to remember a useful bit of information or to recognize a clue related to one of these topics. Using a skill in this way is called making a knowledge check. With the exception of History, these skills can also be used to identify certain kinds of monsters, as noted in a skill's description.

Knowledge Checks

Refer to these rules whenever a creature is making a knowledge check, regardless of the skill it is using.

✦ **Action:** No action. A creature either knows or doesn't know the information.

✦ **DC:** See the Knowledge Checks table. The check DC increases based on the topic and how common the knowledge is. A Dungeon Master might decide that certain information is available only to creatures that have training in the appropriate knowledge skill.

✦ **Success:** The creature recalls a relevant piece of lore in the field of knowledge or recognizes a clue related to it.

✦ **Failure:** The creature doesn't recall any pertinent information. The Dungeon Master might allow a new check if further information comes to light.

KNOWLEDGE CHECKS

Information	DC
General	Easy
Specialized	Moderate
Esoteric	Hard

Monster Knowledge Checks

Refer to these rules whenever a character makes a check to identify a monster, regardless of the knowledge skill he or she is using. The DM typically tells a player which skill to use, based on the creature's origin or relevant keyword. If a monster's origin and keyword suggest the use of two different skills, the DM decides which skill can be used to identify the monster, and might allow the use of either skill. For example, a dracolich is both a natural creature and undead, but the DM might decide that its being undead is more relevant than its natural origin and require the use of Religion. In contrast, an abyssal ghoul is an elemental undead creature, and the DM might allow the use of either Arcana or Religion.

✦ **Action:** No action. A character either knows or doesn't know the information.

✦ **DC:** The DM sets the DC using the Difficulty Class by Level table (page 126), selecting the moderate DC for the monster's level instead of the level of the character making the check.

✦ **Success:** The character identifies the monster and knows its origin, type, typical temperament, and keywords. If the character meets or exceeds the hard DC for the monster's level, he or she also knows the monster's resistances and vulnerabilities, as well as what its powers do.

✦ **Failure:** The character doesn't recall any pertinent information about the monster. The Dungeon Master might allow a new check if further information comes to light.

Monster Origin or Keyword	Skill	Monster Origin or Keyword	Skill
Aberrant	Dungeoneering	Immortal	Religion
Construct	Arcana	Natural	Nature
Elemental	Arcana	Shadow	Arcana
Fey	Arcana	Undead	Religion

SKILL DESCRIPTIONS

The game's skills have many different uses—as many as players and DMs can imagine. Each skill is presented in the following format.

Key Ability: The first line of a skill description after the name of the skill shows the key ability for that skill. Use the ability modifier of a skill's key ability to help determine a creature's skill check modifier for that skill.

Armor Check Penalty: For skills based on Strength, Constitution, and Dexterity, the line containing the key ability also includes a reminder that an adventurer's armor check penalty (page 268) applies to that skill.

Typical Uses and DCs: A skill description describes typical ways that the skill is used. Each description provides sample DCs and specifies the kind of action that is usually required to use the skill. Some of the descriptions specify the consequences of success or failure.

If a skill provides a sample DC that says "easy," "moderate," or "hard," use the DC on the Difficulty Class by Level table that corresponds to the creature's level.

A few skill uses are marked as "Trained Only," which means a creature must have training in the skill to use it in that particular way. For instance, a creature must have training in Acrobatics to make a check to reduce falling damage when it falls.

Improvisation Suggestions: In addition to providing rules for the typical uses of a skill, some skill descriptions include suggestions in sidebars for how players and DMs might use the skill as they improvise various actions in the game. These suggestions include sample DCs.

Skills are meant to be open-ended, and players and DMs are encouraged to use them creatively. Just as for regular uses of a skill, the DM sets the DCs for improvisational uses, decides what sort of action is required for the checks, and determines the consequences of success or failure. The DM also has the final say on what a skill's possible uses are.

Acrobatics

Dexterity (Armor Check Penalty)
Creatures typically use the Acrobatics skill to maintain their balance while walking on narrow or unstable surfaces, to slip free of a grab or restraints, and to take less damage from a fall.

Moving across a surface that is slippery doesn't usually require an Acrobatics check; that surface is instead treated as difficult terrain (page 206). If a surface is extremely slippery, the DM might require an Acrobatics check to cross it.

Balance

Make an Acrobatics check to be able to move across a surface less than 1 foot wide (such as a ledge or a tightrope) or across an unstable surface (such as a wind-tossed rope bridge or a rocking log).

✦ **Action:** The check is usually part of a move action, but it can be part of any of the creature's actions that involve the creature moving.

✦ **DC:** See the Balance table.

✦ **Success:** The creature can move on the surface for the rest of the action, using squares of movement from the action. The creature must spend 1 extra square of movement for each square it enters on the surface. While on the surface, the creature grants combat advantage and might fall if it takes damage (see below).

✦ **Failure by 4 or Less:** The creature can't move any farther on the surface as part of the current action, but it doesn't fall.

+ **Failure by 5 or More:** If the creature is on a narrow surface, the creature falls off it (see "Falling," page 209). If the creature is trying to move across an unstable surface that isn't narrow, it instead falls prone (page 232). Either way, the creature can't move any farther as part of the current action.

Taking Damage while Balancing
While on a narrow or unstable surface, a creature must make a new Acrobatics check whenever it takes any damage.

+ **Action:** Free action. The check is a response to taking damage.
+ **DC:** See the Balance table.
+ **Success:** The creature maintains its balance.
+ **Failure:** If the creature is on a narrow surface, the creature falls off it. If the creature is on an unstable surface that isn't narrow, it instead falls prone.

BALANCE

Surface	Acrobatics DC
Unstable	Moderate
Narrow (less than 1 foot wide)	Moderate (+5 if unstable)
Very narrow (less than 6 inches wide)	Hard (+5 if unstable)

Escape from a Grab

The escape action allows the use of an Acrobatics check to wriggle out of a grab (see "Escape," page 243).

Escape from Restraints

Make an Acrobatics check to slip free of physical restraints such as manacles.

+ **Action:** The check takes 5 minutes of uninterrupted effort. Alternatively, a creature can make the check as a standard action, but doing so increases the DC by 5.
+ **DC:** Hard DC of the creature's level.
+ **Success:** The creature slips free of the restraint.
+ **Failure:** The creature can try again only if someone else provides assistance, most often by using the aid another action.

EVA WIDERMANN

Hop Down

Make an Acrobatics check to hop down 10 feet and land standing.

+ **Action:** The check is usually part of a move action, but it can be part of any of the creature's actions that involve the creature moving.
+ **DC:** DC 15. The creature can make this Acrobatics check only if the drop is no more than 10 feet.
+ **Success:** The creature hops down, lands standing, and takes no falling damage. The downward move uses no movement from the action.
+ **Failure:** The creature falls (see "Falling," page 209).

Reduce Falling Damage (Trained Only)

If a creature that has training in Acrobatics falls, it can make an Acrobatics check to reduce the amount of falling damage it takes. The creature can make this check whether or not the fall is intentional.

+ **Action:** Free action. The check is a response to falling.
+ **Result:** The amount of falling damage that the creature takes is reduced by one-half the check result (rounded down). If the falling damage is reduced to 0, the creature lands standing.

Example: The floor beneath Keira swings open to reveal a pit 40 feet deep. As a rogue, Keira has training in Acrobatics, so she makes an Acrobatics check to reduce the falling damage. When she hits the ground, she takes 24 damage (from a roll of 4d10). Her Acrobatics check result is 21, which is divided in half and rounded down for a result of 10. Keira's check reduces the damage by 10, so she instead takes 14 damage from the fall.

IMPROVISING WITH ACROBATICS

+ Slide down a staircase on a shield while standing (hard DC)
+ Somersault over a creature of the same size (hard DC)
+ Swing from a chandelier (moderate DC)
+ Impress onlookers with an acrobatic performance (moderate DC)

Arcana

Intelligence

The Arcana skill encompasses knowledge about magic-related lore and magical effects. Training in this skill represents academic study, either formalized or as a hobby. This knowledge can touch on any source of magical power—whether arcane, divine, primal, or another one—and extends to information about the following planes of existence, including the creatures native to those planes: the Elemental Chaos, the Feywild, and the Shadowfell. Those that have training

in Arcana also have a chance to know something about the mysterious Far Realm, but not about its creatures (such knowledge falls under the Dungeoneering skill). A creature can sometimes use its knowledge of magic to interact with or manipulate magical phenomena.

Arcana Knowledge

Make an Arcana check to recall a relevant piece of magic-related lore or to recognize a magic-related clue (see "Knowledge Checks," page 129).

A creature must have training in Arcana to possess information about the Far Realm.

Monster Knowledge
Construct, Elemental, Fey, and Shadow

Refer to these rules whenever a character makes a check to identify a mon-ster, regardless of the knowledge skill he or she is using. The DM typically tells a player which skill to use, based on the creature's origin or relevant keyword. If a monster's origin and keyword suggest the use of two different skills, the DM decides which skill can be used to identify the monster, and might allow the use of either skill. For example, a dracolich is both a natu-ral creature and undead, but the DM might decide that its being undead is more relevant than its natural origin and require the use of Religion. In contrast, an abyssal ghoul is an elemental undead creature, and the DM might allow the use of either Arcana or Religion.

MAGICAL RITUALS

Rituals are complex ceremonies that create magical effects, such as raising the dead or opening portals to other planes of existence. To perform such a ritual, a character needs to read from a book or a scroll that contains the ritual.

Ritual books and scrolls await discovery in ancient libraries, laboratories, and vaults, and they are sometimes for sale by purveyors of magic.

A ritual book can be used again and again, but a ritual scroll turns to dust once its ritual is performed. Performing a ritual requires a certain amount of time as well as special ritual components. The one type of component that can be used with almost any ritual is *residuum*, the silvery dust produced when a magic item is disenchanted.

Detect Magic (Trained Only)

Creatures that have training in Arcana can use the skill to identify magical effects and to sense the presence of magic.

Identify Conjuration or Zone

Make an Arcana check to identify a conjuration or a zone.

+ **Action:** Minor action. The creature must be able to perceive the conjuration or the zone.

+ **DC:** Moderate DC of the conjuration's or the zone's level.

+ **Success:** The creature identifies the power used to create the conjuration or the zone and knows the effects and keywords of the conjuration or the zone.

+ **Failure:** The creature can't try to identify the effect again until after a short rest.

Identify Magical Phenomenon

Make an Arcana check to identify a magical phenomenon that was created by a magical ritual or that is part of the environment, such as glowing runes on a cavern wall, an eldritch sign glimmering on an altar, a waterfall that flows upward, or a piece of earth floating in the air. This use of the skill is not normally used to identify powers, magic items, or their effects.

+ **Action:** Standard action. The creature must be able to perceive the phenomenon.

+ **DC:** Hard DC of the phenomenon's level. If it has no level, use the hard DC of the creature's level.

+ **Success:** The creature identifies the phenomenon's power source and other keywords, if any, as well as the phenomenon's basic purpose if it's not obvious. If a magical ritual created the phenomenon, the creature identifies the ritual and is familiar with its effects.

+ **Failure:** The creature can't try to identify the phenomenon again until after an extended rest.

Sense the Presence of Magic

Make an Arcana check to sense the presence of magic in an area. Typically creatures use the skill in this way when no magic is observable, but they suspect it is present.

+ **Action:** Standard action. The creature attempts to detect each source of magical energy within a number of squares equal to 5 + its level, ignoring all barriers.

+ **DC:** Hard DC of the creature's level. The creature automatically succeeds in detecting any source of magical energy within range that is five or more levels lower than its level.

+ **Success:** The creature detects each source of magical energy within range and learns its power sources, if any. If a source of magical energy is within line of sight, the creature pinpoints its location. If it's not within line of sight, the creature knows the direction from which the magical energy emanates but does not know how far away it is.

+ **Failure:** The creature detects nothing, or nothing is within range to detect. The creature can't try again until after a short rest.

IMPROVISING WITH ARCANA

+ Change the visible or audible qualities of one's magical powers when using them (moderate DC)
+ Control a phenomenon by manipulating its magical energy (hard DC)
+ Contribute to a negotiation with an elemental, fey, or shadow creature by exploiting knowledge of its behavior or culture (hard DC)

Athletics

Strength (Armor Check Penalty)

Creatures use the Athletics skill to attempt physical activities that rely on muscular strength, including climbing, escaping from a grab, jumping, and swimming.

Climb

Make an Athletics check to climb up or down a surface. A creature that has a climb speed (page 203) doesn't have to make Athletics checks to climb.

+ **Action:** The check is usually part of a move action, but it can be part of any of the creature's actions that involve the creature moving.

+ **DC:** See the Climb table. If a creature can brace itself between two surfaces, it gains a +5 bonus to the check.

+ **Success:** The creature can climb on the surface for the rest of the action, using squares of movement from the action. The creature must spend 1 extra square of movement for each square it enters on the surface. While climbing, a creature grants combat advantage and might fall if it takes damage (see below).

   When a climber moves from a vertical surface to a horizontal surface, such as when climbing out of a pit, the climber chooses to arrive either standing or prone.

+ **Failure by 4 or Less:** If the creature was already climbing, it doesn't fall. If the creature was trying to start climbing, it fails to do so. Either way, the creature can't move any farther as part of the current action.

+ **Failure by 5 or More:** If the creature was already climbing, it falls (see "Falling," page 209) but can try to catch hold (see below). If the creature was trying to start climbing, it fails to do so. Either way, the creature can't move any farther as part of the current action.

Example: Fargrim the fighter has a speed of 5 and is 2 squares away from a brick wall that he wants to climb. He takes the walk action and moves 2 squares toward the wall. He then makes an Athletics check as part of the same action and gets a result of 20, enough to start climbing. He's able to climb up only 1 square, however, since each square of the climb costs 1 extra square of movement, and he has only 3 squares of movement left. He ends the action 1 square up the wall.

Taking Damage while Climbing
While climbing, a creature must make a new Athletics check if it takes damage.

+ **Action:** Free action. The check is a response to taking damage.
+ **DC:** See the Climb table. If the damage bloodies the creature, the DC increases by 5.
+ **Success:** The creature holds on.
+ **Failure:** The creature falls but can try to catch hold (see below).

Catching Hold
A creature that falls while climbing can make an Athletics check to catch hold of something to stop the fall immediately.

+ **Action:** Free action. The check is a response to falling.
+ **DC:** See the Climb table, and add 5 to the normal DC.
+ **Success:** The creature doesn't fall.
+ **Failure:** The creature falls and can't try to catch hold again as part of this fall.

CLIMB

Surface	Athletics DC
Ladder	0
Rope	10
Uneven surface (cave wall)	15
Rough surface (brick wall)	20
Slippery surface	+5
Unusually smooth surface	+5

EVA WIDERMANN

Escape from a Grab

The escape action allows the use of an Athletics check to muscle out of a grab (see "Escape," page 243).

Jump

Make an Athletics check to jump vertically to reach a dangling rope or a high ledge or to jump horizontally to leap over a pit, a patch of difficult terrain, a low wall, or some other obstacle.

Simply scrambling onto a terrain feature such as a table or a chair doesn't require an Athletics check, because such terrain features are usually difficult terrain (page 206).

High Jump

Make an Athletics check to make a high jump, usually to reach or grab hold of something overhead.

✦ **Action:** The check is usually part of a move action, but it can be part of any of the creature's actions that involve the creature moving.

✦ **Result:** Divide the check result by 10 (round down). This value is the number of feet the creature jumps up, or in other words, the height that the creature's feet clear.

All the squares of the jump, if any, use squares of movement from the action. The High Jump table summarizes the total distances of various high jumps based on Athletics check results. If the creature runs out of movement before landing on something or grabbing onto something, it falls. However, if the jump was part of a move action, the creature can continue the jump as part of a double move (page 205), ending the first move action in midair and continuing the jump as part of the second move action. The creature makes a single Athletics check for the jump but can use squares of movement from both actions for it.

✦ **Running Start:** If the creature moves at least 2 squares as part of the action and then jumps, double the result before dividing by 10 (or simply divide the result by 5).

✦ **Reaching Something:** To determine whether the creature can reach something while jumping, calculate what one-third of the creature's height is (round down to the nearest inch). This extra one-third represents the length of a creature's arms. Add that number to the creature's height and the distance cleared based on its Athletics check.

Example: A 6-foot-tall creature would add 2 for its arms' length for a total of 8 feet, which would then be added to the distance cleared. A 4-foot-tall creature would add 5 feet to the distance.

If a creature jumps and doesn't have a height specified, consult the Vertical Reach table and use the value noted for the creature's size. For example, if a Large creature's height is unknown, add 15 feet to the result of its Athletics check to determine whether it can reach something.

HIGH JUMP

Athletics Result	Distance Cleared
9 or lower	0 feet
10-19	1 foot
20-29	2 feet
30-39	3 feet
40-49	4 feet
And so on . . .	

VERTICAL REACH

Creature Size	Vertical Reach
Tiny	2½ feet
Small	10 feet
Medium	10 feet
Large	15 feet
Huge	25 feet
Gargantuan	35 feet

Example: Dendric, a 6-foot-tall human fighter, attempts a high jump to catch a rope dangling 12 feet overhead. His check result is 26. If Dendric leaps from a standing position, he can't quite reach the end of the rope (26 ÷ 10 = 2 feet plus 1⅓ × his height [8 feet] for a final reach of 10 feet). If Dendric leaps with a running start, he can reach the end of the rope (52 ÷ 10 = 5 feet plus 1⅓ × his height [8 feet] for a final reach of 13 feet).

Long Jump

Make an Athletics check to make a long jump.

+ **Action:** The check is usually part of a move action, but it can be part of any of the creature's actions that involve the creature moving.

+ **Result:** Divide the Athletics check result by 10 (rounded down). This determines the number of squares the creature clears with the jump. The creature lands 1 square beyond the squares it clears. All the squares of the jump, including the landing square, use squares of movement from the action. The Long Jump table summarizes the total distances of various long jumps, including the landing square.

  If the creature ends the movement over a drop, it falls and can't move any farther as part of the current action. If the creature runs out of movement before landing, it also falls. However, if the jump was part of a move action, the creature can continue the jump as part of a double move (page 205), ending the first move action in midair and continuing the jump as part of the second move action. The creature makes a single Athletics check for the jump but can use squares of movement from both actions for it.

+ **Running Start:** If the creature moves at least 2 squares as part of the action and then jumps, double the result before dividing by 10 (or simply divide the result by 5).

✦ **Distance Cleared Vertically:** To determine the number of feet that the creature clears vertically during the long jump, divide the check result by 10 and then add 2 if the result is at least 1. If the creature doesn't jump high enough to clear an obstacle along the way, it hits the obstacle, falls prone (page 232), and can't move any farther as part of the current action.

LONG JUMP

Athletics Result	Distance Cleared	Total Move
9 or lower	0 squares	0 squares
10-19	1 square (3 feet up)	2 squares
20-29	2 squares (4 feet up)	3 squares
30-39	3 squares (5 feet up)	4 squares
40-49	4 squares (6 feet up)	5 squares

And so on . . .

Example: Lyriel the fighter attempts a long jump to leap over a 2-square-wide pit and clear the 5-foot-high wall of thorns beyond it. Her check result is 24. With a running start, she easily jumps the distance [(24 × 2) ÷ 10 = 4 squares] and clears the wall (4 + 2 = 6 feet). If Lyriel jumps from a standing position, she jumps over the pit (24 ÷ 10 = 2 squares) but doesn't clear the wall (2 + 2 = 4 feet). She hits the wall of thorns and falls prone—right into the pit.

Swim

Make an Athletics check to swim, which includes treading water. A creature that has a swim speed (page 203) doesn't have to make Athletics checks to swim or tread water.

Creatures that hold their breath for more than 3 minutes or that take damage while holding their breath risk suffocation (page 180). See the Endurance skill for information on swimming or treading water for an hour or more. See "Currents," page 207, for rules on swimming in a strong current.

✦ **Action:** The check is usually part of a move action, but it can be part of any of the creature's actions that involve the creature moving.

✦ **DC:** See the Swim table.

✦ **Success:** The creature can swim for the rest of the action, using squares of movement from the action. The creature must spend 1 extra square of movement for each square it enters while swimming. Alternatively, the creature simply stays afloat, treading water.

✦ **Failure by 4 or Less:** The creature can't move any farther as part of the current action, but it treads water.

✦ **Failure by 5 or More:** The creature can't move any farther as part of the current action and sinks 1 square.

SWIM

Water	Athletics DC
Calm	10
Rough	15
Stormy	20

IMPROVISING WITH ATHLETICS

✦ Hang onto a wagon while being dragged behind it (hard DC)
✦ Force your way through an earthen tunnel that is too small for you (hard DC)
✦ Move into a strong headwind while flying (moderate DC)

Bluff

Charisma

Characters use the Bluff skill to make what's false seem true, what's outrageous seem plausible, and what's suspicious seem ordinary. A character makes a Bluff check to fast-talk a guard, con a merchant, gamble, pass off a disguise, fake a piece of documentation, or mislead in some other way.

✦ **Action:** Standard action. A Dungeon Master might allow a creature to make a Bluff check as part of another action, depending on what a creature wants to do.

✦ **Opposed Check:** Against a target's passive Insight, or against the target's Insight check if it is actively trying to see through the deception. A creature can make the check against multiple targets at once, opposing the passive Insight of each target with a single Bluff check.

✦ **Success:** The deception is successful against the target that opposed the check.

✦ **Failure:** The target doesn't believe the deception. If the check fails by 5 or more, the DM might rule that additional Bluff checks against the target for the same deception are impossible, or that those checks take a -5 penalty.

Gain Combat Advantage

Make a Bluff check to gain combat advantage against an enemy by feinting.

✦ **Action:** Standard action. A creature can take this action only once per encounter.

✦ **Opposed Check:** Against an adjacent target's passive Insight.

✦ **Success:** The feinting creature gains combat advantage against the target until the end of the feinting creature's next turn.

Create a Diversion to Hide

Make a Bluff check to create a diversion and become hidden using the Stealth skill (page 152).

+ **Action:** Standard action. A creature can take this action only once per encounter.

+ **Opposed Check:** Against a target's passive Insight. The target must be able to see the creature creating the diversion. A creature can make the check against multiple targets at once, opposing the passive Insight of each target with a single Bluff check.

+ **Success:** The creature can immediately make a Stealth check opposed by the passive Perception of any target that failed the opposed Bluff check. If the Stealth check succeeds against a target, the creature becomes hidden from that target until the end of the current turn or until immediately after the hidden creature makes an attack.

IMPROVING WITH BLUFF

+ Entice a guard into leaving its post (hard DC)
+ Impersonate someone's voice convincingly (hard DC)
+ Entertain a crowd with a tall tale (moderate DC)

Diplomacy

Charisma

Creatures use the Diplomacy skill to influence others using tact, subtlety, and social grace. (Monsters rarely make Diplomacy checks.) Make a Diplomacy check to change opinions, inspire good will, haggle with a merchant, demonstrate proper etiquette and decorum, or negotiate a deal in good faith.

+ **Action:** Standard action. A Dungeon Master might allow a creature to make a Diplomacy check as a free action.

+ **DC:** The Dungeon Master sets the DC using the Difficulty Class by Level table. The target's attitude (friendly or unfriendly, peaceful or hostile) and other temporary modifiers (such as what the creature performing the check is seeking to accomplish) might apply to the DC. The DC might also be affected by the number of targets the creature is trying to influence at once.

+ **Success:** The creature achieves the desired influence. This might be the first of several successes—perhaps part of a skill challenge—required to fully influence a target.

HOWARD LYON

IMPROVISING WITH DIPLOMACY

+ Comfort a distraught person (moderate DC)
+ Display proper etiquette at a formal event (moderate DC)
+ Give a pleasing speech (easy DC)
+ Give an inspiring speech (hard DC)

Dungeoneering

Wisdom

The Dungeoneering skill represents knowledge and skills related to dungeon exploration, including finding one's way through underground complexes, navigating winding caverns, recognizing subterranean hazards, and foraging for food in the Underdark.

Training in this skill represents formalized study or extensive experience. Those that have training in the skill can also identify creatures of the Far Realm.

Dungeoneering Knowledge

Make a Dungeoneering check to recall a relevant piece of lore about an underground environment or to recognize an underground hazard or clue (see "Knowledge Checks," page 129).

Examples of dungeoneering knowledge include determining cardinal directions while underground (hard DC), recognizing a dangerous underground plant (moderate DC), spotting new carvings or construction (moderate DC), and noticing a change in depth while exploring an area (moderate DC).

Monster Knowledge

Aberrant

Make a Dungeoneering check to identify a creature that has the aberrant origin (see "Monster Knowledge Checks," page 130).

Forage

Make a Dungeoneering check to locate and gather food and water in an underground environment that includes pools of water, edible fungi or lichen, small vermin, or the like.

+ **Action:** The check takes 1 hour of effort.
+ **DC:** DC 15 to find food and water for one person, or DC 25 for up to five people. The DM might adjust the DC in different environments: 5 lower in a cultivated environment or 5 higher in a barren one.
+ **Success:** The creature finds enough food and water for 24 hours.
+ **Failure:** The creature finds no food or water. The creature must wait 24 hours to try again in the same area.

IMPROVISING WITH DUNGEONEERING

+ Determine how to cause part of a tunnel to collapse (hard DC)
+ Figure out the direction to a source of moving air while underground (moderate DC)
+ Leave well-placed marks to avoid getting lost underground (easy DC)

Endurance

Constitution (Armor Check Penalty)

The Endurance skill is used to stave off ill effects and to push beyond normal physical limits. A creature that has training in Endurance can hold its breath for long periods of time, forestall the debilitating effects of hunger and thirst, and swim or tread water for extended periods. Some hazards—including extreme temperatures, violent weather, and diseases—require creatures to make Endurance checks to resist or delay debilitating effects.

IMPROVISING WITH ENDURANCE

+ Quaff an entire stein of ale in one go (moderate DC)
+ Roll down a steep slope without taking damage (moderate DC)
+ Sustain a swift rowing pace for an extended period (hard DC)

Characters rarely use Endurance actively; the DM directs players to use it in response to certain hazards. Using the skill in that way requires no action, unless otherwise noted. See "Environmental Dangers," page 178, and "Disease," page 184, for some of the situations that require Endurance checks.

Swimming for an Hour or More

A creature that does not have a swim speed (page 203) and swims for more than an hour must make an Endurance check.

+ **Action:** Free action. The creature makes the check at the end of each hour of swimming.
+ **DC:** Use the appropriate DC from the Swim table (page 140) and increase it by 2 for each hour of swimming.
+ **Success:** The creature can continue making Athletics checks to swim.
+ **Failure:** The creature can't make any further Athletics checks to swim until after an extended rest. In addition, the creature sinks 1 square and risks suffocation. The creature can still be dragged along by an ally at half speed.

Heal

Wisdom
The Heal skill is used to help others recover from wounds or debilitating conditions, including disease.

First Aid

Make a Heal check to administer first aid to a subject.

+ **Action:** Standard action. The subject must be adjacent to the creature performing first aid.
+ **DC:** The DC depends on which of the following tasks the creature attempts.

   Grant Second Wind (DC 10): The subject can use its second wind (page 248), if available, without taking an action. The subject doesn't gain the defense bonus normally granted by second wind, but still gains any other benefits associated with its second wind, such as a benefit granted by a class feature or a feat.

   Grant a Saving Throw (DC 15): The subject can either make a saving throw immediately or gain a +2 bonus to a saving throw at the end of its next turn.

IMPROVISING WITH HEAL

+ Ascertain whether a creature is dead (easy DC)
+ Discern whether a seemingly dead or living creature is undead (opposed by Bluff)
+ Deduce what kind of weapon caused an injury (moderate DC)
+ Diagnose a disease affecting a creature (hard DC of the disease's level)

Stabilize the Dying (DC 15): If the subject is dying, the subject stops making death saving throws until it takes damage. Being stabilized does not change the subject's current hit point total.

Treat Disease

Make a Heal check to treat a subject infected by a disease.

+ **Action:** Rather than taking a particular action, the creature must attend the subject periodically throughout an extended rest taken by the subject and make a Heal check when the rest ends. The attending creature can take an extended rest at the same time.
+ **Result:** The check result determines the disease's effects if the result is higher than the result of the Endurance check (or other check) that the subject makes against the disease.

History

Intelligence

The History skill encompasses knowledge related to the history of a region and beyond, including the chronological record of significant events and an explanation of their causes. This knowledge includes information pertaining to royalty and other leaders, wars, legends, important personalities, laws, customs, traditions, and memorable events.

Training in this skill represents academic study, either formalized or as a hobby. Those that have training in the skill are likely to know esoteric historical information.

Make a History check to remember a relevant piece of historical lore or to recognize a historical clue (see "Knowledge Checks," page 129).

IMPROVISING WITH HISTORY

+ Inspire a receptive militia with tales of its heroic ancestors (moderate DC)
+ Locate the secret tomb of a bandit prince by interpreting the chronicles of his final days (hard DC)
+ Recite a canto from one of the epic poems of old (hard DC)
+ Win a game such as chess using historic strategies (hard DC)

Insight

Wisdom

The Insight skill is used to discern intent and decipher body language during social interactions. Characters use the skill to comprehend motives, to read between the lines, to get a sense of moods and attitudes, and to determine how truthful someone is being. (Monsters rarely use Insight.)

Insight is used to oppose Bluff checks and as the social counterpart to the Perception skill. The skill can also be used to gain clues, to figure out how well a social situation is going, and to determine if someone is under the influence of an outside force.

When a creature uses Insight, it is making a best guess about another creature's motives and truthfulness. Insight is not an exact science or a supernatural power; it represents the ability to get a sense of how a person is behaving.

✦ **Action:** Minor action. No action is required when opposing a Bluff check. The creature needs some amount of interaction with a target to interpret its words or behavior.

✦ **DC:** See the Insight table, except when countering a Bluff check, which is an opposed check.

✦ **Success:** The creature counters a Bluff check, gains a clue about a social situation, or senses an outside influence on someone.

✦ **Failure:** The creature can't try again until circumstances change.

INSIGHT

Task	Insight DC
Sense motives or attitude	Moderate DC of the target's level
Sense outside influence	Hard DC of the effect's level

IMPROVISING WITH INSIGHT

✦ Read the mood of a crowd (easy DC)
✦ Discern who among a cagey group is the leader (moderate DC)
✦ Interpret enemies' hand signs (hard DC)
✦ Recognize a creature as illusory (moderate DC of the effect's level)

Intimidate

Charisma

An adventurer can make an Intimidate check to influence others through hostile actions, overt threats, or deadly persuasion. (Monsters can't intimidate adventurers.)

✦ **Action:** Standard action. Outside combat, the DM might allow an adventurer to make the check as part of another action.

+ **Opposed Check:** Against a monster's Will. (Adventurers can also try to intimidate DM-controlled characters.) The monster gains a +5 bonus to Will against the check if it is unfriendly to the adventurer, or a +10 bonus if it is hostile. If an adventurer attempts to intimidate multiple monsters at once, make a separate Intimidate check against each monster's Will. Each monster must be able to see and hear the adventurer.

  If a monster doesn't have defenses specified, the DM should select an appropriate DC from the Difficulty Class by Level table, usually a moderate or a hard DC of the adventurer's level.

  This check fails automatically against a monster that is immune to fear. The DM might decide that this check also fails automatically against a monster, such as a golem or a skeleton, that acts under some form of magical compulsion.

+ **Success:** The adventurer forces a bloodied monster to surrender, gets a monster to reveal a secret, or cows a monster into taking some other action. This skill is not mind control, so a cowed monster is unlikely to take any action that would cause immediate harm to itself.

+ **Failure:** In combat, the adventurer can't try again against the monster during the same encounter.

+ **Target Becomes Hostile:** Whether or not the check succeeds, using this skill against a monster usually makes it unfriendly or hostile toward the adventurer.

IMPROVISING WITH INTIMIDATE

+ Get an unruly crowd to move out of the way (hard DC)
+ Badger allied soldiers into a fighting mood (moderate DC)
+ Goad a person into action (hard DC)

Nature

Wisdom

The Nature skill encompasses knowledge and skills related to nature, including finding ways through wilderness, recognizing natural hazards, dealing with and identifying natural creatures, and living off the land.

Training in this skill represents formalized study or extensive experience. Those that have training in the skill are likely to know esoteric information in the field of study.

Nature Knowledge

Make a Nature check to recall a relevant piece of lore about the natural world—terrain, climate, weather, plants, or seasons—or to recognize a nature-related clue (see "Knowledge Checks," page 129).

Examples of Nature knowledge include determining cardinal directions or finding a path (easy DC), recognizing a dangerous plant or another natural hazard (moderate DC), or predicting a coming change in the weather (moderate DC).

Monster Knowledge
Natural
Make a Nature check to identify a creature that has the natural origin (see "Monster Knowledge Checks," page 130).

Forage
Make a Nature check to locate and gather food and water in the wilderness.

+ **Action:** The check takes 1 hour of effort.
+ **DC:** DC 15 to find food and water for one person, or DC 25 for up to five people. The DM might adjust the DC in different environments: 5 lower in a cultivated environment or 5 higher in a barren one.
+ **Success:** The creature finds enough food and water for 24 hours.
+ **Failure:** The creature finds no food or water. The creature must wait 24 hours to try again in the same area.

Calm Animal
Make a Nature check to calm a natural beast. For instance, a character might use this check to get a wild horse to let him or her ride it.

+ **Action:** Standard action.
+ **DC:** Hard DC of the beast's level. The check fails automatically against a beast that the character's group is fighting.
+ **Success:** The beast is calmed.

Train Animal
Make a Nature check to teach a natural beast a simple trick (come, fetch, heel, stay, and so forth). This use of the skill is usually part of a skill challenge, which might take much longer than an encounter to complete.

IMPROVISING WITH NATURE
+ Camouflage a trap or some other construction in a natural setting (opposed by Perception)
+ Build a shelter that provides some protection against harsh weather (moderate DC)

Perception

Wisdom

The Perception skill encompasses perceiving things, most often by sight or sound. Make a Perception check to notice a clue, detect a secret door, find a trap, follow tracks, listen for sounds behind a closed door, or locate a hidden object.

In most situations, the DM uses passive Perception to determine if a creature notices things. A creature that has fallen asleep naturally (as opposed to being knocked unconscious by a power or other effect) is unconscious, but not totally deprived of awareness; it can use its passive Perception to hear things, but with a –5 penalty.

Perceive Something

Make a Perception check to perceive something, such as a hidden door, a concealed object, a group of creatures talking, or a monster's tracks.

- ✦ **Action:** Minor action. No action is required when the DM is using a creature's passive Perception. Carefully searching an area (the creature's space and squares adjacent to it) requires 1 minute or more.
- ✦ **DC:** The DM chooses a DC from the Listen table, the Spot table, or the Find Tracks table.
- ✦ **Success:** The creature perceives something. If the creature is carefully searching an area, it finds something, assuming there's something to find.

Find a Hidden Creature

Make a Perception check to try to find a hidden creature (see "Stealth," page 152). If a creature finds a hidden creature, it might point the hidden creature out to others, resulting in them knowing its location.

- ✦ **Action:** Minor action.
- ✦ **Opposed Check:** Against a target creature's Stealth check. The DM might apply relevant modifiers from the Listen and Spot tables, depending on how the creature is trying to find a hidden target.
- ✦ **Success:** The target is no longer hidden from the creature. If the creature performing the check cannot see the target for some other reason, such as magical invisibility, it still knows where the target is located.

LISTEN

Noise	Perception DC
Battle	0
Normal conversation	Easy
Whispers	Hard
Through a door	+5
Through a wall	+10
More than 10 squares away	+2

SPOT

Obscured Thing	Perception DC
Barely obscured	Easy
Well obscured	Hard
More than 10 squares away	+2

FIND TRACKS

Find Tracks	Perception DC
Soft ground (snow, loose dirt, mud)	Moderate
Hard ground (wood or stone)	Hard
Rain or snow since tracks were made	+10
Each day since tracks were made	+2
Quarry obscured its tracks	+5
Huge or larger creature	-5
Group of ten or more	-5

IMPROVISING WITH PERCEPTION

✦ Sense the true direction of an echoing sound (hard DC)
✦ Smell a fresh, concealed corpse (hard DC)
✦ Notice that terrain or an object is illusory (moderate DC of the effect's level)

Religion

Intelligence

The Religion skill encompasses knowledge about gods, sacred writings, religious ceremonies, holy symbols, and theology. This knowledge extends to information about the undead and about the Astral Sea, including the creatures of that plane.

Training in this skill represents academic study, either formalized or as a hobby. Those that have training in the skill are likely to know esoteric information in the field of study.

Religion Knowledge

Make a Religion check to recall a piece of relevant religious lore or to recognize a religion-related clue (see "Knowledge Checks," page 129).

Monster Knowledge

Immortal and Undead

Make a Religion check to identify a creature that has the immortal origin or the undead keyword (see "Monster Knowledge Checks," page 130).

IMPROVISING WITH RELIGION
+ Craft a simple nonmagical holy symbol or other sacred object (moderate DC)
+ Preside over a known religious ceremony (moderate DC)
+ Soothe grief-stricken or panicked peasants by chanting a hymn (hard DC)

Stealth

Dexterity (Armor Check Penalty)

Creatures use the Stealth skill to conceal themselves from enemies, slink past guards, slip away without being noticed, and sneak up on others without being detected.

+ **Action:** The check is usually at the end of a move action, but it can be at the end of any of the creature's actions that involve the creature moving.

+ **Opposed Check:** Against the passive Perception of each target creature present. If the creature moves more than 2 squares during the action, it takes a -5 penalty to the Stealth check. If the creature runs (page 248), the penalty is -10.

   A creature can make a Stealth check against a target only if the creature has superior cover (page 219) or total concealment (page 220) against that target or if the creature is outside the target's line of sight. Outside combat, the DM might allow a creature to make a Stealth check against a distracted target, even if the creature doesn't have superior cover or total concealment and isn't outside the target's line of sight. The target might be focused on something in a different direction, allowing the creature to sneak around it.

+ **Success:** The creature becomes hidden from the target. Being hidden means being silent and invisible (see "Invisibility," page 221).

+ **Remaining Hidden:** The creature remains hidden as long as it meets these requirements.

   Keep out of Sight: If the creature no longer has any cover or concealment from a target, it doesn't remain hidden from the target. The creature doesn't need superior cover, total concealment, or to stay outside line of sight, but it at least needs partial cover or partial concealment from a target to remain hidden. A hidden creature can't use another creature as cover to remain hidden.

Keep Quiet: If the creature speaks louder than a whisper or otherwise draws attention to itself with a noise, it doesn't remain hidden from any creature that can hear it.

Keep Still: If the creature moves more than 2 squares during an action, it must make a Stealth check to remain hidden, with a –5 penalty, or a –10 penalty if the creature runs. If any creature's passive Perception beats the check result, it doesn't remain hidden from that creature.

Don't Attack: If the creature makes an attack, it doesn't remain hidden.

✦ **Not Remaining Hidden:** If the creature takes an action that causes it not to remain hidden, the creature retains the benefits of being hidden, such as combat advantage, until the action is resolved. The creature can't become hidden again as part of that same action.

Also, if an enemy tries to enter the creature's space, the creature doesn't remain hidden from that enemy.

Example: After shooting a goblin with her crossbow, Keira uses *acrobatic maneuver* to move 4 squares through a doorway into an adjacent room. From her new position, the goblin does not have line of sight to her, so she can make a Stealth check to become hidden as part of the movement of her *acrobatic maneuver*. Because she moved more than 2 squares, though, she takes a –5 penalty to her Stealth check. She rolls a 12, adds her Stealth check modifier (+9) and subtracts the penalty for movement for a result of 16. Her check result is higher than the goblin's passive Perception of 13, so she is hidden from it. The goblin moves during its turn, but Keira still has partial cover from it even after the goblin's movement, so she remains hidden. During her next turn, Keira uses a rogue power that allows her to move 2 squares before her attack. She moves 2 squares out into the open to get a clear shot and then shoots the goblin. Because her movement and attack are both part of the action that causes her to be no longer hidden, she retains the benefit of being hidden until after the attack is resolved.

She gains combat advantage and deals her Sneak Attack damage to the goblin. Keira can then use her move action to find a new position from which to make a Stealth check to become hidden again.

IMPROVISING WITH STEALTH

✦ Hide an object in a room (opposed by Perception)
✦ Craft a hidden compartment or sheath (moderate DC)
✦ Embed a secret message in a letter (opposed by Insight)

Streetwise

Charisma

The Streetwise skill encompasses knowledge of the ins and outs of life in a settlement (a village, a town, or a city), whether on its main streets or in its back alleys. This knowledge is gleaned from talking to people and observing them as they go about their lives, rather than from studying tomes or maps. A character who has training in this skill is especially adept at getting information out of people living in settlements.

When in a settlement, make a Streetwise check to find out what's going on, who the movers and shakers are, where to get the best deals, and where the dangers are.

- ✦ **Action:** The check takes 1 hour of effort. The DM might allow a creature to use Streetwise as a knowledge skill, in which case the check requires no action; either a creature knows the answer or not.
- ✦ **DC:** See the Streetwise table.
- ✦ **Success:** The creature collects a useful bit of information, gathers rumors, finds out about available jobs, or locates the best deal. The creature usually avoids attracting unwanted attention in gathering this information.
- ✦ **Failure:** The creature can try again but is likely to attract unwanted attention.

HOWARD LYON

STREETWISE

Settlement and Information	Streetwise DC
Familiar settlement	Easy
Unfamiliar but typical settlement	Moderate
Foreign settlement	Hard
Information is secret or closely guarded	+10

IMPROVISING WITH STREETWISE

+ Lose pursuing guards down a series of alleys or in a crowd (opposed by Perception)
+ Deduce a person's profession by his or her dress (moderate DC)
+ Pick up a dialect of a known language (hard DC)
+ Notice that merchandise is counterfeit (hard DC)

Thievery

Dexterity (Armor Check Penalty)

The Thievery skill encompasses various abilities that require nerves of steel and a steady hand: disabling traps, opening locks, picking pockets, and sleight of hand.

The DM might decide that some uses of this skill are so specialized that a creature is required to have training in Thievery to have a chance of succeeding.

Disable Trap

Make a Thievery check to prevent a known trap from triggering. Some traps cannot be disabled using Thievery, as specified in those traps' stat blocks. See "Traps and Hazards," page 180.

+ **Action:** Standard action. Unless otherwise noted, the creature must be adjacent to part of the trap to try to disable it.

+ **DC:** A trap's description normally specifies the DC to disable it, generally the hard DC of its level. The creature gains a +2 bonus to the check if it uses thieves' tools.

+ **Success:** The creature disables the trap. Some traps, however, require multiple checks to be disabled.

+ **Failure by 4 or Less:** Nothing happens, unless the trap's description says otherwise.

+ **Failure by 5 or More:** The creature triggers the trap.

Open Lock

Make a Thievery check to pick a lock.

+ **Action:** Standard action. Unless otherwise noted, the creature must be adjacent to a lock to pick it.
+ **DC:** If a lock has no DC specified, use the hard DC of the creature's level. The DM might decide that a shoddy lock has a moderate DC instead. The creature gains a +2 bonus to the check if it uses thieves' tools.
+ **Success:** The creature picks the lock. A complicated lock might require multiple checks before it can be opened.

Pick Pocket

Make a Thievery check to lift a small object (such as a purse or a key) from a target creature without that creature being aware of the theft.

+ **Action:** Standard action. Unless otherwise noted, the creature must be adjacent to the target, and the target must not be holding the object.
+ **DC:** Hard DC of the target's level.
+ **Success:** The creature lifts a small object from the target without the target noticing.
+ **Failure by 4 or Less:** The creature fails to lift an object, but the target doesn't notice.
+ **Failure by 5 or More:** The creature fails to lift an object, and the target notices the attempt.

Sleight of Hand

Make a Thievery check to perform an act of legerdemain, such as palming an unattended object small enough to fit in the hand (a coin or a ring, for instance).

+ **Action:** Standard action. Unless otherwise noted, the creature performing the check must be adjacent to the object.
+ **Opposed Check:** Against the passive Perception of each creature present.
+ **Success:** The creature pulls off the sleight of hand.
+ **Failure:** The creature performs the sleight of hand but is obvious, unconvincing, or both.

IMPROVISING WITH THIEVERY

+ Fix a broken wagon (easy DC)
+ Craft a standard lock (moderate DC)
+ Bind a creature with rope (check result sets escape DC)

SKILL CHALLENGES

A skill challenge represents a series of tests that adventurers must face. Engaging in an audience with the duke, decoding a mysterious set of sigils in a hidden chamber, finding a safe path through a haunted forest—all of these situations present opportunities for skill challenges, because they take time and a variety of skills to overcome.

From disabling a complex trap to negotiating peace between warring nations, a skill challenge takes complex activities and structures them into a series of skill checks. A skill challenge should not replace the roleplaying, the puzzling, and the ingenuity that players put into handling those situations. Instead, it allows the Dungeon Master to define the adventurers' efforts within the rules structure so that the players understand their options and the DM can more easily adjudicate the outcome.

A skill challenge can stand on its own as a noncombat encounter. For example, a group might have an encounter in which it tries to extract a secret from a stubborn cultist. In another episode of the story, the group might use Nature checks and Perception checks to track the cultists through a jungle, a Religion check to predict a likely spot for their hidden temple, and an Endurance check to fight off the effects of illness and exhaustion over the course of days in the jungle.

Alternatively, a skill challenge can be integrated into a combat encounter. While fighting the cult's leader, some of the adventurers might use a series of Arcana and Religion checks to disrupt a dark ritual that is in progress.

The Basics

To deal with a typical skill challenge, a group of adventurers makes a series of skill checks, sometimes taking a few rounds and sometimes spread over days of game time. The DM either informs the players when the challenge begins or lets it begin quietly, when an adventurer makes a skill check that the DM counts as the first check of the challenge. As the challenge proceeds, the DM might prompt the players to make checks, let them choose when to make checks, or both. The DM can have the adventurers act in initiative order or in some other order of his or her choice. The DM might tell the players which skills to use, let them improvise which ones they use, or both.

The skill challenge is completed either when a specified number of successful skill checks is achieved or when three failures are reached.

If the adventurers complete the challenge through achieving a target number of successes, they succeed at the challenge. Otherwise, they fail the challenge. Whether the adventurers succeed or fail, they complete the challenge, face its consequences, and receive experience points for it.

For example, the adventurers seek a temple in the heart of a jungle—a skill challenge that might occupy them for hours. Achieving six successes means they find their way without too much trouble. Accumulating three failures before achieving the successes, however, indicates that they get lost for part of the search, fight their way through quicksand, and arrive at the temple worn out, having lost some healing surges on the way.

Components of a Skill Challenge

A typical skill challenge includes five main components, whether the challenge is an encounter in its own right or part of another encounter.

1. Goal

Each skill challenge has a goal. Completing a skill challenge almost always results in attaining that goal, regardless of success or failure. If the adventurers succeed at the challenge, they attain the goal more or less unscathed. If they fail the challenge, they typically attain the goal but pay some price for doing so (see "Consequences," below).

Skill challenge goals take many forms: find the lost temple, escape the crumbling tower, disrupt the fiendish ritual, compete in a tournament, and so on. The best skill challenge goals can be achieved with degrees of success or failure, rather than total success or failure.

2. Level and DCs

A skill challenge has a level, which helps determine the DCs of the skill checks involved. A typical skill challenge is of the same level as the adventurers, although the DM might choose to set the level higher or lower.

Most skill checks in a typical challenge are against the moderate DC of the challenge's level (see the Difficulty Class by Level table, page 126). However, after a character has used a particular skill to achieve a success against the moderate DC, later uses of that skill in the challenge by the same character should be against the hard DC.

Group checks (page 128) work differently; they should typically use the easy DC of the challenge's level. Also, in a high-complexity challenge (complexity 3 or higher), adventurers have ways of circumventing the DC guidelines through the use of special advantages. See the "Advantages" sidebar.

A challenge ideally includes at least four ways to gain a success against a moderate DC. Using too many hard DCs threatens to make a challenge too difficult, and using too many easy DCs (except in group checks) makes it trivial.

3. Complexity
The complexity of a skill challenge determines the number of successful checks the adventurers must accumulate to succeed at the challenge.

The Skill Challenge Complexity table lists the five grades of complexity. A complexity 1 challenge requires four skill checks to be completed successfully. Each grade of complexity after the first requires two more successes.

Most challenges (complexity 2 or higher) should involve a mix of moderate and hard DCs. The table suggests a mix for each grade of complexity.

In a high-complexity challenge (complexity 3 or higher), adventurers usually have access to the number of advantages specified in the table. See the "Advantages" sidebar for how advantages work.

SKILL CHALLENGE COMPLEXITY

Complexity	Successes	Advantages	Typical DCs
1	4	—	4 moderate
2	6	—	5 moderate, 1 hard
3	8	2	6 moderate, 2 hard
4	10	4	7 moderate, 3 hard
5	12	6	8 moderate, 4 hard

Succeeding at a complexity 1 challenge is roughly equivalent to defeating a single monster. Adding a grade of complexity is akin to adding a monster to a combat encounter. A complexity 5 challenge has the same weight in an adventure as a typical combat encounter and awards a comparable amount of experience points (see "Consequences," below).

A skill challenge that is part of a combat encounter typically has a complexity of 1 or 2 and replaces one or two monsters of the challenge's level.

4. Primary and Secondary Skills
Each skill challenge has skills associated with it that adventurers can use during the challenge. A skill challenge typically includes a mix of social skills, such as Bluff and Diplomacy; knowledge skills, such as Arcana and Nature; and physical skills, such as Athletics and Acrobatics. Having a mix of skills rewards a group that has a variety of skill specialties.

Whatever skills the DM chooses for a skill challenge, he or she designates them as primary or secondary. A typical skill challenge has a number of

ADVANTAGES

A skill challenge that has a complexity of 3 or higher is considered to have a high complexity. Such a challenge should include ways for the adventurers to gain an advantage of some kind, an edge that lets them remove a failure or gain successes more easily than normal. Without such advantages, the challenge risks becoming an unavoidable failure.

For each success beyond six required in a challenge, one of the following advantages should be available.

✦ A success against a hard DC counts as two successes: a success against both a hard DC and a moderate DC.
✦ A success against a hard DC removes a failure that has already been accumulated in the challenge, instead of counting as a success.
✦ A success against an easy DC counts as a success against a moderate DC.
✦ A success against a moderate DC counts as a success even though the adventurer making the check has already used the same skill to gain a success against a moderate DC.

The DM can mix and match these advantages in a challenge and can use the same one more than once. If the DM prefers one or two of the advantages over the others, he or she can just use the preferred ones.

The DM either determines in advance which of these advantages are available or lets the players' creative use of skills determine when an advantage comes into play. For example, a player might come up with an unusually innovative use for the Endurance skill in a challenge and then meet a hard DC with the skill check. The DM might reward the player's creativity by allowing the success to remove a failure. Similarly, the DM might reward an adventurer for overshooting a DC. If the adventurer makes a skill check against a moderate DC but meets a hard DC, the DM could let that success count as two.

If a published skill challenge has a complexity of 3 or higher but does not include suggestions for granting advantages, the DM should grant an appropriate number of advantages in play. An easy rule of thumb is to count a few checks that meet a hard DC as double successes.

If a group of adventurers has members who can easily achieve the moderate and the hard DCs of a challenge, then fewer of these advantages are necessary in that challenge. In other words, a group of experts needs fewer tricks for avoiding failure.

associated skills equal to the number of adventurers plus two. Usually two or three of those skills are secondary, and the rest are primary.

Primary Skills: The use of certain skills naturally leads to the solution of the problem presented in a skill challenge. These skills serve as the primary skills in the challenge. The DM usually picks the primary skills before a challenge begins and often tells them to the players.

A primary skill can typically be used more than once in a challenge. The DM might limit the number of successes that a particular skill can contribute, up to a maximum that equals the complexity of the challenge. For instance, in a challenge that has a complexity of 2, the DM might decide that each primary skill can contribute no more than two successes.

Secondary Skills: A secondary skill is tangentially related to a skill challenge and can usually contribute only one success. When players improvise creative uses for skills that weren't on the DM's list of skills for the challenge, the DM typically treats them as secondary skills for the challenge.

The DM might decide that a particular secondary skill can't contribute any successes to a challenge but instead provides some other benefit as a result of a successful check: a bonus to a check with a primary skill, a reroll of a different skill check, the addition of a skill to the list of primary skills, and so on.

5. Consequences
Whether adventurers succeed or fail at a skill challenge, there are consequences. One way or another, the adventure goes on.

Success: When adventurers succeed at a skill challenge, they earn rewards specific to the challenge. The reward might boil down to the adventure simply continuing smoothly, or it could be one or more treasures, advantages in future encounters, or useful information.

Failure: Failing a challenge doesn't bring the adventure to a halt. Instead, there is a price to pay. Penalties for failure might include the loss of healing surges or some other lingering penalty, making a later encounter more difficult.

Experience Points: Whether the adventurers succeed or fail, they receive experience points for completing a skill challenge. Generally the adventurers gain experience points as if they had defeated a number of monsters equal to the challenge's complexity and as if the monsters were of the challenge's level.

Example: If the adventurers complete a 7th-level challenge that has a complexity of 1, they receive 300 XP (the award for a single 7th-level monster). If they complete a 7th-level challenge with a complexity of 5, they receive 1,500 XP (the award for five such monsters).

Stages of Success In some skill challenges, each success moves the adventurers toward their goal. Then, even if the adventurers fail, they still achieve some degree of progress. For example, if the goal of a challenge is to extract information from a hostile or wary character, the adventurers get some tidbits of information with each success. The most valuable information comes last (when they achieve the target number of successes for the complexity of the challenge), but even one success followed by three failures gives the adventurers a few pieces of information that keep the adventure moving.

Perhaps the adventurers undertake a skill challenge to weaken a vampire lord before they finally face it in combat. Each success (or every three successes) removes some protective ward or special defense the vampire lord possesses. Thus, even if the adventurers fail the challenge—and are thrust into combat with the vampire—they have still weakened it a little, and the fight is measurably easier than if they had achieved no successes at all.

Stages of Failure One way that some skill challenges remain lively is by providing immediate consequences for each failed check in the challenge. Each time an adventurer fails, the consequences become gradually worse, climaxing in the termination of the skill challenge after three failures.

Here are some typical consequences that can occur in response to a failure:

✦ The adventurer who failed the check either loses a healing surge outside combat or takes damage in combat.

✦ The adventurers must spend time or money making up for the failure.

✦ For the rest of the challenge, no adventurer can achieve a success using the same skill that was used for the failed check.

✦ The next check using a specified skill takes a penalty. For instance, if an adventurer fails an Intimidate check in the midst of a complex negotiation, the next adventurer who attempts a Diplomacy check takes a -2 penalty.

Example of Play

This example shows a DM running a skill challenge for five adventurers: Valenae (an eladrin cleric), Dendric (a human fighter), Uldane (a halfling rogue), Kathra (a dwarf wizard), and Shara (a human fighter). After a battle with a demonic creature that attempted to slay their friend, the priest Pendergraf, the adventurers must determine where the monster came from to prevent another attack.

This 1st-level challenge has a complexity of 1 and requires four successes against DC 12, the moderate DC for 1st level. The goal of the challenge is to find the spot where the adventurers' enemy, a wizard named Garan, summoned the demon. Garan has hired some thugs to beat up anyone they spot snooping around. If the adventurers fail the challenge, the thugs find them and attack.

DM: You're left with the last misty remnants of the strange creature's corpse and a handful of frightened witnesses. "What was that thing?" Pendergraf asks. "And where did it come from?"

Kathra: Can I make an Arcana check to see if I know anything about it?

DM: Sure.

Kathra: I got a 14.

DM (*marking down a success for the characters*): Okay, you know that the creature was some sort of demon, not native to the world.

Uldane: Can I look around and see if I can tell which way it came from?

DM: Sure, make a Perception check.

Uldane: Ouch, a 9. Someone remind me to open my eyes the next time I try looking around.

DM (*marking the first failure*): It takes you quite a bit of work to uncover the tracks. It looks like they head to the east side of town.

Valenae: Let's follow the tracks. If we want to protect Pendergraf and the other priests of Pelor, we need to find and destroy whoever summoned that thing.

DM: The tracks continue for a block or two before they twist and turn around. You realize that you confused the monster's tracks with a horse's, double back, and finally find the trail. It leads to the river quarter, the roughest part of town. The trail ends outside a rundown tavern. Three thuggish-looking men sit on a bench by the front door. They glare at you as you approach.

Notice how the failed check didn't stop the action. The adventurers wasted some time, giving the thugs more time to find them, but eventually found the trail.

Kathra: I'd like to talk to the men to see if any of them saw the demon come by here. How about a Diplomacy check—an 11.

DM (marking the second failure): The thugs make a show of ignoring you as you approach. Then one of them snarls: "Around here, folks know better than to stick their noses where they're not wanted." He puts a hand on the hilt of his dagger.

Shara: I put a hand on my greatsword and growl back at them, "I'll stick my sword where it's not wanted if you keep up that attitude." I got a 21 on my Intimidate check.

DM (marking the second success): The thug turns pale in fear as his friends bolt back into the tavern. He points at the building behind you before darting after them.

Dendric: What's the place look like? Is it a shop, or a private residence?

DM: Someone make a Streetwise check.

Uldane: Using aid another, I try to assist Dendric, since he has the highest Streetwise. I got a 12, so Dendric gets a +2 bonus.

Dendric: Thanks, Uldane. Here's my check . . . great, a natural 1. That's a 10, even with Uldane's assistance.

DM (marking the third and final failure): It looks like an old shop that's been closed and boarded up. You heard something about this place before, but you can't quite remember it. As you look the place over, the tavern door opens up behind you. A hulk of a half-orc lumbers out, followed by the thugs you talked to earlier. "I heard you thought you could push my crew around. Well, let's see you talk tough through a set of broken teeth." Roll for initiative!

Unfortunately for the adventurers, they failed the skill challenge. If they had succeeded on the last check, they would have remembered stories of a secret entrance into the building and had a chance to find the hidden laboratory where Garan summoned the demon. They can question the half-orc after combat and learn something about their foe, but not as much they would have learned from finding the laboratory. Perhaps they can still find the laboratory, but the delay caused by the fight gives Garan a head start in escaping.

CHAPTER 5

EXPLORATION AND THE ENVIRONMENT

A significant part of DUNGEONS & DRAGONS adventures is exploration, which takes place between encounters. Exploring adventurers make their way through unmapped dungeon corridors, untracked wilderness, or a sprawling city, investigating the environment's dangers and wonders.

While they are exploring, adventurers need to know what they can see, particularly in dark dungeons, and how far they can move between encounters. During a journey or an adventure into a dangerous location, they must rest and recover. Interaction with the environment produces both discoveries and threats, whether through the actions of the adventurers or the nature of their surroundings. This chapter provides guidelines for dealing with the environment.

+ **Vision and Light:** How ambient light and characters' vision affect what can see and be seen. This section also summarizes common light sources and describes special senses.

+ **Movement between Encounters:** Exploration usually involves movement. This section provides guidance on distances and travel times when adventurers aren't in a fight.

Adventurers investigate dangers and wonders.

+ **Rest and Recovery:** During or after an adventure into a dangerous location, adventurers become exhausted, injured, or both. These rules describe how they can rest and recover expended resources.

+ **Interacting with the Environment:** During exploration, adventurers interact with the environment in various ways: searching rooms, climbing walls, breaking down doors, and smashing open chests. Rules for performing such actions appear in this section.

+ **Environmental Dangers:** Threats posed by adverse weather, malign influence, and other harmful effects of the environment. This section also provides guidance for using the Endurance skill to withstand environmental hazards, as well as resisting starvation, thirst, and suffocation.

+ **Traps and Hazards:** Whether constructed with malign intent or simply dangerous terrain features, traps and hazards are common challenges during exploration. This section describes how adventurers deal with them.

+ **Disease:** A polluted environment, a magical plague, or a rat's filth-encrusted teeth can infect explorers with disease. Here's how diseases are handled in the game.

ADAM PAQUETTE

VISION AND LIGHT

As adventurers explore an environment, the DM tells the players what their characters see, starting with the obvious, such as the dimensions of a corridor. If the adventurers are perceptive, they might also notice something hidden, such as a trap.

Creatures automatically see anything that is conspicuous, but they  use the Perception skill to try to see something less obvious. If adventurers aren't actively searching an area, the DM determines whether they notice hard-to-see objects or creatures by using the passive Perception of each adventurer.

Creatures normally can't see anything without some light. Many dungeons and other indoor areas are lit, since only a few monsters are at home in utter darkness. Illumination might be provided by torches (sometimes magical ones that never stop burning), ceiling panels magically imbued with light, great oil-filled braziers or stone channels that burn continuously, or even magic globes of light that drift through the air. Natural caverns might be filled with phosphorescent fungi or lichen, extraordinary mineral veins that glimmer in the dark, streams of glowing lava, or eerie auroralike veils of magic fire undulating high above a cavern floor.

Categories of Light

Light in the DUNGEONS & DRAGONS game is defined by three categories. See "Vision and Special Senses," below, for how these categories affect a creature.

- ✦ **Bright Light:** This category includes daylight, as well as the light provided by most portable light sources or cast by surrounding fires or lava.

- ✦ **Dim Light:** This category includes moonlight, the light provided by a candle or another dim light source, indirect illumination (such as in the interior of a cave whose entrance is nearby or in a subterranean passageway that has narrow shafts extending to the surface), and the light cast by things such as phosphorescent fungi.

- ✦ **Darkness:** Darkness prevails outside on a moonless night and in lightless rooms.

WILLIAM O'CONNOR

Light Sources

Even though many dungeons are adequately lit, the cautious adventurer brings a torch or a sunrod when venturing into a cavern or an underground complex.

Common light sources are described in the Light Sources table. Assuming nothing blocks a creature's view, the creature can see most light sources from at least a quarter of a mile away, and it can see exceptionally bright sources from up to a mile away.

LIGHT SOURCES

Source	Brightness	Radius	Duration
Bonfire	Bright	20 squares	4 hours
Campfire	Bright	10 squares	8 hours
Candle	Dim	2 squares	1 hour
Fireplace	Bright	5 squares	8 hours per load of fuel
Forge	Bright	2 squares	8 hours per load of fuel
Lantern	Bright	10 squares	8 hours per pint of oil
Magma	Bright	40 squares	Ongoing
Phosphorescent fungi	Dim	10 squares	Ongoing
Sunrod	Bright	20 squares	4 hours
Torch	Bright	5 squares	1 hour

Brightness: Most light sources provide an area of bright light around them.

Radius: A light source illuminates its space (or a creature's space if the creature is carrying the light source) and all squares within the stated radius. For example, if a character carries a torch, bright light illuminates his or her space and 5 squares in every direction.

Duration: Most light sources last only so long because they require a fuel source.

Vision and Special Senses

Many creatures see in the dark much better than humans do. Some can even see in utter lightlessness. Other creatures get along in the dark by using other senses: uncanny hearing, sensitivity to vibrations and air movement, or an acute sense of smell.

A creature's vision determines how it is affected by obscured squares (see "Concealment," page 220). Unless otherwise noted, a creature has normal vision. Some creatures have special senses that are noted in their race entries or stat blocks. For example, a human typically has normal vision, whereas an elf has low-light vision.

Radius: If a creature has a special sense followed by a number, that number is the sense's radius. Beyond that radius, a creature relies on its normal senses. For instance, if a creature has blindsight 6, the blindsight extends only 6 squares in every direction. If no radius is specified, the special sense extends as far as the creature can see.

Normal Vision: A creature that has normal vision can see normally in areas of bright light. Areas of dim light are lightly obscured to the creature, and areas of darkness are totally obscured to it.

Low-Light Vision: A creature that has low-light vision can see normally in areas of bright light and dim light, but areas of darkness are totally obscured to it. The creature ignores concealment that is a result of dim light.

Darkvision: A creature that has darkvision can see normally regardless of light. It ignores concealment that is a result of dim light or darkness.

Blindsight: A creature that has blindsight can see normally regardless of how obscured an area is and regardless of whether creatures or objects are invisible. Blindsight usually has a radius, beyond which the creature relies on its other senses.

Tremorsense: A creature that has tremorsense can see normally regardless of how obscured an area is and regardless of whether creatures or objects are invisible or outside line of effect, but both they and the creature must be in contact with the ground or the same substance, such as water or a web. For instance, tremorsense allows a creature to sense something on the other side of a wall, as long as the creature and the thing are both in contact with the ground or the wall. Tremorsense usually has a radius, beyond which the creature relies on its other senses.

MOVEMENT BETWEEN ENCOUNTERS

Movement is what gets adventurers from encounter to encounter and from one place to another within an encounter. This section provides rules for movement between encounters; "Movement, Distance, and Terrain," page 199, explains movement during a combat encounter. Movement in a noncombat encounter rarely needs to be precise and can simply be described by the DM and the players. If a particular encounter requires such precision, use the movement rules for combat.

Often a DM summarizes the adventurers' movement between encounters without having to figure out exact distances or travel times: "You travel for three days and reach the dungeon entrance." Even in a dungeon—particularly a large complex or a cave network—the DM can summarize movement between encounters: "After killing the guardian at the entrance to the ancient dwarven stronghold, you wander through miles of echoing corridors before you arrive at a chasm bridged by a narrow stone arch, which is broken in the middle."

The DM might evocatively describe the terrain the adventurers pass through, but the encounters along the way are the focus of the game. Sometimes it's important, however, to know how long it takes to get from one encounter to another, whether the answer is in days, hours, or minutes. The rules to figure out travel time depend on two factors: speed and terrain.

Exploration Speed

The Base Exploration Speed table shows how much distance a creature that has a given speed covers in a day, an hour, or a minute of travel. A group of travelers moves at the slowest traveler's pace, so most groups use the table's first row (to accommodate dwarves and heavily armored members).

The table includes the four most common speeds. Here's how to calculate the exploration speed of a creature that has a speed not on the table. To figure out how many miles a creature can typically cover during a 10-hour day of exploration and travel, multiply the creature's speed by 5. Divide that result by 10 to figure out how many miles the creature can cover per hour, and multiply that result by 10 to figure out how many feet it can cover per minute.

BASE EXPLORATION SPEED

Speed	Per Day	Per Hour	Per Minute
5	25 miles	2½ miles	250 feet
6	30 miles	3 miles	300 feet
7	35 miles	3½ miles	350 feet
8	40 miles	4 miles	400 feet

Speed per Day: A creature can sustain a normal walking pace for 10 hours of travel per day without tiring out (people who aren't adventurers can rarely walk for more than 6 or 8 hours in a day). Beyond that limit, the creature must make an Endurance check at the end of each hour (or part of an hour) of walking, until it takes an extended rest. The DC for the check is 20 at the end of the first hour and increases by 5 at the end of each subsequent hour of walking. Whenever a creature fails this check, the creature loses a healing surge, or it takes damage equal to its level if it has no healing surges left.

Speed per Hour: A creature's speed per hour assumes a walking pace. A creature can move at twice this speed for an hour. If the creature maintains the faster pace beyond that time, the creature loses a healing surge at the end of each subsequent hour (or part of an hour) at that pace, or it takes damage equal to its level if it has no healing surges left.

Speed per Minute: A creature's speed per minute assumes a walking pace and is intended for travel that takes less than an hour. If a creature is in a hurry, it can move at twice this speed.

Terrain and Travel

The distances on the Base Exploration Speed table assume relatively clear terrain: roads, open plains, or dungeon corridors that aren't choked with rubble. Other terrain can slow progress. How much? That depends on the prevalence of difficult terrain in the area.

TERRAIN AND TRAVEL

Distance Multiplier	Terrain
× 0.5	Difficult terrain predominates (dense forests, mountains, deep swamps, rubble-choked ruins)
× 0.75	Difficult terrain is widespread (forests, hills, swamps, crumbling ruins, caves, city streets)
× 1	Difficult terrain is rare (open fields, plains, roads, clear dungeon corridors)

To figure out how far creatures travel per day, hour, or minute, multiply the distance they would normally travel, as shown on the Base Exploration Speed table, by the distance multiplier shown on the Terrain and Travel table.

Flying creatures and airborne vehicles ignore distance multipliers for difficult terrain.

MARCHING ORDER

It's a good idea for adventurers to establish a standard marching order, which describes the way they are normally arranged when traveling. They can change their marching order any time, but having it established before an encounter lets the DM know exactly where everyone is when an encounter begins.

Players can record the marching order any way they like: They might write it on paper or a whiteboard, or arrange the adventurers' miniatures or tokens on the battle grid to show their relative positions. Different marching orders can be created for different situations—one for corridors that are 2 squares wide and one for open areas, for example.

Danger in a dungeon environment often comes from up ahead, so it's a good idea to put a defender at the front of the marching order, protecting the group's controllers. Leaders make a good choice for the back of the group, since they're tough enough to withstand an ambush from behind. Strikers might scout ahead, but most prefer to stay closer to the middle of a group.

Find a balance between clustering and spreading out. Staying close ensures that everyone can get to the action quickly when an encounter begins, but being bunched up leaves characters vulnerable to area attacks from traps or ambushers.

Mounts and Vehicles

When traveling long distances outdoors, characters can use mounts or vehicles to increase their speed, their carrying capacity, or both. The Mounts and Vehicles table shows the effective speed of common mounts and vehicles, as well as their typical carrying capacities. For mounts, the carrying capacity is the normal load, the heavy load, and the maximum drag load for the creature (see "Carrying, Lifting, or Dragging," page 265). For vehicles, it's the maximum weight of goods that the vehicle can carry.

The table assumes a day of travel is 10 hours long, although sailing ships and airships can travel up to 24 hours a day if properly crewed.

MOUNTS AND VEHICLES

Mount or Vehicle	Speed	Per Day	Per Hour	Per Minute	Carrying Capacity
Airship	15	180 miles	7½ miles	750 feet	20 tons
Cart or wagon	5	25 miles	2½ miles	250 feet	1 ton
Riding horse	10	50 miles	5 miles	500 feet	237/475/1,187 pounds
Rowboat	3	15 miles	1½ miles	150 feet	600 pounds
Downstream	4-6	20-30 miles	2-3 miles	200-300 feet	600 pounds
Sailing ship	7	84 miles	3½ miles	350 feet	150 tons
Warhorse	8	40 miles	4 miles	400 feet	262/525/1,312 pounds

BEN WOOTTEN

Rest and Recovery

Sooner or later, even the toughest adventurers need to rest. When not in an encounter, characters can take one of two types of rest: a short rest or an extended rest. Unless a monster survives a combat encounter, a DM rarely has to keep track of it resting.

About 5 minutes long, a short rest consists of catching one's breath after an encounter. At least 6 hours long, an extended rest includes relaxation, sometimes a meal, and usually sleep.

Short Rest

A short rest allows a creature to regain the use of encounter powers and spend healing surges to regain hit points. Short rests follow these rules.

Duration: A short rest is about 5 minutes long.

No Limit per Day: A creature can take an unlimited number of short rests per day.

No Strenuous Activity: Resting means just that. The creature can stand guard, sit in place, ride on a wagon or other vehicle, or do other tasks that don't require much exertion.

Regain the Use of Powers: After a short rest, a creature regains the use of expended encounter powers.

Spend Healing Surges: After a short rest, a creature can spend as many healing surges as desired (see "Hit Points and Healing," page 255). A creature that runs out of healing surges must take an extended rest to regain them.

Using Powers during the Rest: If a creature uses an encounter power (such as a healing power) during a short rest, it needs another short rest to regain the use of that power.

Interruptions: If a creature's short rest is interrupted, the creature needs to rest for another 5 minutes to get the benefits of a short rest.

Extended Rest

Once per day, a creature can gain the benefits of an extended rest.

Duration: An extended rest is at least 6 hours long.

Once per Day: After a creature finishes an extended rest, it has to wait 12 hours before beginning another one.

No Strenuous Activity: A creature normally sleeps during an extended rest but doesn't have to. The creature can engage in light activity that doesn't require much exertion.

Regain Hit Points and Healing Surges: At the end of an extended rest, a creature regains all lost hit points and all spent healing surges.

Regain the Use of Powers: At the end of an extended rest, a creature regains the use of expended encounter powers and daily powers.

Action Points: At the end of an extended rest, a creature loses any unspent action points, but starts fresh with 1 action point.

Interruptions: If anything interrupts a creature's extended rest, such as an attack, add the time spent dealing with the interruption to the total time the creature needs to spend in the extended rest.

Sleeping and Waking Up

A creature needs at least 6 hours of sleep every day to keep functioning well. If, at the end of an extended rest, a creature hasn't slept at least 6 hours in the last 24, it gains no benefit from that extended rest.

While asleep, a creature is unconscious. The creature wakes up if it takes damage or hears sounds of danger (making a passive Perception check with a -5 penalty). Another creature can wake the sleeper by shaking it (a standard action) or by shouting (a free action).

KEEPING WATCH

Adventurers typically take turns keeping watch while their companions sleep. If five characters are in a group, each of them can take a turn on watch duty for 1½ hours and sleep for 6 hours, so that they spend a total of 7½ hours resting.

An adventurer who's taking a turn on watch is actively looking for signs of danger. At the start of the shift on watch, make a Perception check. If something occurs during the shift, the DM uses the result of the Perception check to determine whether the adventurer notices.

If everyone in a group sleeps at the same time without setting a watch, the DM uses each character's passive Perception, counting the -5 penalty for being asleep, to determine whether he or she hears approaching danger and wakes up.

INTERACTING WITH THE ENVIRONMENT

A typical adventure environment is full of dangers, surprises, and puzzles. A dungeon room might hold a complex bank of mysterious levers, a statue positioned over a trap door, a locked chest, or a teleportation circle. Sometimes an adventurer needs to cut through a rope, break a chain, bash down a door, lift a portcullis, or smash the Golden Orb of Khadros the Reaver before the villain can use it.

An adventurer's interaction with the environment is often simple to resolve in the game. The player tells the DM that the character is moving the lever on the right, and the DM says what happens, if anything. The lever might be part of a fiendishly clever puzzle that requires several levers to be pulled in the correct order before the room completely fills with water, testing adventurers' ingenuity to the limit, but rules aren't necessary for the simple act of pulling the lever.

Searching

Adventurers must often look carefully to find concealed objects, such as secret doors, disguised treasures, or crucial clues that will lead them to the next stage of the adventure. They make Perception checks to find such items of interest. Unless the group is under a time constraint, the DM should assume that the best searcher is going to roll a 20 eventually and should therefore use the best possible Perception check result that any member of the group can achieve. (In other words, add 20 to the best Perception check modifier in the party.) The adventurers spend a couple of minutes searching, and the DM tells them what they find.

A published adventure tells the DM what can be found in a room and how hard it is to find. For a DM creating his or her own adventures, the following examples provide guidelines for setting the Perception DC to find a secret object.

PERCEPTION CHECK

DC	Examples
Easy	Anything valuable in a chest full of junk; something very small or subtle but otherwise in sight
Moderate	A valuable item tucked away in an unlikely place; a secret latch or compartment
Hard	A secret door

Consult the Difficulty Class by Level table, page 126, and use the appropriate DC of the adventurers' level.

Climbing, Jumping, and Swimming

Adventurers frequently encounter terrain that prevents them from simply walking across a room or a battlefield. Craggy stone walls, deep crevasses, and raging rivers typically require successful Athletics checks to overcome them.

A published adventure tells the DM what obstacles exist in a room and how hard they are to navigate. When the DM creates his or her own adventures, the Athletics skill provides guidelines for setting the DCs to overcome obstacles.

Breaking and Forcing Things

Adventurers have a habit of breaking down doors and smashing other objects they encounter. The rules can't anticipate every situation, but the following guidelines and examples should help the DM find the right numbers to use.

The tables below provide some sample DCs for forcing open a door or breaking an object. A given DC is usually the moderate DC for the midpoint of the specified target levels, meaning that the task is straightforward for a creature with a high Strength score but difficult for anyone else (and more difficult for creatures lower in level than the target). For more challenging tasks, the DCs are 5 higher than the moderate DCs for that level, meaning that a strong creature of the appropriate level has about a one-in-three chance of success.

Forcing Open Doors

Usually a creature can open a door simply by using a minor action (see "Action Types," page 194). Sometimes, though, adventurers encounter doors that are stuck or locked. Forcing open a stuck or a locked door requires a standard action and a successful Strength check.

The Force Open Doors table shows some sample doors and includes the Strength check DC to force or break them open.

FORCE OPEN DOORS

Strength Check to . . .	DC
Break down wooden door	13
Break down reinforced door	16
Break down barred door	20
Break down iron door	23
Break down adamantine door	27
Break through force portal	30
Force open wooden portcullis	21
Force open iron portcullis	28
Force open adamantine portcullis	35

Breaking Objects

The rules can't cover every possible object that adventurers might decide needs destruction, but some common items and situations are given in the Break Objects table.

Some objects can be broken simply with a successful Strength check (usually a standard action). If an adventurer could conceivably break an object with his or her bare hands (or with a well-placed kick or shoulder), the DM should assign a Strength DC using the following examples as a baseline.

BREAK OBJECTS

Strength Check to . . .	DC
Smash wooden chest	16
Smash iron box	23
Smash adamantine box	30
Burst rope bonds	21
Burst iron chains	28
Burst adamantine chains	35
Break through wooden wall (6 inches thick)	25
Break through masonry wall (1 foot thick)	35

Attacking Objects

Sometimes a Strength check isn't sufficient to damage or destroy an object, often because of the object's size, durability, or both. Alternatively, a character might need to destroy an object from across the room. In such cases, attacking an object with a power can provide the answer. At the DM's discretion, any power that targets one or more creatures can target one or more objects (see "Choosing Targets," page 105).

Object Defenses and Hit Points

Like creatures, objects have hit points. They also have defenses: AC, Fortitude, and Reflex. Objects don't have Will, however (see "Object Immunities," below).

Determining Defenses: An object's AC, Fortitude, and Reflex depend entirely on its size, as noted in the Object Properties table. These defenses are typically very low, so it's pretty easy to hit an object—so easy, in fact, that many DMs skip the attack roll against an object unless the situation is particularly dramatic.

Determining Hit Points: An object's hit point total generally depends on two factors: the object's size and its material. As a rule, larger or thicker objects have more hit points than smaller or thinner ones. Objects made of stone or metal have more hit points than those made of wood or glass.

Exceptions to this general rule abound. An object that's big but full of delicate moving parts might have fewer hit points than a smaller, more solid object, because it doesn't take as much damage to render the complex object functionally useless.

To determine an object's hit points, first find its size on the Object Properties table. Then consult the Object Hit Point Multipliers table and apply the appropriate multipliers based on the object's material, composition, or both. If more than one multiplier is appropriate, the order doesn't matter. A Large iron clockwork contraption, for instance, should have around 60 hit points (40 for Large, × 3 for iron, × 0.5 for intricate construction).

An object reduced to 0 hit points is destroyed or otherwise rendered useless. At the DM's discretion, the object might remain more or less whole, but its functionality is ruined—a door knocked from its hinges or a clockwork mechanism broken internally, for instance.

Even though an object has hit points, it is never considered to be bloodied. The DM can certainly describe when the object has less than half of its hit points remaining ("The door is barely holding together now," for instance), but effects that are triggered by a target being bloodied are not triggered by an object.

OBJECT PROPERTIES

Size	AC/Reflex	Fortitude	Base HP	Examples
Tiny	10	5	5	Bottle, book
Small	8	8	10	Treasure chest, manacles
Medium	5	10	20	Door, statue
Large	4	12	40	Wagon, vault door
Huge	3	15	100	Big statue
Gargantuan	2	20	200	Even bigger statue

OBJECT HIT POINT MULTIPLIERS

Multiplier	Material/Composition
× 0.25	Very fragile
× 0.5	Fragile or intricate
× 1.5	Reinforced
× 0.1	Paper or cloth
× 0.25	Glass or ice
× 0.5	Leather or hide
× 1	Wood
× 2	Stone
× 3	Iron or steel
× 5	Adamantine

Object Immunities

Unless otherwise noted, an object has immunity to the following:

+ necrotic damage
+ poison damage
+ psychic damage
+ any attack that targets Will

The DM might decide that a particular object is immune to other damage types. For instance, a magic altar might be immune to fire.

Object Resistances and Vulnerabilities

Objects don't have any universal resistances or vulnerabilities, but the DM might rule that some kinds of damage are particularly effective against a certain object—the object has vulnerability to that damage. For instance, a gauzy curtain or a pile of dry papers might have vulnerable 5 fire because any spark is likely to destroy it.

Similarly, the DM might occasionally decide that an unusual material resists a type of damage, typically having resist 5 or 10 to that damage.

Environmental Dangers

In addition to offering interesting terrain features to complicate combat, the wilderness poses a particular sort of risk: the environment itself. Polar travelers risk frostbite and exposure, desert explorers face heatstroke, and mountaineers must contend with the perils of high altitude.

In the Dungeons & Dragons world, cataclysmic magical events can render entire regions hostile. For example, the dead-gray mist bordering the Mournland in Eberron saps the life force of those who pass through it, and the Smoldering Duke's Dungeon of Ash in the Elemental Chaos can steal the last breath from even a hardy adventurer.

Using the Endurance Skill

The Endurance skill determines how well a creature can withstand many environmental dangers. Usually, this skill applies to adventurers; monsters are usually native to the environment and inured to its harmful effects. In general, each day or night of exposure to a harsh environment requires a adventurer to succeed on an Endurance check or lose a healing surge. If the adventurer has no healing surges left, he or she instead loses hit points equal to his or her level. Healing surges lost to such a failed Endurance check can't be regained until the adventurer completes an extended rest outside the harsh environment.

For simplicity, each character can make the Endurance check at the end of each day of adventuring, and again after each extended rest. A published adventure sets the DC for the check. The Endurance Check table provides some benchmark DCs, based on the Difficulty Class by Level table (page 126).

ENDURANCE CHECK

DC	Examples
Easy	Driving rain, moderately high altitude, unusually hot or cold temperature
Moderate	Freezing rain, pervasive smoke, extremely high altitude, arctic or tropical temperature
Hard	Pervasive ash clouds, necromantic energy, unearthly temperature

Weather

As adventurers explore the wilderness, weather can present significant challenges. Drizzling rain obscures their foes; gusting wind hampers movement in combat. Blinding snow can complicate a climb through a mountain pass, or a living storm might attack at random as the party scrambles for cover.

Rain, Fog, and Falling Snow: These weather conditions create lightly or heavily obscured squares (see "Concealment," page 220). At the DM's discretion, they might also create difficult terrain on the ground—as a result of snow accumulation or flooding, for instance. Blinding snow might force travelers to make Endurance checks every hour, or Acrobatics checks to avoid slipping.

THE WILD

When adventurers leave the relative safety of towns and cities, they quickly enter a world of monsters and raiders, where the land can be actively hostile. Even if they're traversing only a few miles between a village and a nearby dungeon, the wilderness is a force to be reckoned with.

Wilderness areas fall into three broad categories. Formerly settled regions have been reclaimed by the forces of nature—overgrown with forest, swallowed into swamp, or worn into rubble by desert wind and scouring sand. Once-busy roadways are now nothing but fragments of stone littering the ground. Even in the peak of the great empires of the past, the lands between cities were wild, and only frequent patrols kept trade routes safe. Now those lands are full of monster-haunted ruins, including the crumbled remains of those ancient cities. Quests might lead adventurers to these ruins searching for lost libraries or artifacts, investigating a rumor of a surviving settlement buried in the wilderness, or looking for treasure.

Other regions have never been settled. These consist primarily of inhospitable terrain: deserts, mountains, tundras, jungles, and swamps. These areas hold no ruins from the ancient empires of the world, except the occasional hint of a short-lived colony that failed to tame the wilderness around it. These regions hold more fantastic terrain—places where magic gathers in pools or where parts of the Feywild, the Shadowfell, or the Elemental Chaos overlap the world and alter nature with their proximity. Adventurers might find a foundry built by fire archons or a snow-capped mountain torn from its roots and suspended in the air. Their quests might lead them to seek a font of magical power on a forbidding peak, or a city that appears in the desert once every century.

Even in these days of fallen empires, colonists and pioneers fight back the wilderness on the frontier, hoping to spread the light of civilization and found new kingdoms. The world's largest city-states establish colonies at the edges of their spheres of influence, and brave and hardy souls build hardscrabble villages near sources of minerals or other resources. Devotees of Erathis seek to tame the wilderness, and followers of Avandra roam in search of new frontiers. These tiny outposts of civilization barely shed a glimmer of light into the surrounding wilds, but they can be home bases for adventurers who have reason to venture out. A city-state might send them on a quest to find or save a colony that has broken contact, or adventurers who serve Erathis might undertake a quest to found a colony of their own.

Gusting Wind: Functioning as difficult terrain, gusts can slow creatures down. In a narrow mountain pass, the wind might be a constant force that acts like a strong water current (page 207).

Starvation, Thirst, and Suffocation

When a character is deprived of food, water, or air, the rule of three applies. An adventurer can handle 3 weeks without food, 3 days without water, and 3 minutes without air. After that, such deprivation is a significant test of an adventurer's stamina. (People who aren't adventurers are far less hardy.)

Endurance Check: At the end of the time period (3 weeks, 3 days, or 3 minutes), the character must make a DC 20 Endurance check.

Success: Success buys the character another day (if hungry or thirsty) or round (if unable to breathe). Then the check is repeated against DC 25, then against DC 30, and so on.

Failure: When a character fails the check, he or she loses a healing surge and must continue to make checks against DC 25, then against DC 30, and so on. A character who fails a check and has no healing surges takes damage equal to his or her level.

A character cannot regain healing surges lost to starvation, thirst, or suffocation until he or she eats a meal, drinks, or gains access to air again, respectively.

A character who has 0 hit points or fewer and continues to be subject to one of these effects keeps taking damage as described above until he or she dies or is rescued.

Suffocation in Strenuous Situations: In strenuous situations, such as combat, going without air is very hard. A character holding his or her breath during underwater combat, for instance, must make a DC 20 Endurance check at the end of his or her turn in a round in which he or she takes damage.

TRAPS AND HAZARDS

One wrong step in an ancient tomb triggers a series of scything blades that cleave through armor and bone. The seemingly innocuous vines that hang over a cave entrance grasp at and choke anyone foolish enough to push through them. A narrow stone bridge leads over a pit filled with hissing, sputtering acid. In the DUNGEONS & DRAGONS game, monsters are only one of many challenges that adventurers face. If something can hurt the adventurers, but it isn't a monster, it's usually either a trap or a hazard.

Traps and hazards fit into an encounter much like additional monsters. Every trap or hazard has a level and an appropriate XP value for that level. See Appendix 1 and Appendix 2 for more information.

Trap or Hazard?

What's the difference between a trap and a hazard? Traps are constructed with the intent to damage, harry, or impede intruders. Hazards are natural or supernatural in origin, but typically lack the malicious intent of a trap. Though both feature similar risks, a pit covered with a goblin-constructed false floor is a trap, while a deep chasm between two sections of a troglodyte cave constitutes a hazard.

Traps tend to be hidden, and their danger is apparent only when they are discovered with keen senses or a misplaced step. The danger of a hazard is usually out in the open, and its challenge ascertained by the senses (sometimes far too late) or deduced by those knowledgeable about the hazard's environs.

The common link between traps and hazards revolves around peril—both to adventurers and monsters. Because of this similarity, traps and hazards feature similar rules, conventions, and presentations.

Basic Rules

A few basic rules govern a trap or a hazard, unless otherwise noted.

Targeting a Trap or a Hazard:
A trap or a hazard is usually an object or a terrain feature, but most powers target creatures, enemies, and allies. Despite that fact, a trap or a hazard counts as a creature for the purpose of targeting. The DM might decide that certain powers cannot be used on a trap or a hazard, regardless of this rule.

HOWARD LYON

Some traps and hazards have no defenses, whereas others have some defenses but not others. A trap or a hazard is immune to attacks against any defense it lacks. For instance, if a trap has no Will, it is immune to attacks against Will.

No Opportunity Attacks Provoked: Traps and hazards don't provoke opportunity attacks (page 246). Provoking such an attack usually represents dropping one's guard, and the attentiveness of a trap or a hazard does not vary.

How to Read a Trap/Hazard Stat Block

The stat block below presents an example trap, a spear gauntlet. Five hidden spears thrust upward from the floor in response to pressure, each in a separate square. When a creature steps on a trigger plate or starts its turn on one, all five spears thrust upward.

Spear Gauntlet	Level 2 Trap
Object	XP 125

Detect Perception DC 20   **Initiative** —
HP 10 per spear, 30 per trigger plate
AC 13, **Fortitude** 10, **Reflex** 10, **Will** —
Immune necrotic, poison, psychic, forced movement, all conditions, ongoing damage

TRIGGERED ACTIONS

⚔ **Attack** ✦ **At-Will**
Trigger: A creature enters one of the trigger squares or starts its turn there.
Attack (Opportunity Action): Melee 1 (each creature on a trigger square); +7 vs. AC
Hit: 2d8 + 6 damage.

COUNTERMEASURES

✦ **Disable:** Thievery DC 20. *Success:* A single trigger square and its associated spear no longer function.

Role   Some traps and hazards have roles: minion, elite, or solo. A minion is typically inert after it makes a single attack (unlike a monster minion, a trap or hazard minion might have more than 1 hit point). An elite trap or hazard is about as dangerous as two standard traps or hazards of the same level, and a solo trap or hazard is about as dangerous as five of the same level.

Perceiving Traps and Hazards   When an adventurer is within line of sight of a trap or a hazard, the DM compares the adventurer's passive Perception to the Detect DC of the trap. The spear gauntlet trap presented here requires a passive Perception of 20 or higher to detect. A character whose passive Perception is equal to or higher than the DC notices the trap or some part of it. Other skills might play a role in allowing characters to notice traps or hazards, such as Arcana, Dungeoneering, and Nature. An exceptional trap or hazard might even be undetectable to Perception.

Characters have the option of making Perception checks to find traps or hazards. They usually do so only when the DM has given some hint that a trap or a hazard might be present.

Triggering Traps and Hazards

Traps and hazards act without a hint of intelligence. A trap is constructed to be triggered when certain conditions are met. The description of a trap or a hazard explains when and how it activates. The spear gauntlet trap presented here is triggered when a creature enters one of the trigger squares or starts its turn on one.

Powers

Traps and hazards have powers, just as monsters do, and their powers follow the normal rules for powers (see Chapter 3). Most trap powers and hazard powers are attack powers. A blade cuts across the corridor, making melee attacks. Flames shoot out in close blasts. Rubble drops from the ceiling in an area burst. Arrows shoot out from the wall, making ranged attacks. In the sample trap presented here, the spears make melee attacks against any creatures on trigger squares.

Countermeasures

The best way to counter a trap or a hazard is to avoid it, but sometimes that's not possible to do. In such a situation, adventurers have three approaches to countering the obstacle: break it, disable it, or avoid it.

Destroying a trap or a hazard with an attack is often difficult, if not impossible—arrow traps are typically protected by walls or shielding, magic traps have a habit of blowing up when attacked, and very few attacks can counter that huge boulder rumbling down the corridor. But attacking and destroying a trap might be the best way to defeat it in a pinch. A trap or a hazard can be attacked only if its stat block contains defenses.

Most traps can be disabled with the Thievery skill. Sometimes other skills and abilities can supplement the Thievery check. Disabling a trap takes the trap out of commission until someone makes the effort to repair or reset it. While it's disabled, the trap effectively isn't there. A trap's stat block notes if it can be disabled and provides the DC for doing so. The spear gauntlet trap presented here requires a character to succeed on a DC 20 Thievery check to disable a trigger square.

Characters can also avoid a trap or a hazard. Figuring out a trap's location is a sure way of doing this, but more subtle and interesting methods sometimes apply. Many traps have interesting countermeasures other than destroying or disabling them that make it possible for a variety of characters to foil them.

DISEASE

When creatures are exposed to a disease—whether by the bite of a plague-bearing monster, immersion in filthy swamp water, infected food, or something else—they risk contracting the disease. The transmission and effects of a disease follow three steps: exposure, infection, and progression.

Filth fever is an example of a disease. It is commonly transmitted by creatures that inhabit unsanitary environments, such as rats and otyughs.

Filth Fever	Variable Level Disease

Those infected by this disease waste away as they alternately suffer chills and hot flashes.

Stage 0: The target recovers from the disease.
Stage 1: While affected by stage 1, the target loses a healing surge.
Stage 2: While affected by stage 2, the target loses a healing surge. The target also takes a -2 penalty to AC, Fortitude, and Reflex.
Stage 3: While affected by stage 3, the target loses all healing surges and cannot regain hit points. The target also takes a -2 penalty to AC, Fortitude, and Reflex.
Check: At the end of each extended rest, the target makes an Endurance check if it is at stage 1 or 2.
Lower than Easy DC: The stage of the disease increases by 1.
Easy DC: No change.
Moderate DC: The stage of the disease decreases by 1.

1. Exposure

A creature that is exposed to a disease risks contracting it. A creature is typically exposed to a disease in one of two ways.

✦ **Monster Attack:** A monster has an attack power that includes a disease (such as filth fever) as one of its effects.

✦ **Environmental Exposure:** A phenomenon or environmental feature that a creature touches, ingests, or inhales includes a disease. The phenomenon's description specifies whether exposure to the disease is automatic or requires a successful attack roll against the creature.

Unless the disease-inducing attack power or environmental description says otherwise, a creature exposed to the disease does not automatically contract it. Instead, the creature makes a saving throw at the end of the encounter to determine if the exposure leads to infection. If the saving throw fails, the creature is infected.

If a creature is exposed to the same disease multiple times in an encounter, it makes a single saving throw at the end of the encounter to determine if it contracts the disease. For instance, if Uldane is bitten over and over by dire rats carrying the filth fever disease, he makes a single saving throw against that disease at the end of encounter, not multiple saving throws.

2. Infection

Each disease has stages of increasing severity. Typically a disease has four stages:

+ Stage 0 (the disease ends)
+ Stage 1 (usually the initial effect of the disease)
+ Stage 2 (a more severe version of stage 1)
+ Stage 3 (usually the final state of the disease)

The effect that exposes a creature to a disease specifies the stage of the disease that applies when the creature is infected. As soon as the creature contracts the disease, the creature is subjected to that stage's effects. For instance, an attack power might say that a creature contracts filth fever (stage 1), which means the creature has the effects of stage 1 upon infection. If no stage is specified for a disease, the creature starts at stage 1.

Unless the disease is removed from the creature—with a power, a magical ritual, or something else—the disease might progress at the end of the creature's next extended rest.

3. Progression

While infected by a disease, a creature faces the possibility of the disease getting worse. However, the creature also has a chance to rally against it. Adventurers often help one another combat a disease by using the Heal skill on one another's behalf.

Endurance Checks: Until the disease ends, the creature must make an Endurance check at the end of each extended rest to determine if the disease's stage changes or stays the same. A disease typically specifies two DCs. A check result that equals or exceeds the higher DC causes the stage of the disease to decrease by 1 (in other words, the creature's health improves). If the check result equals the lower DC or a number between it and the higher DC, the disease remains at its current stage. A lower check result causes the stage of the disease to increase by 1 (in other words, the creature's health worsens).

Some diseases have more than two DCs, require a skill other than Endurance, or require checks at different times. For instance, a disease might require a creature to make an Endurance check against it at the end of each short rest.

Reaching a New Stage: When a creature reaches a new stage of the disease, it is subjected to the effects of the new stage right away. Unless a disease description says otherwise, the effects of the new stage replace the effects of the old one.

Final Stage: When a creature reaches the highest stage of a disease (usually stage 3), it stops making checks against the disease. The creature is now stuck with the disease until cured by a power, a magical ritual, or something else.

A particular disease might specify an unusual way to cure the creature (drink from a particular magic stream, for instance), and another disease might be mild enough that it has no final stage.

CHAPTER 6

COMBAT

Whether it's a skirmish against a handful of orcs or an all-out battle with a demon prince, combat is a staple of a DUNGEONS & DRAGONS adventure.

Combat encounters usually begin when adventurers enter an area containing monsters. Sometimes the monsters enter instead—when werewolves attack the adventurers' camp at night, for example—or the adventurers and the monsters stumble upon one another.

Skirmish or all-out battle, combat is a game staple.

This chapter details the rules for combat.

✦ **The Combat Sequence:** The cycle of rounds and turns that make up a battle. This section includes rules for surprise and rolling initiative.

✦ **Action Types:** The different types of actions that a creature can take on its turn and on other creatures' turns.

✦ **The Structure of a Turn:** What to do at the start of a turn, during a turn, and at the end of a turn.

✦ **Movement, Distance, and Terrain:** Rules for speed, special movement modes, difficult terrain, obstacles, flanking, teleportation, forced movement, and aerial combat.

✦ **Making Attacks:** How to make an attack roll and score a critical hit.

✦ **Attack Roll Modifiers:** Various factors that affect attack rolls, including combat advantage, cover, and concealment.

✦ **Damage:** Rules for dealing damage, including ongoing damage, extra damage, resistance, and vulnerability.

✦ **Durations:** How long does that effect last? This section answers that question.

✦ **Saving Throws:** How and when to make a saving throw to avoid or end ongoing damage and other continuing effects.

✦ **Conditions:** Rules and definitions for conditions imposed by attack powers and other effects.

✦ **Actions in Combat:** The most common actions in a battle, from spending an action point to walking.

✦ **Mounted Combat:** Rules for using a mount in combat.

✦ **Aquatic Combat:** Rules for battles underwater.

✦ **Hit Points and Healing:** Rules on hit points, healing surges, temporary hit points, and regeneration.

✦ **Dying and Death:** What happens when a creature drops to 0 hit points and how to escape death.

WILLIAM O'CONNOR

VISUALIZING THE ACTION

When a combat encounter starts, it's time to turn your attention to the battle grid. The combat rules assume that your group uses *D&D Dungeon Tiles,* a poster map, a gridded whiteboard, or an erasable, gridded mat to show the area where a battle takes place. The rules also assume that you use miniatures or tokens to represent the adventurers and the enemies they face.

A 1-inch square on the battle grid represents a 5-foot square in the game world. So a dungeon room that is 8 squares by 10 squares on the grid would be 40 feet by 50 feet, which is a huge room but a good size for a battle.

Characters and monsters are represented on the grid with pieces of some sort. These might be cardboard tokens, such as those included in the DUNGEONS & DRAGONS *Fantasy Roleplaying Game Starter Set,* or miniature figures molded in metal or plastic, such as *D&D Miniatures.* You can also use coins, beads, or other markers. Don't worry about not having the exact miniature for a creature: If your character is a dwarf cleric with a mace, and all the available dwarf miniatures have axes or swords (or you don't have any dwarf miniatures), choose the figure you like best. Just make sure that everyone at the table knows which object on the grid stands for which creature.

Miniatures for human-sized characters and monsters are a little more than 1 inch tall (about 32 millimeters) and stand on a base that fits in a 1-inch square. Plenty of creatures in the game aren't human-sized, though. Larger creatures take up more space on the battle grid. Creature sizes on the battle grid are discussed in "Creature Size and Space," page 199.

A combat encounter can be played without such visual representations, but there are good reasons to use them.

+ **Position is everything.** With a battle grid, players can easily determine whether an adventurer can see a monster, whether a monster has cover, and whether one combatant flanks another.
+ **Combat can be complex.** With five adventurers and a bunch of monsters involved, having tokens or miniatures on the table helps everyone remember which monsters are down, who's attacking whom, and where everyone is.
+ **Terrain matters.** An exciting combat encounter includes terrain features and hazards that make the environment an important part of the encounter. If adventurers want to claim the magic circle or avoid the cursed stone, the players need to know where that feature or hazard is.
+ **Imagination sometimes needs help.** The DM might describe a room with bubbling lava, a narrow stone bridge, overlooking ledges, and acid pits. It's a great scene, but sometimes it's a little hard to imagine how all those pieces fit together. The battle grid helps by showing exactly where all the elements of the scene are in relation to one another.

THE COMBAT SEQUENCE

A typical combat encounter is a clash between two sides, a flurry of weapon swings, feints, parries, footwork, and spellcasting. The DUNGEONS & DRAGONS game organizes the chaos of combat into a cycle of rounds and turns.

The actions in a combat encounter happen almost simultaneously in the game world, but to make combat manageable, creatures take turns acting—like taking turns in a board game. If a character's turn comes up before an enemy's, that character's actions take place before the enemy's actions do. The order of turns is determined at the beginning of a combat encounter, when everyone rolls initiative.

A combat encounter follows these steps.

1. **Determine surprise.** The DM determines whether anyone involved in the combat encounter is surprised. If any creatures notice enemies without being noticed in return, the aware creatures gain a surprise round (see "The Surprise Round," below).

2. **Establish positions.** The DM decides where the creatures are positioned on the battle grid. For example, if the adventurers have just opened a door into a room, the DM might draw or arrange a depiction of the door and the room on the battle grid and then ask the players to arrange their miniatures or tokens near the door. Then the DM places miniatures or tokens that represent the monsters in the room.

3. **Roll initiative.** Everyone involved in a combat encounter rolls initiative, determining the order of combatants' turns. Rolling initiative happens only at the beginning of a combat encounter.

KEY TERMS

The rules for the combat sequence rely on several key terms.

round: A round represents about 6 seconds in the game world. In a round, every combatant takes a turn.

turn: On a creature's turn, it takes actions: a standard action, a move action, a minor action, and any number of free actions, in any order it wishes. See "Action Types," page 194, for what can be done with these different actions.

once per round: Some effects are usable only once per round. For example, if a creature uses an effect (such as a class feature) that is usable only once per turn, it can't use that effect again until the start of the creature's next turn.

once per turn: Some effects can occur only once per turn. If a creature can use an effect (such as a class feature) only once per turn, that effect can be used no more than once during each turn in a round—not only during that creature's turn.

4. **Take surprise round actions.** If any creatures gained a surprise round, they act in initiative order, each taking a single action. (Surprised creatures take no actions during the surprise round.) The surprise round then ends, and the first regular round of combat begins.

5. **Take turns.** In initiative order, every combatant takes a turn, which includes various actions. (Creatures can also take certain actions on one another's turns.)

6. **Begin the next round.** When everyone involved in the combat has had a turn, the round ends. Begin the next round with whoever has the highest initiative.

7. **End the encounter.** Repeat steps 5 and 6 until one side stops fighting—for instance, all the monsters are captured, fleeing, unconscious, or dead.

WHEN IS AN ENCOUNTER OVER?

A combat encounter usually ends when the monsters or enemy characters stop fighting (often because they are dead, or captured, or have fled the battle). Typically, encounters are separated by a short rest, during which the adventurers regain hit points and refresh encounter powers, and some amount of travel time—even if it's as little as crossing a room to open the next door. The next encounter begins when the adventurers engage new opponents. An encounter might instead be followed by an extended rest.

Effects that last "until the end of the encounter" never carry over from one encounter to another, as long as those encounters are separated by a short rest. Such effects actually last about 5 minutes, if no rest intervenes after their use. Thus, if adventurers use them outside combat, or plow through multiple encounters without taking a short rest, they enjoy their effects for the full 5 minutes.

What if the adventurers don't take a short rest? Sometimes they feel as though they can't—they have to get to the high priest's chamber before the assassin strikes! Sometimes they just choose not to, perhaps because they hope to enjoy the benefit of an effect that lasts until the encounter ends. In any event, starting a new encounter without the benefit of a short rest after the last one makes the new encounter more challenging.

The Surprise Round

Some combat encounters begin with a surprise round, which occurs if any creatures are caught completely off guard at the start of battle. If even one creature is surprised, a surprise round occurs, and all creatures that aren't surprised act in initiative order during that round. Surprised creatures can't act at all during the surprise round.

Special Rules Two special rules apply to the surprise round.

Limited Action: If a creature is not surprised, it can take only one of the following actions on its turn during the surprise round: a standard action, a move action, or a minor action. The creature can also take free actions, but it cannot spend an action point. During the surprise round (but not on its turn), the creature can take an immediate action, as well as opportunity actions. See "Action Types," page 194, for definitions of these terms.

After every creature that is not surprised has acted, the surprise round ends, and creatures can act normally in subsequent rounds.

Surprised: If a creature is surprised, it can't take any actions, not even free actions, during the surprise round. The creature also grants combat advantage (page 217). As soon as the surprise round ends, the creature is no longer surprised.

Surprised is one of many conditions that can be applied to a creature. See "Conditions," later in this chapter.

Determining Surprise Determining surprise is usually straightforward. If one side in a battle notices the other side without being noticed in return, it has the advantage of surprise.

In many situations, surprise is extremely unlikely. Two groups traveling an open road or blundering through the woods notice each other, with no need for Perception checks of any kind. Neither group surprises the other.

Surprise can happen when creatures are actively hiding. Adventurers try to sneak past the giants guarding the outskirts of the enemy encampment. Kobolds hide along a well-traveled road, hoping to ambush travelers. A displacer beast stalks through the forest, hunting for prey.

A group that is actively trying to avoid detection might surprise its foes. In such a situation, the DM typically has each group member make a Stealth check (see "Group Checks," page 128). Alternatively, the group member who has the lowest Stealth modifier might have to make one check for the entire group. (If any member is at least 10 squares away from the rest of the group, however, that member can also make a separate check.) Whichever method is used, the DM compares the check result, or results, to the passive Perceptions of any creatures that might notice the group. Creatures that fail to notice the group are surprised if the group attacks.

Initiative

Before the first round of combat, each combatant rolls initiative. Rolling initiative follows the normal rules for making a check:

1. Roll a d20.

2. For an adventurer, add his or her initiative modifier (page 80), which is typically just his or her Dexterity modifier. For a monster, add the initiative modifier noted in its statistics block.

3. Add any bonuses or penalties that apply.

The result of the check determines the creature's initiative for the encounter.

Initiative Order Throughout a battle, creatures act in order, from

highest initiative to lowest. The order in which creatures take their turns is called the initiative order. The initiative order remains the same from round to round, although a creature's position in the order can change after delaying or readying an action (see "Actions in Combat," page 235).

Ties: When two creatures have the same initiative, the one with the higher initiative modifier goes before the other. If their modifiers are the same, their players can roll a die or flip a coin to break the tie.

Rolling for Different Combatants: Each player rolls initiative for his or her adventurer, and the DM rolls once for each distinct kind of monster or enemy character in the encounter.

Example: In an encounter with one orc storm shaman, two orc reavers, two orc rampagers, and four orc savages, the DM makes one initiative roll for each of the four kinds of orcs. As the combat progresses, all the orc savages act at once, both the orc reavers go together, and so on. The DM can choose to roll for each individual monster, but that could slow down play.

JIM NELSON

TRACKING INITIATIVE

Different play groups use different methods to track initiative order. If you're the DM, choose the method that works best for your group. Two factors come into play when deciding how to keep track of initiative: how you handle readying actions and delaying, and whether the players can see the order.

Combat Cards: One effective method of tracking initiative and other details of combat is to use index cards, blank playing cards, or a similar device. Create a card for each adventurer and for each group of identical monsters. When the players announce their characters' initiative check results, write the numbers on their combat cards and arrange them in order with the highest result on top, then insert the monsters' cards in initiative order. Then flip through the stack of cards, starting at the top. After each combatant acts, move that card to the bottom of the stack.

If a creature delays or readies an action, you might want to keep track of that by shifting the position of the card; turning it so it sticks out from the stack, for example. Then when the creature acts, you can easily pull the card from the stack and reinsert it in its new place. Alternatively, if an adventurer readies an action or delays, you can hand the combat card to the player, who returns it when his or her adventurer jumps back into the action.

With combat cards, the players don't know much about the order of play. They don't know where the monsters are in the initiative order until they act, which some DMs enjoy. On the other hand, they might also forget when their turns come up. You can help them plan ahead by saying who's up next when you call out the name of the character whose turn it is.

Visible List: This method uses a whiteboard, chalkboard, or easel tablet to track initiative where everyone can see the order. As the players call out their initiative check results, write them on the board in order (highest to lowest), leaving room between each name. You can either write the monster results on the list at the same time or add each monster to the list on its first turn.

If a creature delays or readies an action, make a mark next to that creature's name in the order. When the creature acts, erase its name from the list and then write it in the new position.

A visible list lets everyone see the order of play as they go. Players know when their turns are coming up, and they can start planning their actions in advance. On the downside, a visible list involves erasing and rewriting, which can slow down the action in complicated battles. Alternatively, you can use magnets on a whiteboard with names written on them, which make moving those elements around easier.

A variation on the visible list is having one of the players keep track of initiative, either on a board or on a piece of paper that the other players can see. This method reduces your mental processing load, freeing you up to think about the rest of what's going on at the table. On the other hand, it can be hard for you to remember when the monsters' turns are coming up.

List behind the Screen: This method tracks initiative on a list the players can't see, written on your own private whiteboard or a piece of scratch paper. Some argue that doing this combines the worst features of the other two methods: Players can't see the order, and keeping track involves erasing and rewriting. However, some DMs prefer it because it keeps control of the battle where they feel it belongs—solidly in their hands.

ACTION TYPES

A combat round is made up of actions. Firing an arrow, casting a spell, running across a room, opening a door—each of these activities, along with many others, is an action. Different action types are used to do different things. For instance, most attack powers are standard actions, and moving from one spot on the battlefield to another is normally a move action. Each power in the game specifies the type of action that is required to use it.

Actions help organize what creatures do during a battle and put a limit on how much a creature can do on a particular turn, since each creature can take only so many actions at a time. Certain conditions, such as dazed and unconscious, limit or prevent the actions a creature would otherwise be able to take.

After reading this section, see "Taking a Turn" and "Actions in Combat," discussed later in this chapter, for more about actions and game terms used here.

The Main Action Types

A typical turn in combat includes at least one of three actions, if not all three: a standard action, a move action, and a minor action. Unless a power or other effect says otherwise, a creature can take these types of actions only on its turn.

Standard Action: A standard action requires more effort than any other type and is usually the main action of a creature's turn. *Examples:* Most attack powers, using one's second wind, administering first aid to an ally.

Move Action: Move actions involve movement from one place to another. *Examples:* Walking, running, shifting.

Minor Action: As the name implies, minor actions are simple and quick. *Examples:* Pulling an item from a pouch or a sheath, opening a door or a treasure chest, picking up an item.

Free Actions

Free actions take almost no time or effort. A creature can usually take as many free actions as it wants during any turn, including other creatures' turns. *Examples:* Speaking a few sentences, dropping a held item, letting go of a grabbed creature.

There is an exception to this rule: A creature can take a free action to use an attack power only once per turn. Creatures don't normally have attack powers that can be used as free actions, but some powers and other effects grant the ability to use an attack power (usually a basic attack) as a free action. For instance, a character might have two different abilities that let him or her make a melee basic attack as a free action when their respective triggers occur. If both abilities are triggered on the same turn, the character can make only one of the melee basic attacks during that turn. This limitation does not apply to free actions that a creature is forced to take by an enemy.

In certain circumstances, the DM might decide to limit the use of free actions further. For instance, if an adventurer has already used free actions during a particular turn to talk, drop things, and use a class feature, the DM might rule that the adventurer can use no more free actions during that turn.

Triggered Actions

A triggered action is any action that can be taken only when a specific trigger occurs. A trigger is an action, an event, or an effect that allows the use of a triggered action.

Two action types—immediate actions and opportunity actions—always have triggers. Free actions sometimes have triggers as well, as do some powers and effects that require no action at all.

Whatever the type of action (or non-action), if it has a trigger, it cannot be used unless the trigger occurs. For instance, a wizard's *shield* power is triggered by the wizard being hit. Only when that trigger occurs does the wizard have the option of using the power.

Immediate Actions
There are two kinds of immediate actions: interrupts and reactions. The following rules govern both kinds of immediate action.

Trigger: Each immediate action—usually a power—defines its trigger. The one type of immediate action that every creature can take is a readied action (see "Ready an Action," page 247).

Someone Else's Turn: A creature cannot take an immediate action on its own turn. The action interrupts some event on another creature's turn or responds to that event.

Once per Round: A creature can take only one immediate action per round, either an immediate interrupt or an immediate reaction. Therefore, if a creature takes an immediate action, it can't take another one until the start of its next turn.

Interrupts
An immediate interrupt jumps in when its trigger occurs, taking place before the trigger finishes. If an interrupt invalidates a triggering action, the triggering action is lost.

Example: An enemy makes a melee attack against Keira the rogue, but Keira uses a power that lets her shift away as an immediate interrupt. If the enemy can no longer reach her, its attack action is lost. Similarly, Albanon the wizard might use *shield* in response to being hit and turn that hit into a miss, or Keira might use the immediate interrupt *heroic escape* to evade an enemy's attack before it can deal damage.

Reactions An immediate reaction lets a creature act in response to a trigger. The triggering action or event occurs and is completely resolved before the reaction takes place.

An immediate reaction waits for its trigger to finish, not necessarily for the action that contains the trigger to finish.

Example: An elder dragon's *claw* attack power is a standard action that allows two attack rolls against the same target. The dragon faces Fargrim the fighter, who has an immediate reaction (*veteran gambit*) that is triggered by being hit with a melee attack. If the dragon uses *claw* and hits Fargrim with the first attack roll, he can use *veteran gambit* in response to that hit. In that case, the immediate reaction waits for that hit to be resolved, but does not wait for the entire power to be resolved.

Likewise, an immediate reaction can interrupt movement. Here's how: If a creature triggers an immediate reaction while moving (by coming into range, for instance), the reaction can take place before the creature finishes moving, but after it has moved at least 1 square. In other words, an immediate reaction can be in response to a square of movement, rather than to an entire move action.

Opportunity Actions
An opportunity action is similar to an immediate interrupt, but it can be taken once per turn, rather than once per round.

Trigger: Each opportunity action—usually a power—defines its trigger. The one type of opportunity action that every creature can take is an opportunity attack (page 246).

Someone Else's Turn: A creature cannot take an opportunity action on its own turn. The action interrupts some event on another creature's turn.

Once per Turn: A creature can take no more than one opportunity action per turn (but it can take one on each other creature's turn).

Interrupt: Just like an immediate interrupt, an opportunity action interrupts its trigger, taking place before the trigger finishes.

Other Triggered Effects
If an effect has a trigger but is neither an immediate action nor an opportunity action, assume that it behaves like an immediate reaction, waiting for its trigger to completely resolve. However, ignore this guideline when the effect has to interrupt its trigger to function. For instance, if a triggered power allows an adventurer to use a free action to reroll an attack roll, with the hope of turning a miss into a hit, the power must interrupt the trigger ("You miss with an attack") to function; otherwise the attack would be resolved as a miss.

THE STRUCTURE OF A TURN
When a creature's turn comes up in the initiative order, it can do things. A creature's turn has three parts: the start of the turn; the actions of the turn, if any; and the end of the turn. Of course, if a creature is destroyed, it has no turns!

The Start of a Turn
Each creature has a start of each turn: a phase that takes no time in the game world but is used to keep track of certain effects. The start of a creature's turn always takes place, even if the creature is unable to act.

+ **No Actions:** A creature can't take any actions at the start of its turn. However, other creatures might have abilities that they can use at the start of that creature's turn.

+ **Ongoing Damage:** If a creature is affected by ongoing damage (page 224), it takes the damage now.

+ **Regeneration:** If the creature has regeneration (page 260), it regains hit points now.

+ **End Effects:** Some effects end automatically now ("at the start of your next turn").

+ **Any Order:** The creature can choose the order in which things happen at the start of its turn. For instance, if the creature has regeneration and is taking ongoing damage, it can choose to take the ongoing damage and then use its regeneration or the other way around.

The Actions of a Turn

During a creature's turn, the creature can take a few actions. Players decide what to do with their adventurers' actions while the DM determines the monsters' actions, considering what can help achieve victory and create an exciting scene.

✦ **Three Main Actions:** A creature gets the following three actions on its turn:
   Standard action
   Move action
   Minor action

✦ **Free Actions:** The creature can also take any number of free actions on its turn.

✦ **Any Order:** The creature can take its actions in any order and can skip any of them.

✦ **Action Points:** If a creature has any action points (page 235), it can take an extra action on its turn by spending an action point as a free action.

The End of a Turn

Each creature has an end of each turn: a phase that takes no time in the game world but is used to keep track of certain effects. The end of a creature's turn always takes place, even if the creature is unable to act.

✦ **No Actions:** A creature can't take any actions at the end of its turn. However, other creatures might have abilities that they can use at the end of that creature's turn.

✦ **Saving Throws:** A creature now makes a saving throw (page 227) against each effect on it that a save can end.

SUBSTITUTING ACTIONS

A move action or a minor action can replace a standard action, and a minor action can replace a move action. By substituting actions in this way, a creature can vary the actions that it takes on its turn quite a bit.

Here are the action options for a turn, in addition to free actions.

Option A
Standard action
Move action
Minor action

Option B
Standard action
Two minor actions

Option C
Two move actions
Minor action

Option D
Move action
Two minor actions

Option E
Three minor actions

+ **End Effects:** Some effects end automatically now ("at the end of your next turn").
+ **Any Order:** The creature can choose the order in which things happen at the end of its turn. For instance, if the creature has saving throws to make and is subjected to an effect that damages it at the end of its turn, the creature can choose to take the damage and then make the saving throws or the other way around.

Actions on Other Turns

Most of a creature's actions take place on its turn. But a creature can take free actions on anyone's turn, and an event or another combatant's actions might provide an opportunity to take an immediate action or an opportunity action on someone else's turn.

MOVEMENT, DISTANCE, AND TERRAIN

In a battle, adventurers and monsters are in constant motion. Keira the rogue skirts the melee, looking for a chance to set up a deadly flanking attack. Albanon the wizard stays away from the enemy, trying to find a position from which he can make the best use of area attacks, while goblin archers move to get clear shots with their bows. Creatures can gain the edge in battle by using movement and position to their advantage.

Creatures use actions—most often move actions—to reposition themselves, and they sometimes move other creatures forcibly. Terrain affects where a creature can move and how quickly it can get there. Wherever a creature is positioned, it takes up a certain amount of space based on its size.

Creature Size and Space

Each creature falls into one of six size categories. A creature's size determines its space and affects its reach.

Size	Space	Reach
Tiny	1/2 × 1/2	0
Small	1 × 1	1
Medium	1 × 1	1
Large	2 × 2	1 or 2
Huge	3 × 3	2 or 3
Gargantuan	4 × 4 or larger	3 or 4

KEY TERMS

The rules for movement, range, and terrain rely on several general terms. These terms often appear in descriptions of powers, feats, and other game elements.

battle grid: The network of 1-inch squares that represents an encounter area.

enter a square: Move into a square on the battle grid by any means, whether willingly or unwillingly.

filling a square: When something fills a square, that thing functions as blocking terrain (page 206). Unless otherwise noted, a creature or an object such as a chair does not fill squares in its space.

forced movement: Movement that a creature is compelled to do, specifically a pull, a push, or a slide. A creature can be moved in other ways, such as through teleportation, but only pulls, pushes, and slides are technically forced movement.

leave a square: Move out of a square on the battle grid by any means, whether willingly or unwillingly.

move: Any instance of movement, whether it is done willingly or unwillingly. Whenever a creature, an object, or an effect leaves a square to enter another, it is moving. Shifting, teleporting, and being pushed are all examples of moves.

occupied space or square: A space or square occupied by a creature.

position: The location of a creature, an object, or an effect on the battle grid.

size: One of six categories that determines the extent of a creature's space.

space: The square area that a creature occupies or the squares where an object or a phenomenon is located. A typical adventurer's space is a single square.

speed: The distance (in squares) that a creature can move using the walk action.

square: A 1-inch square on the battle grid, which is equivalent to a 5-foot square in the game world. The square is the main unit of measurement in the game.

unoccupied space or square: A space or square that is neither occupied by a creature nor filled by an object.

willing movement: Movement of any sort that a creature does of its own free will. Any other sort of movement, such as forced movement, is unwilling.

Space: A creature's space is the area, measured in squares, that the creature occupies on the battle grid. This area represents the three-dimensional space that the creature needs to take part in an encounter, allowing it to turn around, attack, fall prone, and so on. Despite the cubic shape of its space, a creature is not actually a cube (unless it's a gelatinous cube).

Reach: A creature's size affects its reach, which is measured in squares. A creature's reach can influence several things in the game, such as how far the creature can reach out to touch or grab something as well as the range of some of its melee powers. See "Melee Powers," page 99, for how reach can affect the range of certain melee powers.

Facing: A creature that is taking part in an encounter is assumed to be in constant motion, looking here and turning there. Because of this assumption, no one ever has to keep track of which direction a creature is facing.

The Size Categories

Tiny: Four individual Tiny creatures can fit in a square, and a Tiny creature can enter a larger creature's space and end its turn there. Having a reach of 0 means a Tiny creature cannot make melee attacks against targets outside its own space, unless otherwise noted. *Examples:* mundane animals such as cats and crows.

Small: Small creatures occupy the same space as Medium creatures, but they face some restrictions in the weapons they can wield (see "Weapons and Size," page 270). *Examples:* gnomes, goblins, halflings.

Medium: This is the size of a typical human and serves as a standard in the game. This category has no special rules. *Examples:* humans, dwarves, elves, orcs.

Large, Huge, and Gargantuan: Creatures larger than Medium take up more than 1 square. For instance, an ogre takes up a space that is 2 squares by 2 squares. Most Large and larger creatures also have a reach greater than 1, which means they can make melee attacks against creatures that aren't adjacent to them. A creature's basic body shape usually determines its reach; a Large ogre has a reach of 2, but a Large horse has a reach of 1. *Examples:* dragons, giants, trolls.

Determining Distance

Whether a creature wants to dash from one position on the battlefield to another or target a foe with an attack, everyone needs to know how to determine distance between things on the battle grid. Here are the basic rules related to distance.

Adjacent Squares: Two squares are adjacent if a side or a corner of one touches a side or a corner of the other. Two creatures or objects are adjacent if one of them is in a square adjacent to a square occupied or filled by the other, or if they are in the same square.

Counting Distance: To determine how far away one square is from another, start counting from any square adjacent to one of the squares (even one that is diagonally adjacent but around a corner), then count around blocking terrain (page 206) and end up in the other square. Make sure to use the shortest path.

Nearest Creature or Square: Sometimes a creature uses a power or another effect that refers to the nearest creature or square. To determine the nearest creature or square, count distance normally. When two or more creatures or squares are equally close, the creature's player can pick either one as the nearest.

Determining Distance

The monster is 5 squares away from the adventurer.

Speed

Each creature has a speed that is measured in squares. This speed represents how far a creature can move using the walk action (although it can choose not to move any distance at all). For instance, Keira has a speed of 6, so she can move up to 6 squares (or 30 feet) when she walks.

The most common way that a creature moves is by taking a move action, such as the walk or the run action, that is based on its speed. Powers, feats, and other effects also refer to a creature's speed. Keira might use a power that lets her shift up to her speed, for instance.

Determining Speed
A character's speed is determined by the character's race and any bonuses and penalties. A monster's speed is noted in its stat block.

The most common penalty to speed comes from certain types of armor. For instance, an elf starts with a speed of 7. But Lyriel the elf fighter wears plate armor, so her speed drops to 6, since the armor imposes a –1 penalty to speed.

Special Movement Modes
In addition to walking, some creatures have other movement modes that allow them to burrow, climb, fly, or swim. A creature's stat block specifies which of these movement modes it can use, if any, and its speed when using one of those modes. Creatures can also temporarily gain access to special movement modes from powers and other effects.

DEFAULT MOVE ACTIONS

These are the three most common move actions, available to every creature.

✦ **Walk:** A creature uses a move action to move up to its speed.

✦ **Shift:** A creature uses a move action to move 1 square (certain powers allow a creature to shift more than 1 square). Shifting doesn't provoke opportunity actions.

✦ **Run:** A creature uses a move action to move its speed plus up to 2 additional squares. As soon as a creature starts running, it both grants combat advantage and takes a -5 penalty to attack rolls until the start of its next turn.

Two other common move actions are usable only by creatures that are prone.

✦ **Crawl:** A creature uses a move action to move up to half its speed while it is prone.

✦ **Stand Up:** A creature uses a move action to stand up, which ends the prone condition on it.

For more about these actions, see "Actions in Combat," page 235.

If a creature can use a special movement mode, it can take the walk or the run action using its speed (or simply stand still) with that movement mode instead of its walking speed. It might also be able to charge, shift, or use other move actions while using that movement mode. For instance, a creature that has a fly speed can take the walk action to fly instead of walk, and it can shift while flying.

Burrow Speed: A creature that has a burrow speed, such as a purple worm or an umber hulk, can move through loose earth at the stated speed and through solid stone at half that speed. The creature can't shift or charge while burrowing.

Climb Speed: A creature that has a climb speed, such as a spider or a carrion crawler, doesn't have to make Athletics checks to climb. It can simply climb up and down a surface using its climb speed, doing so as part of any of its actions that involve it moving. In addition, the creature ignores difficult terrain during the climb and doesn't grant combat advantage because of climbing. For rules on climbing, see "Athletics," page 136.

Fly Speed: A creature that has a fly speed, such as an angel or a dragon, can move through the air. See "Flying," page 210.

Swim Speed: A creature that has a swim speed, such as a crocodile or a black dragon, doesn't have to make Athletics checks to swim. It can simply move through water using its swim speed, doing so as part of any of its actions that involve it moving. For rules on swimming, see "Athletics," page 136.

Combining Movement Modes

Sometimes a creature can combine one movement mode with another in a single move. For instance, a creature that has a climb speed can take the walk action to move a few squares toward a wall using its normal speed, and then climb up the wall using its climb speed.

When a creature combines movement modes in this way, two rules govern the combination.

✦ **Use Highest Speed:** The highest speed among the movement modes used determines the number of squares that the creature can move with the action. Don't add the speeds together.

✦ **Maximum for Each Movement Mode:** The speed of each movement mode determines the maximum number of squares that the creature can move during the segment of the action that movement mode applies to.

Example: A vampire wants to walk to a nearby wall and then climb up, both during the same move action. It has a walking speed of 7 and a climb speed of 4. If the vampire takes the walk action, it can move a total of 7 squares, since 7 is the higher of the two speeds, but no more than 4 of those squares can be part of the climb.

Basic Movement Rules

Movement is governed by the following rules, unless otherwise noted.

Diagonal Movement

Moving diagonally works the same as other movement, except that a creature can't cross the corner of an obstacle, such as a stone wall, that fills its space. A creature can move diagonally past creatures, since they don't fill their squares.

Ending a Move

A creature must have enough movement to enter its destination space. A creature can't enter a square partway: If it doesn't have enough movement or runs out on the way, its move ends in the last square it could get to.

Example: If a creature has a speed of 6, it can normally choose to end its move in a square 6 squares away. However, if that square costs 1 extra square of movement to enter, the creature cannot end its move there but must choose a different square (or stop where it is).

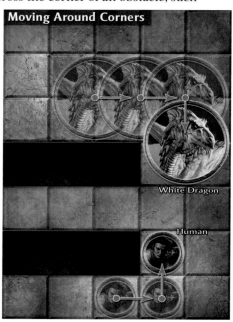

Moving Around Corners

White Dragon

Human

Occupied Squares
A creature occupies all the squares of its space. The rules for moving through occupied squares depend on whether the squares belong to an ally or an enemy.

Ally: A creature can enter an ally's space, but it can end its move in an ally's space only if the ally is prone (page 232).

Enemy: A creature can't enter an enemy's space unless that enemy is helpless (page 231) or two size categories larger or smaller than it. A creature can end its move in an enemy's space only if the enemy is helpless.

Tiny Creatures: A Tiny creature can enter a larger creature's space and end its move there, regardless of whether the larger creature is an ally or enemy.

Prone Creatures: A prone creature that ends up in the same square as another creature has two main options for moving itself out of that square: crawl or stand up.

Double Move
A creature can move twice on its turn if it takes another move action instead of a standard action. Taking the same move action twice in a row is called taking a double move.

Same Move Action Twice: To take a double move, a creature must take the same move action twice in a row on the same turn—two walks, two runs, two shifts, or two crawls.

Combined Speed: During a double move, first add the speeds of the two move actions together. The creature moves using the combined speed.

Because of this greater speed, the creature can sometimes move into a square that it would otherwise be unable to enter.

Example: A creature whose speed is 5 can enter only 2 squares of difficult terrain (see below) when it takes a single move action to walk. If it takes a double move by walking twice in a row, it can move a total of 10 squares, so it can enter 5 squares of difficult terrain instead of only 4.

Occupied Squares: During a double move, a creature's first move action can end in an ally's space, since the creature is not stopping. The second move action follows the normal rules for where the creature can end the move.

Terrain and Obstacles
Most battles don't take place in bare rooms or featureless plains. Adventurers fight monsters across boulder-strewn caverns, in briar-choked forests, and on steep staircases. Each battleground offers its own combination of challenges, such as cover, concealment, and poor footing. Appendix 3 describes various forms of terrain, both mundane and fantastic.

MOVEMENT IN THREE DIMENSIONS

Aquatic and aerial encounters force players to think in three dimensions, as well as creating the awkward situation of trying to stack several figures in one square. Here are some ideas for dealing with these situations.

To begin with, define an arbitrary elevation as "ground" level, preferably the one where most of the encounter takes place. Creatures are all positioned above or below the action relative to that altitude.

Placing a small d6 or d4 next to a miniature or token is a good way to measure its distance above or below ground level. The number on the die shows how many squares the creature is above or below that level. Use dice of one color to mark creatures below ground level and another color for those above.

When a monster is directly above or below an adventurer, its miniature or token can share the same square on the battle grid. Although crowded, two miniatures can usually fit well enough in one square. To avoid knocking figures over or accidentally pushing them into the wrong squares, instead set the miniatures or tokens aside and use smaller proxies, such as the dice that measure elevation, in their place.

Determining the distance between creatures above or below one another is straightforward: First, count squares between the two creatures as if they were at the same elevation, then count the difference between their elevations. Use the higher of these two numbers.

Blocking Terrain
Walls, doors, large pillars, and various obstacles that fill squares on the battle grid are blocking terrain, which prevents movement.

Blocks Movement: Creatures can't enter squares of blocking terrain. A typical square of blocking terrain is completely filled, which prevents diagonal movement across its corners.

No Line of Effect or Line of Sight: Blocking terrain blocks line of effect. It blocks line of sight as well, unless the terrain is transparent.

Cover: A creature can gain cover by positioning itself near blocking terrain. See "Cover and Concealment," page 219.

Difficult Terrain
Rubble, undergrowth, shallow bogs, steep stairs, low furniture, and many sorts of other impediments are difficult terrain, which hampers movement.

Costs 1 Extra Square: Each square of difficult terrain costs 1 extra square of movement to enter. Some difficult terrain, such as a low wall, is on the line between two squares, rather than in the squares themselves. Entering a square by crossing that line costs 1 extra square of movement.

Because difficult terrain costs that extra square of movement to enter, a creature can't normally shift into it. However, if a power or some other effect lets a creature shift 2 squares, the creature can shift into a square of difficult terrain.

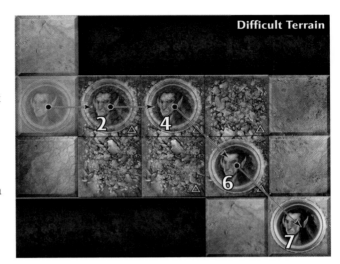

Large, Huge, and Gargantuan Creatures: If a Large or larger creature enters two or more squares that have different kinds of terrain, count that square of movement according to the most difficult terrain. Count only squares the creature is entering for the first time, not squares it already occupies.

Terrain Walk: Some creatures have a trait called terrain walk, which allows them to ignore difficult terrain in specific kinds of environments. See the "Movement-Related Traits" sidebar for definitions of the different kinds of terrain walk.

Hindering Terrain

Pits, electrifying runes, lava, extremely deep water, and other harmful environmental phenomena are hindering terrain, which punishes creatures that are in it or try to enter it.

Saving Throw: A creature can make a saving throw to avoid being forced into hindering terrain, whether it is pulled, pushed, slid, teleported, or otherwise moved against its will. See "Forced Movement" and "Teleportation," discussed later in this section.

Damage: Hindering terrain almost always has the potential to harm creatures that enter it, either by causing them to fall or by dealing damage to them directly. (Some hindering terrain might impose a penalty or a harmful condition without dealing damage.)

Currents

Currents come into play when creatures are moving or fighting in swift-flowing water (see "Aquatic Combat," page 255) or battling strong winds while flying.

A current drags creatures along its path. When a creature enters a current or starts its turn in one, it moves a distance and direction according to the current's strength (as specified in an adventure or as determined by the DM) and in the direction it flows. This movement is a slide effect (page 211), with the distance and direction determined by the current.

A creature that wants to fight against a current can spend squares of movement to reduce the distance the current slides it. The creature can reduce the distance partially, or decrease it to 0, provided that the creature has enough movement to do so.

If a current slides a creature through another square that has a current, the creature ignores that other current. If a creature starts its turn in a square that contains more than one current, the strongest current applies. If the currents have the same strength, the creature chooses which one applies.

MOVEMENT-RELATED TRAITS

The following traits modify movement in various ways. They are innate to some creatures (noted in their stat blocks), whereas other creatures gain such traits temporarily from powers and other effects.

Clumsy: Some creatures are clumsy while using a specific movement mode (noted next to that mode in the creature's stat block), and others are clumsy while on the ground (noted next to the creature's speed). While a creature is clumsy, it takes a –4 penalty to attack rolls and all defenses.

Terrain Walk: The following traits are all kinds of terrain walk.

Earth Walk: A creature that has earth walk ignores difficult terrain that is rubble, uneven stone, or an earthen construction.

Forest Walk: A creature that has forest walk ignores difficult terrain that is part of a tree, underbrush, or some other forest growth.

Ice Walk: A creature that has ice walk ignores difficult terrain that is icy or snowy.

Swamp Walk: A creature that has swamp walk ignores difficult terrain that is mud or shallow water.

Phasing: While a creature is phasing, it ignores difficult terrain, and it can enter squares containing blocking terrain, obstacles, and enemy creatures. The creature follows the normal rules for where it must end its movement (normally an unoccupied space).

Spider Climb: A creature that has spider climb can use its climb speed to move across overhanging horizontal surfaces (such as ceilings) without making Athletics checks.

Tunneling: A creature that has tunneling leaves tunnels behind it as it moves using its burrow speed. The creature, as well as smaller creatures, can move through these tunnels without any reduction in speed. Creatures of the same size as the tunneling creature must squeeze (page 249) to move through these tunnels, and larger creatures cannot move through them at all.

Falling

Some kinds of terrain present a unique danger: a precipitous drop. When a creature falls at least 10 feet, it is likely to take damage. Most often, a creature falls because of forced movement (page 211).

Falling Damage: A creature takes 1d10 damage for each 10 feet it falls, to a maximum of 50d10. The creature falls prone when it lands, unless it somehow takes no damage from the fall.

    Fast Alternative: If a creature falls more than 50 feet, it takes 25 damage per 50 feet, plus 1d10 damage for each 10 extra feet.

Large, Huge, and Gargantuan Creatures: If only part of a creature's space is over a pit or a precipice, the creature doesn't fall. (Normally a creature ends up in such a position as a result of forced movement.) On the creature's next turn, it must either move to an unoccupied space that is at least as large as it is or squeeze (page 249) if it wants to remain on the edge of the drop.

Reducing Falling Damage: If a creature has training in Acrobatics, it can make a check to reduce the damage of a fall.

No Opportunity Actions Triggered: When a creature falls past an enemy, the creature does not trigger opportunity actions, such as opportunity attacks, from that enemy that are triggered by movement.

High-Altitude Falls: Some encounters take place very high above the ground. In such an encounter, it is possible for a creature to spend more than 1 round falling to the ground. As a rule of thumb, such a creature falls 500 feet during its first turn of falling. If it is still falling at the start of its turn, it can take actions on that turn as normal. If none of those actions expressly halts the fall, the creature falls 500 feet at the end of the turn. This sequence continues until the creature lands.

Flying Creatures: If a creature falls while it is flying (see below), it descends the full distance of the fall but is likely to take less damage than a creature that can't fly. Multiply the creature's fly speed by 5 and subtract that value from the distance of the fall, then figure out falling damage. If the difference is 0 or less, the creature lands without taking damage from the fall. For instance, if a red dragon falls when it is 40 feet in the air, subtract its fly speed of 8 (8 squares = 40 feet) from its altitude. The difference is 0, so the dragon lands safely and is not prone.

    If a creature is flying when it starts a high-altitude fall, it has one chance to halt the fall by making a DC 30 Athletics check as an immediate reaction, with a bonus to the check equal to the creature's fly speed. On a success, the creature falls 100 feet and then stops falling. On a failure, the creature falls as normal.

Flying

Some creatures have the innate ability to fly, whereas others gain the ability through powers, magic items, or other attributes. The rules for flight emphasize abstraction and simplicity over simulation. In real life, a flying creature's ability to turn, the speed it must maintain to stay aloft, and other factors put a strict limit on flight. In the game, flying creatures face far fewer limitations.

Flight follows the basic movement rules, with the following clarifications.

Fly Speed: To fly, a creature takes the walk, run, or charge action but uses its fly speed in place of its walking speed. A creature that has a fly speed can also shift and take other move actions, as appropriate, while flying.

Moving Up and Down: While flying, a creature can move straight up, straight down, or diagonally up or down. There is no additional cost for moving up or down.

Falling Prone: If a creature is knocked prone while it is flying, it falls. This means a flying creature falls when it becomes unconscious or is subject to any other effect that knocks it prone. The creature isn't actually prone until it lands and takes falling damage.

Remaining in the Air: A flying creature does not need to take any particular action to remain aloft; the creature is assumed to be flying as it fights, moves, and takes other actions. However, a flying creature falls the instant it is stunned, unless it can hover (see the "Flight Traits" sidebar).

Landing: If a creature flies to a surface it can hold onto or rest on, the creature can land safely.

Terrain: Terrain on the ground does not affect a flying creature if the terrain isn't tall enough to reach it. Because of this rule, flying creatures can easily bypass typical difficult terrain, such as a patch of ice on the ground. Aerial terrain (see below) can affect flying creatures.

FLIGHT TRAITS

Many flying creatures have traits related to flight, which are noted in a creature's stat block.

Altitude Limit: If a creature has a specified altitude limit, the creature falls at the end of its turn if it is flying higher than that limit. For example, a creature that has an altitude limit of 2 falls at the end of its turn if it is flying higher than 2 squares.

Hover: A creature that can hover, such as a beholder, can remain in the air even when it is stunned.

Aerial Terrain Difficult terrain for a flying creature includes airborne debris, swirling winds, and other factors that interfere with flight, including surface features that reach to a great height. Clouds provide concealment, while towers, floating castles, and other structures provide cover. Strong gusts of wind work like currents in water, following the rules under "Current," earlier in this chapter.

Forced Movement

Certain powers and effects allow a creature to move a target forcibly, whether the target is willing or unwilling. (Other effects, such as traps or zones, can also force targets to move.) The three kinds of forced movement are pull, push, and slide. Teleporting a creature does not count as forced movement for the purpose of these rules.

✦ **Pull:** Pulling a target means that each square of the forced movement must bring the target closer to the creature or effect that is pulling it.

✦ **Push:** Pushing a target means that each square of the forced movement must move the target farther away from the creature or effect that is pushing it.

✦ **Slide:** Sliding a target can move it in any direction. Sometimes a creature can swap places with a target. Doing so is a special kind of slide; the creature slides the target into its space and then shifts so that its space includes at least 1 square that the target just left.

ADAM PAQUETTE

The following rules govern all three kinds of forced movement. A particular instance of forced movement might contain exceptions to these rules.

Distance, Specific Destination, or Both: The power or other effect that produces forced movement specifies a distance in squares, a specified destination square, or both for the movement.

When a distance is specified, it is a maximum; the creature or effect producing the forced movement can move its target up to that number of squares (or none at all). For instance, a character's power might say, "You slide the target 4 squares (or "up to 4 squares"); both mean the character can move the target up to 4 squares or not move it at all.

When a destination is specified, it is absolute; the creature or effect must either move the target to that destination or not move it at all. Often a destination is combined with a distance, which means the target can be moved to the destination only if it is no farther away than the specified distance. For instance, a character's power might say, "You slide the target up to 5 squares to a square adjacent to you (or "5 squares to a square adjacent to you)," both of which mean the character can move the target up to 5 squares but only if the move ends in a square adjacent to that character.

Line of Effect: A creature must have line of effect to any square that it pulls, pushes, or slides a target into. Also, a target cannot be forced through blocking terrain.

Ignores Difficult Terrain: Forced movement isn't hindered by difficult terrain.

Ignores Speed: A target's speed is irrelevant to the distance it is forced to move, and the target expends none of its own actions for the movement.

Destination Space: The destination of the forced movement must be an unoccupied space that is at least the same size as the target. For instance, a Large creature cannot be pushed into a space that is only 1 square wide.

No Opportunity Actions Triggered: When a target is pulled, pushed, or slid, it does not trigger opportunity actions, such as opportunity attacks, that are triggered by movement.

Catching Oneself: If a target is forced over a precipice or into hindering

terrain, such as lava or a pit, the target can immediately make a saving throw to avoid going over the edge or entering that terrain. If the creature saves, it falls prone in the last square it occupied before it would have fallen or entered the terrain. Otherwise, it falls over the edge or enters the terrain. Once the saving throw is resolved, the forced movement ends.

Two-Dimensional: Forced movement is normally two-dimensional; all the squares of the movement must be on the same horizontal plane. Forced movement can become three-dimensional when the target is flying, is moved through a substance such as water, or is on a non-horizontal surface, such as an incline, that supports it. This means an earthbound target cannot normally be pushed to a square in the air, but a hovering target can be. Similarly, a target can be pulled down a flight of stairs, and it can be slid in any direction underwater.

Immobilized or Restrained: Being immobilized doesn't prevent a target from being pulled, pushed, or slid, but being restrained does. See "Conditions," discussed later in this chapter, for more.

Teleportation

Teleportation allows instant movement from one location to another. Typically, a creature teleports by means of a magical power, such as the wizard spell *dimension door*.

Unless the description of a power or other effect says otherwise, use the following rules when a creature uses a teleportation power on a target, which might be itself, another creature, or an object.

Instantaneous: Teleportation takes no time. The target disappears and immediately appears in the destination that the teleporting creature chooses. The movement is unhindered by intervening creatures, objects, or terrain.

Destination Space: The destination of the teleportation must be an unoccupied space that is at least the same size as the target. For instance, a Large creature cannot be teleported into a space that is only 1 square wide.

If arriving in the destination space would cause the target to fall or if that space is hindering terrain, the target can immediately make a saving throw. On a save, the teleportation is negated. Otherwise, the target arrives in the destination space.

If a prone creature teleports, it arrives in the destination space still prone.

Line of Sight: The user of the teleportation power must have line of sight to the destination space.

No Line of Effect Required: Neither the user of the teleportation power nor the target needs line of effect to the destination space.

No Opportunity Actions Triggered: When a target teleports, it doesn't provoke opportunity actions, such as opportunity attacks, that are triggered by movement.

Immobilized or Restrained: Being immobilized or restrained doesn't prevent a target from teleporting. If a target teleports away from a physical restraint, a monster's grasp, or some other immobilizing effect that is located in a specific space, the target is no longer immobilized or restrained. Otherwise, the target teleports but is still immobilized or restrained when it reaches the destination space.

Not Forced Movement: Teleporting a creature, even an unwilling one, does not count as forced movement (page 211).

MAKING ATTACKS

DUNGEONS & DRAGONS battles are won through cleverly chosen attacks, able defenses, and luck. On a typical turn, a monster takes a standard action to use an attack power, as does an adventurer, whether he or she is a stalwart fighter, a wily rogue, a devout cleric, or a clever wizard. All creatures' defenses are tested by foes' attacks.

Every creature has a number of attacks to choose from. The exact attack powers available to an adventurer depend on the player's choices at character creation and as the adventurer gains levels, and a monster's attack powers are specified in its stat block.

Each attack power has a type—melee, ranged, close, or area—that determines how the power interacts with a number of rules in the game. Whatever type of attack power a creature uses, the process for making an attack is almost always the same.

1. Choose an attack power, keeping in mind the rules for its type.
2. Choose targets. Each target must be within the power's range and must be within line of effect. See "Choosing Targets," page 105, for how to determine whether a creature can be targeted by a power.
3. Make an attack roll, rolling a d20 and adding the appropriate bonuses and penalties.
4. Compare the attack roll's result to the target's defense. The attack specifies what defense to check. If the result is equal to the specified defense or higher, the attack hits the target. Otherwise, it misses. (However, if the d20 shows a 20, the attack automatically hits the target, and if it shows a 1, the attack automatically misses.)

5. When an attack hits, it usually deals damage, and many attacks produce some other effect, such as forced movement or a condition. An attack power's description specifies what happens on a hit. Most attack powers do nothing on a miss, but some specify an effect, such as half damage, on a miss.

6. If the attack power has more than one target, repeat steps 3 through 5 for each of them.

Some attack powers don't include attack rolls. Such powers automatically deal damage, impose conditions, or harm enemies in some other way.

Attack Rolls

Making an attack roll follows the normal rules for making a check. An adventurer's attack power specifies which ability modifier to use for the check. For instance, "Strength vs. AC" means use the adventurer's Strength modifier, plus one-half the adventurer's level. In contrast, a monster's attack power simply states a number to add to the die roll.

DEFAULT ATTACK POWERS

Any creature can use the following attack powers, each of which is detailed in "Actions in Combat," later in this chapter.

✦ **Melee Basic Attack:** The attacker makes a simple attack using a melee weapon, which can be an unarmed strike or an improvised weapon such as a chair.

✦ **Ranged Basic Attack:** The attacker makes a simple attack using a ranged weapon, which can be an improvised weapon such as a mug.

✦ **Opportunity Attack:** The attacker takes an opportunity action to make a melee basic attack against an adjacent enemy that moves or uses an area or a ranged power.

✦ **Bull Rush:** The attacker tries to push a target back and follow it.

✦ **Grab:** The attacker tries to seize a target and immobilize it.

Class powers, monster powers, and other powers are almost always better than these default powers, but sometimes the defaults are the best options tactically. For example, Keira is crossing swords with a bandit on the edge of a precipice. She might not have a rogue class power that could push the bandit over the edge, but *bull rush* could do the trick.

These default powers, particularly melee basic attacks, are used by many other powers and actions in the game. For example, the charge action allows a creature to take a standard action to move up to its speed and then use *bull rush* or make a melee basic attack against a target.

All attack powers specify which of a target's defenses to compare the check result to. For instance, "Intelligence vs. Reflex" means the attack roll is against the target's Reflex.

When making an attack roll for a creature, add the following to the d20 roll:

+ The modifier for the attack power the creature is using. For an adventurer, this number equals the specified ability modifier plus one-half the adventurer's level. For a monster, this modifier is specified in the power description.

+ Any other bonuses or penalties that apply, such as a bonus granted by a power or the enhancement bonus from a magic weapon.

+ Any temporary attack roll modifiers that apply, such as a bonus for combat advantage or a penalty for the target having cover. See the "Attack Roll Modifiers" table, below.

Automatic Hits
Some attacks are so lucky or well timed that bonuses, penalties, and other factors don't matter. The attacks simply hit.

Natural 20: When a creature makes an attack roll against a target and a 20 comes up on the d20 (this is called getting a natural 20), the power automatically hits the target. Bonuses and penalties don't matter; the target is simply hit.

Critical Hit: An automatic hit is almost always a critical hit as well (see below).

Automatic Misses
Sometimes misfortune plagues an attack: The attacker stumbles slightly, makes a poorly timed weapon swing, or otherwise completely misses the mark. No bonus can turn the attack into a hit. It simply misses.

Natural 1: When a creature makes an attack roll against a target and a 1 comes up on the d20 (this is called getting a natural 1), the power automatically misses the target. Bonuses and penalties don't matter; the target is simply missed.

Critical Hits
Occasionally an attack is a bull's-eye: It hits so well that a target takes more damage than normal. Such a lucky result is called a critical hit (sometimes shortened to "crit").

Natural 20: When an attack roll against a target gets a natural 20, the power not only automatically hits the target, but also scores a critical hit if the attack roll result is high enough to hit the target's defense. If the result is too low to hit the defense, the power still hits the target automatically, but without scoring a critical hit.

Precision: Some powers and other abilities allow a creature to score a critical hit on a roll other than 20, but only a natural 20 is an automatic hit.

Maximum Damage: When an attack scores a critical hit against a target, the target takes the maximum damage possible from the attack. Don't make a damage roll. Instead, the target takes damage as if the maximum result had been rolled for damage. However, attacks that don't deal damage still don't deal damage on a critical hit.

Extra Damage: Magic weapons and implements, as well as high crit weapons (page 269), can increase the damage dealt on a critical hit by contributing extra damage. If this extra damage is a die roll, it is not automatically maximum damage; roll the specified dice and add the result to the critical hit's damage.

Example: Dendric the fighter is wielding a magic longsword that deals 1d8 extra damage on a critical hit. His player rolls a d8 and adds the result to the damage Dendric deals on a critical hit with the longsword.

ATTACK ROLL MODIFIERS

Combat rarely consists of foes standing toe to toe and bashing each other. Movement and position are important; if one archer can fire from behind a tree at an enemy archer out in the open, the one using the tree for cover enjoys an advantage. Similarly, the use of magic or special abilities often creates opportunities that creatures can exploit. If Albanon the wizard turns his ally Keira invisible, she can easily evade her enemies, but if an enemy wizard stuns Keira with a spell, she drops her guard so that enemies can easily gang up on her.

Temporary advantages and disadvantages in combat are reflected in a set of common attack roll modifiers. An attack roll modifier is a bonus or a penalty that applies to an attack roll in certain circumstances, as determined by the DM.

ATTACK ROLL MODIFIERS

Circumstance	Modifier
Combat advantage against target	+2
Attacker is prone	-2
Attacker is restrained	-2
Target has partial cover	-2
Target has superior cover	-5
Target has partial concealment (melee and ranged only)	-2
Target has total concealment (melee and ranged only)	-5
Long range (weapon attacks only)	-2

Combat Advantage

One of the most common attack roll modifiers is combat advantage, which represents a situation in which a target can't give full attention to defense. The target is pressed by multiple enemies at the same time, stunned, distracted, or otherwise caught off guard. Combat advantage has two rules.

+2 Bonus to Attack Rolls: A creature gains a +2 bonus to attack rolls against a target granting combat advantage to it.

Able to See Target: A creature must be able to see a target to gain combat advantage against it. This rule means a blinded creature cannot have combat advantage against anyone.

Once per encounter, a creature can try to gain combat advantage against a target by making a Bluff check.

Combat advantage is relative. In any given pair of combatants, either, both, or neither might have combat advantage against the other. It's possible for a single creature to be adjacent to one enemy that has combat advantage against it and a second enemy that does not.

Flanking
One of the simplest ways for two allied creatures to gain combat advantage is for them to take up flanking positions adjacent to an enemy.

Combat Advantage: A creature has combat advantage against any enemy it flanks.

Opposite Sides: To flank an enemy, a creature and at least one of its allies must be adjacent to the enemy and on opposite sides or corners of the enemy's space.

When in doubt about whether two creatures flank an enemy, trace an imaginary line between the centers of the creatures' spaces. If the line passes through opposite sides or corners of the enemy's space, the enemy is flanked.

Large, Huge, and Gargantuan Creatures: A Large or larger creature is flanking as long as at least one square of its space qualifies for flanking.

Restrictions: A creature cannot flank an enemy that it can't see. A creature also cannot flank while it is subject to any effect that prevents it from taking actions. If no line of effect exists between a creature and its enemy, the creature cannot flank the enemy.

Cover and Concealment

Many types of terrain offer places to hide or obstructions that combatants can duck behind to avoid attacks. Cover means solid obstructions that can physically deflect or stop objects. Concealment means objects or effects that don't physically impede an attack but instead hide a creature from view.

Cover

Targets behind a low wall, around a corner, or behind a tree enjoy some amount of cover. They can't be hit as easily as normal—the attacker takes a penalty to attack rolls against them. There are two degrees of cover.

✦ **Partial Cover (-2 Penalty to Attack Rolls):** An attacker takes a -2 penalty to attack rolls against a target that has partial cover (sometimes simply called "cover"). The target is around a corner or protected by terrain. For instance, the target might be in the same square as a small tree, obstructed by a small pillar or a large piece of furniture, or crouching behind a low wall.

✦ **Superior Cover (-5 Penalty to Attack Rolls):** An attacker takes a -5 penalty to attack rolls against a target that has superior cover. The target is protected by a significant terrain advantage, such as when fighting from behind a window, a portcullis, a grate, or an arrow slit.

The following rules govern both degrees of cover.

Determining Cover: To determine if a target has cover, choose a corner of a square the attacker occupies, or a corner of the attack's origin square, and trace imaginary lines from that corner to every corner of any one square that the target occupies. If one or two of those lines are blocked by an obstacle or an enemy, the target has partial cover. (A line isn't blocked if it runs along the edge of an obstacle's or an enemy's square.) If three or four of those lines are blocked yet line of effect remains—such as when a target is behind an arrow slit—the target has superior cover.

Reach: If a creature that has reach (see "Creature Size and Space," page 199) attacks through terrain that would grant cover if the target were in it, the target has cover. For

instance, even if a target isn't in the same square as a small pillar, it has cover against the *greatclub* attack of an ogre on the other side of the pillar.

Area Attacks and Close Attacks: Against an area attack or a close attack, a target has cover only if there is an obstruction between it and the attack's origin square.

Creatures and Cover: When a creature makes a ranged attack against an enemy target and other enemies are in the way, the target has partial cover. A creature's allies never grant cover to the creature's enemies, and neither allies nor enemies grant cover against melee, close, or area attacks.

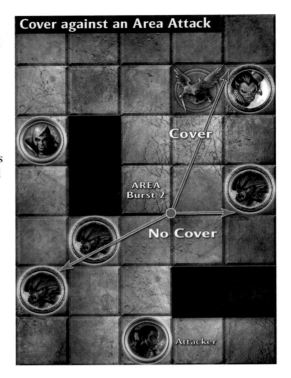

Cover against an Area Attack

Concealment
If an attacker can't get a good look at a target, the target has concealment: The attacker takes a penalty to melee and ranged attack rolls against that target. The battle might be in an area of dim light, in a chamber filled with smoke or mist, or among terrain features, such as foliage, that get in the way of vision.

Unless otherwise noted, area powers and close powers are not affected by concealment. Such powers often produce explosions or great weapon swings that don't depend on vision.

Obscured Squares The degree to which a square is obscured helps determine how much concealment a target has while in that square.

✦ **Lightly Obscured:** Squares of dim light, foliage, fog, smoke, heavy falling snow, or rain are lightly obscured.

✦ **Heavily Obscured:** Squares of heavy fog, thick smoke, or dense foliage are heavily obscured.

✦ **Totally Obscured:** Squares of darkness are totally obscured.

Degrees of Concealment There are two degrees of concealment.

✦ **Partial Concealment (-2 Penalty to Attack Rolls):** An attacker takes a -2 penalty to melee and ranged attack rolls against a target that has partial concealment (sometimes simply called "concealment"). The target is in a lightly obscured square or in a heavily obscured square and adjacent to the attacker.

✦ **Total Concealment (-5 Penalty to Attack Rolls):** An attacker takes a -5 penalty to melee and ranged attack rolls against a target that has total concealment. The attacker can't see the target: It is invisible, in a totally obscured square, or in a heavily obscured square and not adjacent to the attacker.

Invisibility A variety of powers and other effects can turn a creature invisible, effectively giving it total concealment. Sometimes invisibility is magical, and other times it is mundane. The most common way to become invisible is to use the Stealth skill to become hidden.

An invisible creature can take advantage of several benefits.

✦ It can't be seen by normal forms of vision.

✦ It has total concealment against any enemy that can't see it.

✦ It has combat advantage against any enemy that can't see it (but it still has to be able to see the enemy).

✦ It doesn't provoke opportunity attacks from enemies that can't see it.

TARGETING WHAT YOU CAN'T SEE

Sometimes a creature attacks an enemy it can't see—the enemy is invisible, the attacking creature is blinded, or the fight is taking place in impenetrable darkness. In these situations, the attacker has to target a square rather than the enemy. It also has to figure out which square to attack.

Invisible Creatures and Stealth: If an invisible creature is hidden from the attacker (see "Stealth," page 152), the attacker can neither hear nor see it, and it has to guess the creature's position. If the invisible creature is not hidden from the attacker, the attacker can hear it or sense some other sign of its presence and therefore knows where it is, although it still can't see the creature.

Make a Perception Check: On its turn, the attacker can make a Perception check as a minor action to try to determine the location of an invisible creature that is hidden from it.

Pick a Square and Attack: The attacker chooses a square to attack, using whatever information it has gleaned about the enemy's location. It makes the attack roll normally (taking the -5 penalty for attacking a target that has total concealment). If the attacker picks the wrong square, that attack automatically misses, but only the DM knows whether the attacker guessed wrong or simply rolled too low to hit.

Close or Area Attacks: An attacker can make a close attack or an area attack that includes the square it thinks (or knows) an invisible creature is in. The attack roll doesn't take a penalty from the target's concealment.

DAMAGE

When a typical attack hits a target, the attack deals damage to it, reducing the target's hit points. Each attack specifies how much damage it deals, if any, and under what circumstances: on a hit, on a miss, or automatically. Most attack powers deal more damage than basic attacks do, and high-level powers generally deal more damage than low-level ones do.

Damage is almost always instantaneous. The most common exception is ongoing damage (see below). Regardless of how a creature loses hit points, it regains them through healing (see "Hit Points and Healing," page 255), and some creatures take more or less damage in certain circumstances because of immunity, resistance, or vulnerability to particular damage types.

Damage Rolls

When most attacks deal damage, they do so through a damage roll: a roll of dice to determine damage. Whenever a power or other effect requires a damage roll, it specifies which dice to roll and how many of them. For instance, an attack might indicate that it deals 2d8 + 4 damage on a hit. When a creature hits with that attack, roll 2 eight-sided dice and add 4 to determine how much damage it deals.

A damage roll can be modified by a number of factors. Monsters' damage rolls are rarely modified by anything but temporary bonuses or penalties, such as those applied by powers. The following bonuses are the most common for an adventurer's damage rolls.

+ A specific ability modifier. A typical attack power used by an adventurer specifies an ability modifier to add to the damage roll. The ability modifier is usually the same one added to the power's attack roll.

+ An enhancement bonus (usually from a magic weapon or an implement).

+ A feat bonus.

+ An item bonus.

+ A power bonus.

Modifiers to Damage Rolls
Many powers, feats, and other game features grant bonuses or penalties to damage rolls. A bonus to a damage roll is added to the damage roll as a whole, not to each die roll within it.

Example: A warlock has a +4 bonus to damage rolls. If that warlock uses an attack power that deals 2d10 damage, the warlock adds 4 to the total of the two d10s. He does not add 4 to each d10.

Also, an attack power might contain multiple damage rolls, such as a melee attack power against multiple targets. If a creature has a bonus to damage rolls and uses such a power, the creature applies the bonus to every damage roll of that power.

ROLLING ATTACKS AND DAMAGE

Players are often accustomed to rolling the attack roll first and then the damage roll. If players make attack rolls and damage rolls at the same time, things move a little faster around the table than if each player waits to roll damage after finding out if an attack hits.

The DM might prefer for players to say how much damage an attack did, wait until the damage is recorded, and then mention any additional conditions and effects of the attack, such as stunning or knocking prone.

When making area attacks or close attacks, which use a single damage roll but a separate attack roll for each target, rolling damage first is helpful. Once it's established how much damage the effect deals on a hit (and on a miss), run through attack rolls against the targets one at a time.

Weapon Damage Dice In a damage roll expression, [W] is a variable that stands for the damage die of the weapon used to deal the damage. The number before the [W] indicates the number of times to roll the damage die. This sort of damage roll expression typically appears only in adventurer powers.

Example: If a power deals 2[W] + Strength modifier damage and the attacker uses a dagger (1d4 damage die), roll 2 four-sided dice (2d4), then add the attacker's Strength modifier. If the attacker uses a maul (2d6 damage die), roll 4d6, then add the attacker's Strength modifier.

Damage Types

Powers and other effects often deal specific types of damage. For instance, a red dragon's breath deals fire damage, a scorpion's sting deals poison damage, a mind flayer's telepathic blast deals psychic damage, and a wraith's touch deals necrotic damage.

If a power doesn't specify a damage type, the damage has no type. Most weapon attack powers deal damage that has no type. It is simply physical damage.

See page 114 for information on damage type keywords.

Extra Damage

Many powers and other effects grant the ability to deal extra damage. Extra damage is always in addition to other damage and is of the same type or types as that damage, unless otherwise noted. Because of this rule, an effect that deals no damage cannot deal extra damage. However, a power doesn't necessarily have to hit a target to deal extra damage—it needs only to deal damage to the target.

Example: Valenae the cleric might have an ability that causes her to deal 5 extra radiant damage to undead creatures. That ability means she deals 5 extra radiant damage whenever she deals damage to an undead creature.

Ongoing Damage

Some powers deal damage on consecutive turns after the initial attack. Such damage is called ongoing damage. An efreet might hit a creature with a burst of fire that sets it alight, dealing ongoing fire damage. When a snake's venom courses through a creature's blood, it deals ongoing poison damage. A royal mummy's *plague chant* deals ongoing necrotic damage.

Start of a Creature's Turn: When a creature is subjected to ongoing damage, it does not take the damage right away. Instead, the creature takes the specified damage at the start of each of its turns until the ongoing damage ends. For instance, a creature that is subjected to ongoing 5 fire damage takes 5 fire damage at the start of each of its turns.

Save Ends: Unless otherwise noted, an instance of ongoing damage lasts on a creature until the creature makes a successful saving throw against it. See "Saving Throws," page 227.

Different Types of Ongoing Damage: If a creature is subjected to ongoing damage of different types (including no type) at the same time, it takes damage of each of those types every round, and it must make a separate saving throw against each damage type.

> *Example:* If a creature is taking ongoing 5 damage (which has no type) when a power causes it to take ongoing 5 lightning damage, it is now taking ongoing 5 damage and ongoing 5 lightning damage, and it must make saving throws against each effect.

Same Type of Ongoing Damage: If a creature is subject to multiple instances of ongoing damage of the same type at the same time (including no type), only the highest number applies.

> *Example:* If a creature is taking ongoing 5 damage (which has no type) when a power causes it to take ongoing 10 damage, the creature is now taking ongoing 10 damage, not 15.

Resistance

Resistance means a creature takes less damage from a specific damage type. Resistance appears in a stat block or power as "Resist x," where x is the amount that the damage is reduced, followed by the type of damage that is being resisted. Damage cannot be reduced below 0. For example, a creature that has resist 5 fire takes 5 less fire damage whenever it takes that type of damage.

Some creatures are inherently resistant to certain damage types, as noted in their stat blocks, and some powers and other effects grant temporary resistance.

Against Combined Damage Types
A creature's resistance is ineffective against combined damage types unless the creature has resistance to each of the damage types, and then only the weakest of the resistances applies.

Example: A creature has resist 10 lightning and resist 5 thunder, and an attack deals 15 lightning and thunder damage to it. The creature takes 10 lightning and thunder damage, because the resistance to the combined damage types is limited to the lesser of the two (in this case, 5 thunder). If the creature had only resist 10 lightning, it would take all 15 damage from the attack.

Not Cumulative
Resistances against the same damage type are not cumulative. Only the highest resistance applies.

Example: If a creature has resist 5 cold and then gains resist 10 cold, it now has resist 10 cold, not resist 15 cold. Similarly, if a creature has resist 5 cold and then gains resist 2 to all damage, the creature still has resist 5 cold, not resist 7 cold.

Combined with Vulnerability
If a creature has resistance and vulnerability to the same type of damage, they both apply. Subtract the smaller value from the larger one and apply the result. For instance, a creature that has resist 5 fire and vulnerable 10 fire is treated as if it has vulnerable 5 fire.

IMMUNITY

Some creatures are immune to certain effects. If a creature is immune to a damage type (such as cold or fire), it doesn't take that type of damage. If a creature is immune to charm, fear, illusion, or poison, it is unaffected by the non-damaging effects of a power that has that keyword. A creature that is immune to a condition or another effect (such as the dazed condition or forced movement) is unaffected by the stated effect.

Immunity to one part of a power does not make a creature immune to other parts of the power. For example, when a creature that is immune to thunder is hit by a power that both deals thunder damage and pushes the target, the creature takes no damage, but the power can still push it.

Vulnerability

Being vulnerable to a damage type means a creature takes extra damage from that damage type. Vulnerability appears in a stat block or power as "Vulnerable x," where x is the amount of the extra damage. For instance, if a creature has vulnerable 5 fire, it takes 5 extra fire damage whenever it takes that type of damage.

Against Combined Damage Types
Vulnerability to a specific damage type applies even when that damage type is combined with another. For instance, if a creature has vulnerable 5 fire, the creature takes 5 extra fire damage when it takes ongoing fire and radiant damage.

Not Cumulative Vulnerabilities to the same damage type are not cumulative. Only the highest vulnerability applies.

Example: If a creature has vulnerable 5 psychic and then gains vulnerable 10 psychic, it has vulnerable 10 psychic, not vulnerable 15 psychic. Similarly, if a creature has vulnerable 5 psychic and then gains vulnerable 2 to all damage, the creature still has vulnerable 5 psychic, not vulnerable 7 psychic.

Combined with Resistance If a creature has vulnerability and resistance to the same type of damage, they both apply. Subtract the smaller value from the larger one and apply the result. For instance, a creature that has vulnerable 5 fire and resist 10 fire is treated as if it has resist 5 fire.

Half Damage

Some powers deal half damage when they miss, and some effects, such as the weakened condition, cause damage to be halved. When a power or other effect deals half damage, first apply all modifiers to the damage, including resistances and vulnerabilities, and then divide the damage in half (rounded down).

Example: Albanon the wizard is weakened and uses *ice storm*, which deals 16 cold damage to a fire giant that has vulnerable 5 cold. First add 5 to the 16 cold damage for the vulnerability, giving a result of 21. Then divide that result in half for the weakened condition. The giant ends up taking 10 cold damage.

Insubstantial Some creatures, such as wraiths, are naturally insubstantial, and some powers can make a creature insubstantial. While a creature is insubstantial, it takes half damage from any attack that deals damage to it. Ongoing damage is also halved.

DURATIONS

Many effects in the game are instantaneous, as brief as a sword swing or a fiery explosion. Some effects last for a round or more, however. Such an effect has a duration, a specific amount of time that the effect lasts. There are two types of durations: conditional and sustained.

Conditional Durations

An effect that has a conditional duration lasts until a specific event occurs. Three conditional durations appear more than any other in the game.

✦ **Until the Start/End of Someone's Next Turn:** The effect ends when a specific creature's next turn starts or ends. The creature is usually the one who produced the effect or else the target of the effect.

✦ **Until the End of the Encounter:** The effect ends at the end of the current encounter or after 5 minutes, whichever comes first.

✦ **Save Ends:** The effect ends when the target makes a successful saving throw against it. See "Saving Throws," below.

Sustained Durations

Some effects can be sustained for multiple rounds. Such an effect is labeled with the word "Sustain." That word is followed by the name of an action type: "Sustain standard," "Sustain move," "Sustain minor," and the like.

How to Sustain: On the turn that a creature creates a sustainable effect, the creature can do nothing to sustain it; the effect automatically lasts until the end of the creature's next turn, unless otherwise noted. Starting on that next turn, the creature can begin sustaining the effect.

To sustain the effect, the creature must take the type of action indicated in the effect's label. For instance, if the effect is labeled "Sustain minor," the creature must take a minor action to sustain it.

Consequences of Sustaining: When the creature sustains the effect, the effect lasts until the end of the creature's next turn, unless otherwise noted. Sustaining an effect often has consequences beyond extending the duration. An effect might let the creature attack each time it is sustained, for instance. The description of a sustainable effect notes any such consequences.

Limitations: The creature can sustain a particular effect only once per round and for no more than 5 minutes. During that time, the creature cannot take a short or an extended rest.

Overlapping Durations

When a creature is subject to identical effects that end at different times, it ignores all but the effect that has the most time remaining. For instance, if Dendric the fighter is slowed by a monster until the end of the encounter and is then slowed by another monster until the end of his next turn, he ignores the second effect, since it has less time remaining than the first.

Effects that a save can end (labeled "save ends") work differently, since it's not possible to know when they're going to end. Therefore, effects that a save can end are tracked separately from those that end at specific times.

SAVING THROWS

A saving throw is a special d20 roll, unmodified by a creature's level or ability scores, which is used to avoid or end certain effects. Some perils, such as being pushed into a pit, can be avoided with a save, and many effects last until the affected creature saves against them.

How to Make a Saving Throw

To make a saving throw, roll a d20 without adding any modifiers, unless the creature has bonuses or penalties that specifically apply to saving throws. On a roll of 9 or lower, the saving throw fails. A roll of 10 or higher is a successful saving throw, called a **save**. Because a saving throw is usually an unmodified roll, it gives slightly better than even odds to avoid or shake off an effect.

When to Make Saving Throws

The game rules explain when to make a saving throw immediately to avoid a peril, such as avoiding being pushed into a pit. See "Falling," page 209, for an example.

If a creature is subject to an effect that a save can end, the creature makes a saving throw against that effect at the end of each of its turns. An effect that a save can end includes one of the following notations: "save ends," "save ends both," or "save ends all."

When two effects are followed by the notation "save ends both," they are treated as a single effect when making saving throws against them. For instance, if a creature is "weakened and slowed (save ends both)," the creature makes a single saving throw against those two conditions whenever the time comes for it to make saving throws. Similarly, effects that are followed by the notation "save ends all" are treated as a single effect when saving throws are made against them. However, if a creature is subject to separate "weakened (save ends)" and "slowed (save ends)" effects, it must save against each separately. When a creature makes saving throws against multiple effects that a save can end, its player chooses the order of the saving throws.

Sometimes a power or other game feature allows a character to make a saving throw immediately against an effect that a save can end. If the character is allowed to make a single saving throw but is subject to multiple effects that a save can end, the player chooses which of those effects to make the saving throw against.

Identical Effects that a Save Can End

If a character is subject to identical effects that a save can end, ignore all but one of those effects. For instance, if the character is dazed (save ends) and then is attacked and again becomes dazed (save ends), ignore the second effect, since it is identical to the first one.

Identical effects never require multiple saving throws. A creature does make separate saving throws against effects that aren't identical, even if they contain the same condition. For instance, "dazed (save ends)" and "dazed and immobilized (save ends both)" are not identical effects, so separate saving throws are made against each of them.

CONDITIONS

Conditions are states imposed on creatures by various effects, including powers, traps, and the environment. A condition is usually temporary, imposing a penalty, a vulnerability, a hindrance, or a combination of effects.

Duration: The effect that imposes a condition on a creature specifies how long the condition lasts. For instance, a cleric might use an attack power that makes its target blinded (save ends). However, some conditions have built-in rules for when they end. For instance, the prone condition ends on a character who stands up, and the dying condition ends on a character who regains hit points.

No Degrees of Effect: Conditions don't have degrees of effect; either a creature has a condition, or it doesn't. Putting the same condition on a creature more than once doesn't change the condition's effect on that creature. For instance, if a weakened creature is subjected to the weakened condition again, the creature still deals half damage, not one-quarter damage.

Definitions

The following definitions specify the effects of each condition while a creature is subject to it.

Some conditions include other conditions within their effects. For instance, an unconscious creature is also helpless and prone.

Blinded

+ The creature can't see, which means its targets have total concealment against it.
+ The creature takes a -10 penalty to Perception checks.
+ The creature grants combat advantage.
+ The creature can't flank.

A blinded creature cannot have combat advantage against anyone.

This condition applies to creatures that have been temporarily blinded, such as by exposure to brilliant light or a magical darkness clouding their eyes. It doesn't apply to creatures that are naturally blind (such as oozes).

Dazed

+ The creature doesn't get its normal complement of actions on its turn; it can take either a standard, a move, or a minor action. The creature can still take free actions.
+ The creature can't take immediate actions or opportunity actions.
+ The creature grants combat advantage.
+ The creature can't flank.

The dazed condition is a common way of representing a general state of stupor. Dazed creatures don't act as quickly as normal or respond to danger as readily. A creature might be dazed because it took a hard blow to the head, a spell assaulted its mind, or a prayer called forth a clap of thunder around it.

Deafened

- ✦ The creature can't hear.
- ✦ The creature takes a -10 penalty to Perception checks.

This condition applies to creatures that have temporarily lost their normal sense of hearing, not to creatures that normally can't hear. The game effects of the condition are relatively minor, but being deafened can be a flavorful result of a thunder power.

Dominated

- ✦ The creature can't take actions voluntarily. Instead, the dominator chooses a single action for the creature to take on the creature's turn: a standard, a move, a minor, or a free action. The only powers and other game features that the dominator can make the creature use are ones that can be used at will, such as at-will powers. For example, anything that is limited to being used only once per encounter or once per day does not qualify.
- ✦ The creature grants combat advantage.
- ✦ The creature can't flank.

In spite of this condition, the creature's allies remain its allies, and its enemies remain its enemies. If the dominator tries to force the creature to throw itself into a pit or to move into some other form of hindering terrain, the creature gets a saving throw to resist entering the terrain.

A wide variety of creatures and powers can impose this condition. Just as in myth and legend, vampires and fey creatures are adept at controlling the minds of others, but the specific limitations of this condition prevent such creatures from forcing player characters to expend their best powers.

Dying

✦ The creature is unconscious.

✦ The creature must make death saving throws.

✦ This condition ends immediately on the creature when it regains hit points.

Dropping to 0 hit points or fewer subjects an adventurer to this condition. Monsters normally die when they drop to 0 hit points, so this condition applies to them only in exceptional situations. See "Dying and Death," page 259.

Grabbed

✦ The creature is immobilized.

✦ Maintaining this condition on the creature occupies whatever appendage, object, or effect the grabber used to initiate the grab.

✦ This condition ends immediately on the creature if the grabber is subjected to an effect that prevents it from taking actions, or if the creature ends up outside the range of the grabbing power or effect.

A grabbed creature can take the escape action to try to get away. Other common tactics for escaping a grab are to teleport away or to be pulled, pushed, or slid out of the grabber's reach. Using forced movement on the grabber can also end a grab, as long as the movement results in the grabbed creature being out of the grabbing effect's range.

While a creature is grabbed, the grabber can try to move it (see "Moving a Grabbed Target," page 244).

Helpless

✦ The creature grants combat advantage.

This condition is a precondition for certain things such as the coup de grace action. Normally, a creature is affected by this condition because it is unconscious, but the DM might rule that a creature is so firmly bound that it is effectively helpless.

Immobilized

✦ The creature can't move, unless it teleports or is pulled, pushed, or slid.

An immobilized creature can't reposition itself on the battle grid, but it's not paralyzed. It can still stand up when it's prone, pull an item from a backpack, or attack normally. It might have taken a serious, but temporary, injury to the legs, or it could be stuck to the ground by a huge cobweb.

A creature wrapped up in animated vines might be restrained instead (see below); that condition imposes more restrictions on the creature's ability to attack and defend itself. A creature that is actually paralyzed, such as by the bite of a ghoul, might be stunned rather than immobilized or restrained.

Marked

✦ The creature takes a -2 penalty to attack rolls for any attack that doesn't include the marking creature as a target.

✦ A creature can be subjected to only one mark at a time, and a new mark supersedes an old one.

✦ A mark ends immediately when its creator dies or falls unconscious.

This condition reflects the ability of some creatures to claim the attention of a chosen target in battle. When a target is marked, it has a hard time ignoring the creature that marked it. Most marking effects have very short durations, or else they require the marking creature to remain a threat to the marked target.

Petrified

✦ The creature is unconscious.

✦ The creature has resist 20 to all damage.

✦ The creature doesn't age.

Usually a creature is subjected to this condition when it is turned to stone, such as by a medusa. Often the only way to end this condition is by using a power or a magical ritual.

Normally, a creature falls prone when it becomes unconscious. The DM might decide that a petrified creature instead remains upright, posed like a statue.

Prone

✦ The creature is lying down. However, if the creature is climbing or flying, it falls.

✦ The only way the creature can move is by crawling, teleporting, or being pulled, pushed, or slid.

✦ The creature takes a -2 penalty to attack rolls.

✦ The creature grants combat advantage to attackers making melee attacks against it, but it gains a +2 bonus to all defenses against ranged attacks from attackers that aren't adjacent to it.

A creature can end this condition on itself by standing up. A creature can drop prone as a minor action.

This condition can affect limbless creatures, such as fish and snakes, as well as amorphous creatures, such as oozes. When such a creature falls prone, imagine it is writhing or unsteady, rather than literally lying down. The game effect on that creature is the same as for other creatures.

Removed from Play

✦ The creature can't take actions.

✦ The creature has neither line of sight nor line of effect to anything, and nothing has line of sight or line of effect to it.

An effect that removes a creature from play specifies where the creature reappears when it returns to play. Typically the creature reappears in the space it left, or in the nearest unoccupied space if that space is now occupied.

A creature is normally subjected to this condition because it has been transported to another plane of existence or is engulfed or swallowed. Whatever the cause, the creature's turns start and end as normal.

Restrained

✦ The creature can't move, unless it teleports. It can't even be pulled, pushed, or slid.

✦ The creature takes a -2 penalty to attack rolls.

✦ The creature grants combat advantage.

This condition is similar to the immobilized condition (see above), but it puts more restrictions on the creature's ability to attack or defend itself. This condition usually results from being held in place by something: vines, tentacles, manacles attached to a wall, strands of webbing, or a monster's gaping jaws. Whatever is holding the creature in place interferes with its ability to move around freely.

Slowed

✦ The creature's speed becomes 2 if it was higher than that. This speed applies to all of the creature's movement modes (walking, flying, swimming, and so on), but it does not apply to forced movement against it, teleportation, or any other movement that doesn't use the creature's speed. If a creature is subjected to this condition while it is moving using any of its speeds, it must stop if it has already moved at least 2 squares.

+ The creature cannot benefit from bonuses to speed, although it can use powers and take actions, such as the run action, that allow it to move farther than its speed.

A variety of different effects can cause a creature to become slowed. A creature subject to this condition might have taken an injury to the legs (or other limbs used for locomotion), or it might be entangled in something. The creature could also be poisoned, beset by wracking pain that hampers its movement, encased in frost, or slowly turning to stone.

Stunned

+ The creature can't take actions.
+ The creature grants combat advantage.
+ The creature can't flank.
+ The creature falls if it is flying, unless it can hover.

Usually a creature is subjected to this condition because of significant physical or mental trauma. It might be on the brink of succumbing to a deadly poison, completely paralyzed by a ghoul's bite, reeling under the mental assault of a mind flayer, or battered by an extremely powerful blow.

Surprised

+ The creature can't take actions.
+ The creature grants combat advantage.
+ The creature can't flank.

Normally a creature is subjected to this condition only during a surprise round (page 190), at the end of which the condition ends.

Unconscious

+ The creature is helpless.
+ The creature can't take actions.
+ The creature takes a –5 penalty to all defenses.
+ The creature is unaware of its surroundings.
+ The creature falls prone, if possible.
+ The creature can't flank.

This condition applies when a creature is knocked out, cast into a magical slumber, or otherwise incapacitated totally.

A creature that has fallen asleep naturally—as opposed to being knocked unconscious by a power or other effect—is unconscious but not totally deprived of awareness; it can use its passive Perception to hear things, but with a -5 penalty.

Weakened

✦ The creature's attacks deal half damage. Two kinds of damage that it deals are not affected, however: ongoing damage and damage that isn't generated by an attack roll.

When a creature is weakened, it can't exert force as well as normal. Not only physical attacks are affected; the creature's magical powers are hampered just as much. The creature's might is diminished in every way, usually as a result of the life-sapping effects of necrotic damage or other deathly magic.

ACTIONS IN COMBAT

During a creature's turn, it can choose from a wide variety of actions. Usually, the most important decision a player makes in combat is what to do with an adventurer's standard action each turn. Does he or she use a power? If so, which one? Or does the situation demand a different approach, such as using that standard action to charge, try to talk to foes, or instead get a second move action this turn? This section describes how to perform typical actions in combat.

The list that follows isn't exhaustive; a creature can try to do anything imaginable in the game world. The rules in this section cover the most common actions, and they can serve as a guide for figuring out what happens when a character or a creature tries something that's not in the rules.

Action Points

Action points allow creatures to take more actions than normal. Adventurers each start with 1 action point, and some monsters have action points, as noted in their stat blocks. Typically an adventurer spends an action point to pull off an extra attack, to move farther than normal, to take the second wind action in the same turn that he or she attacks, and so on.

Spend an Action Point

✦ **Action:** Free action. A creature must have an action point in order to take this action. Also, the creature can take this action only during its turn, and never during a surprise round.

✦ **Gain an Extra Action:** The creature gains an extra action to use during its current turn. The action can be a standard, a move, or a minor action. Some creatures have special abilities that trigger when they spend action points, and some have the option of gaining a benefit other than an extra action when they spend their points.

✦ **Once per Encounter or Round:** An adventurer can spend an action point only once per encounter. In contrast, a monster that has action points can spend more than 1 action point during an encounter, but only 1 per round.

✦ **Gone When Spent:** An action point is gone when spent, regardless of the success of the action taken.

Earning Action Points
Adventurers earn action points as they complete more and more encounters. Each adventurer gains 1 action point whenever he or she reaches a milestone (page 291) by completing two encounters without taking an extended rest. Sometimes a DM awards an action point to each adventurer who completes an unusually difficult encounter.

Regardless of milestones, a creature's action point total reverts to its starting value whenever the creature completes an extended rest, so an adventurer has 1 action point, and only 1, at the end of an extended rest. Because of this rule, a creature benefits most from spending its action points as often as possible.

STANDARD ACTIONS

Action	Description
Administer a potion	Help an unconscious creature consume a potion
Aid another	Improve an ally's skill check or ability check
Aid attack	Improve an ally's attack roll
Aid defense	Improve an ally's defenses
Basic attack	Make a basic attack
Bull rush	Push a target 1 square and shift into the vacated space
Charge	Move and then make a melee basic attack or a bull rush
Coup de grace	Make a critical hit against a helpless enemy
Equip or stow a shield	Use a shield or put it away
Grab	Seize and hold an enemy
Ready an action	Ready an action to perform when a specified trigger occurs
Second wind	Spend a healing surge and gain a bonus to defenses (once per encounter)
Total defense	Gain a +2 bonus to all defenses until next turn

MOVE ACTIONS

Action	Description
Crawl	While prone, move up to half speed
Escape	Escape a grab and shift 1 square
Run	Move up to speed + 2; grant combat advantage until next turn and take a -5 penalty to attack rolls
Stand up	Stand up from prone
Shift	Move 1 square without provoking opportunity attacks
Squeeze	Reduce size by one category, move up to half speed, and grant combat advantage
Walk	Move up to walking speed

MINOR ACTIONS

Action	Description
Draw or sheathe a weapon	Use or put away a weapon
Drink a potion	Consume a potion
Drop prone	Drop down to lie on the ground
Load a crossbow	Load a bolt into a crossbow to fire it
Open or close a door	Open or close a door or container that isn't locked or stuck
Pick up an item	Pick up an object in one's space or in an unoccupied square within reach
Retrieve or stow Item	Retrieve or stow an item on self

IMMEDIATE ACTION

Action	Description
Readied action	Take readied action when its trigger occurs

OPPORTUNITY ACTION

Action	Description
Opportunity attack	Make a melee basic attack against an enemy that provokes an opportunity attack

FREE ACTIONS

Action	Description
Delay	Put off a turn until later in the initiative order
Drop held items	Drop any items currently held
End a grab	Let go of an enemy
Spend an action point	Spend an action point to take an extra action (once per encounter, not in a surprise round)
Talk	Speak a few sentences

Aid Another

A creature can use a standard action to try to aid an adjacent creature's skill check or ability check. See "Aid Another," page 128.

Aid Attack

A creature can aid an ally's attack against an enemy. This action represents a feint, a distraction, or some other action that makes it easier for the ally to hit the enemy.

Aid an Ally's Attack

✦ **Action:** Standard action. When a creature takes this action, it chooses an enemy adjacent to it.

✦ **Grant Bonus to Attack Roll:** The creature chooses an ally. That ally gains a +2 bonus to its next attack roll against the chosen enemy. This bonus ends if it is not used by the end of the aiding creature's next turn. A creature can take the aid attack action only once to affect a particular attack roll. However, up to four creatures can take the action to affect the same attack roll.

Aid Defense

A creature can try to protect an ally against an enemy. This action represents a parry, a shield block, or some other action that makes it harder for the enemy to hit the ally.

Aid an Ally's Defenses

✦ **Action:** Standard action. When a creature takes this action, it chooses an enemy adjacent to it.

✦ **Grant Bonus to Defenses:** The creature chooses an ally. That ally gains a +2 bonus to all defenses against the chosen enemy's next attack against it. This bonus ends if it is not used by the end of the aiding creature's next turn. A creature can take the aid defense action only once to affect a particular ally's defenses. However, up to four creatures can take the action to affect the same ally's defenses.

Basic Attack

Sometimes a creature just wants to hit something. The following two basic attack powers—one melee and one ranged—are powers that everyone can use, regardless of class (see Chapter 3 for how to read a power). Using either of these powers is usually referred to as making a basic attack. Some classes provide alternatives to these default powers, and each monster has its own basic attack power, which is noted in its stat block with a circle around the power's icon.

When a power or other effect allows a creature to make a basic attack, the creature can make either a melee basic attack or a ranged basic attack. If the power or other effect specifically calls for a melee basic attack or a ranged basic attack, the creature must use that type. For instance, a power might read, "Each ally within 5 squares of you can make a basic attack as a free action," which means each of those allies can make either a melee or a ranged basic attack, and they can each do so as a free action, rather than a standard action.

Melee Basic Attack

Basic Attack

You resort to the simple attack you learned when you first picked up a melee weapon.

At-Will ✦ Weapon
Standard Action   **Melee** weapon
Target: One creature
Attack: Strength vs. AC
Hit: 1[W] + Strength modifier damage.
  Level 21: 2[W] + Strength modifier damage.

A creature uses a melee basic attack to make an opportunity attack or to make a charge attack. Even if it has no weapon equipped, it can make a melee basic attack using an unarmed strike (such as a kick or punch) or another improvised weapon (page 272).

Ranged Basic Attack

Basic Attack

You resort to the simple attack you learned when you first picked up a ranged weapon.

At-Will ✦ Weapon
Standard Action   **Ranged** weapon
Target: One creature
Attack: Dexterity vs. AC
Hit: 1[W] + Dexterity modifier damage.
  Level 21: 2[W] + Dexterity modifier damage.

A creature can make a ranged basic attack as long as it has something to throw or shoot. Even if it has no ranged weapon equipped, it can make a ranged basic attack using an improvised weapon (page 272). If it makes the attack using a weapon that has the heavy thrown property, the attack uses the creature's Strength instead of Dexterity for the attack roll and the damage roll (see "Weapon Properties," page 269).

Bull Rush

When a creature wants to push another creature away, the *bull rush* power is a good option. Although many classes and monsters have powers that can push a target farther, the advantage of *bull rush* is that anyone can use it, regardless of class.

The *bull rush* power is useful for forcing an enemy out of a defensive position or into a dangerous one, such as into a pool of lava or over a cliff. It can also do useful things such as pushing an ally out of an enemy's grasp.

Bull Rush

Attack

You hurl yourself at your foe and push it back.

At-Will
Standard Action   **Melee** 1
Target: One creature
Attack: Strength vs. Fortitude
Hit: You push the target 1 square and then shift 1 square into the space it left.

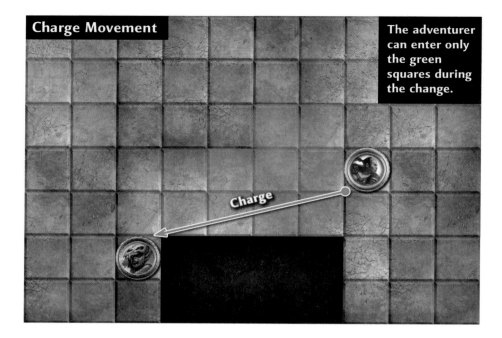

Charge Movement

The adventurer can enter only the green squares during the change.

Charge

A creature uses the charge action when it wants to dash forward and launch an attack with a single action. Such an attack is sometimes referred to as a charge attack.

Charge a Target

✦ **Action:** Standard action. When a creature takes this action, it chooses a target. Figure out how far away the creature is from the target—even counting through squares of blocking terrain—and then follow these steps.

1. Move: The creature moves up to its speed toward the target. Each square of movement must bring the creature closer to the target, and the creature must end the move at least 2 squares away from its starting position.

2. Attack: The creature either makes a melee basic attack against the target or uses *bull rush* against it. The creature gains a +1 bonus to the attack roll.

3. No Further Actions: The creature can't take any further actions during this turn, except free actions.

A creature's turn usually ends after it charges. However, it can extend its turn by taking certain free actions.

Some powers allow a creature to use them in place of a melee basic attack when charging. When a creature uses such a power, the creature retains all the normal benefits of a charge and must follow all the same rules. For instance, it still must end the move at least 2 squares away from its starting position, and it still gains the +1 bonus to attack rolls.

Coup de Grace

Sometimes a creature has the chance to attack a foe who is completely defenseless. Doing so isn't chivalrous, but it is viciously effective. This action is known as a coup de grace.

Perform a Coup de Grace

+ **Action:** Standard action.
+ **Attack Helpless Target:** The creature uses one of its attack powers against an adjacent target that is helpless. If the attack hits, it automatically scores a critical hit against the target.
+ **Slaying the Target Outright:** If the critical hit deals damage greater than or equal to the target's bloodied value, the target dies.

The most common way for a target to be helpless is to be unconscious; thus, the coup de grace action is typically used against sleeping foes.

Crawl

When a creature is prone, crawling is one of the only ways it can move.

Crawl

+ **Action:** Move action. A creature must be prone to take this action.
+ **Move:** The creature moves up to half its speed.

Standing up and then moving is usually preferable to crawling, but sometimes a prone creature wants to move and doesn't have enough actions to stand up first. In that situation, crawling and teleporting are the best options.

Delay

A creature can choose to wait to take its turn until later in a round. It might want to see what actions its allies take so that it can plan tactics, or it could be waiting for enemies to move into range.

Delay Turn

+ **Action:** Free action. A creature can take this action only when its turn is about to start.

+ **Delay until Later Initiative:** The creature delays its turn until it decides to act later in the initiative order. However, parts of the creature's turn occur the moment the creature delays, as detailed below.

+ **Returning to the Initiative Order:** After any turn has been completed, the creature can step back into the initiative order and take its turn. The creature's initiative changes to this new position in the initiative order.

+ **Start of Turn:** The start of the creature's turn occurs when the creature delays, not when it later takes its turn. Thus, effects that are triggered by the start of the turn still take place–they can't be avoided by delaying.

+ **End of Turn:** The end of the creature's turn gets split in two: One part occurs when the creature delays, and the second part when it later takes its delayed turn. Different things occur at each of those times.

    End of Turn when the Creature Delays: At the moment the creature delays, any effect that it has been sustaining ends. In addition, effects that last until the end of the creature's turn now end if they are beneficial to it and its allies–they cannot be prolonged by delaying. For instance, if the creature stunned an enemy until the end of its next turn, the stunned condition ends as soon as the creature delays.

    End of Turn after the Creature Acts: After the creature returns to the initiative order and takes its delayed turn, it makes the saving throws it normally makes at the end of its turn. In addition, harmful effects that last until the end of the creature's turn now end–they cannot be avoided by delaying. For instance, if the creature is weakened until the end of its next turn, the weakened condition ends only after it acts.

+ **Losing a Delayed Turn:** If the creature doesn't take its delayed turn before its initiative comes back up in the order, it loses the delayed turn, and its initiative remains where it was.

Drop Prone

Sometimes a creature wants to be prone–to avoid ranged attacks, for instance, or to play dead.

Drop Prone

+ **Action:** Minor action.
+ **Prone:** The creature is now prone.

Escape

A creature can attempt to escape when it is grabbed. Other immobilizing effects might also let a creature try to escape.

Escape a Grab or Immobilizing Effect

+ **Action:** Move action.
+ **Acrobatics or Athletics Check:** The creature makes either an Acrobatics or an Athletics check. Normally, the immobilizing effect specifies the DC for the check. If no DC is specified, an Acrobatics check is opposed by the Reflex of the immobilizing creature or effect, and an Athletics check is opposed by its Fortitude.
+ **Against Multiple Grabbers:** If the creature is trying to escape and is grabbed by more than one source at once, the creature makes a single check against the highest of the grab DCs. The DC increases by 2 for each grabber beyond the first, to a maximum increase of 8.
+ **Success:** If the check succeeds, the immobilizing effect ends on the creature, which can then shift 1 square.

Grab

By using the *grab* power, any creature can try to seize a target bodily and keep it from moving. Although class powers and monster powers are usually more effective than *grab* at locking a target down, the advantage of *grab* is that anyone can use it, regardless of class.

Grab	Attack

You reach out and grasp your foe, preventing it from moving.

At-Will
Standard Action   **Melee** touch
Requirement: You must have a hand free.
Target: One creature that is no more than one size category larger than you
Attack: Strength vs. Reflex
Hit: You grab the target until the end of your next turn. You can end the grab as a free action.
Sustain Minor: The grab persists until the end of your next turn.

Moving a Grabbed Target A creature can try to move a target it is grabbing, whether or not it used the *grab* power to grab the target.

Move a Grabbed Target

+ **Action:** Standard action.
+ **Strength Check:** The creature makes a Strength check opposed by the Fortitude of a target it is grabbing. The check automatically succeeds if the target is a helpless ally of the creature.
+ **Success:** The creature can move up to half its speed and pull the target with it. The creature's movement doesn't provoke an opportunity attack from the grabbed target, but the movement otherwise provokes opportunity attacks as normal.

Manipulating Objects

Creatures can pick up or drop items, draw or sheathe weapons, strap shields to their arms or sling them on their backs, open and close doors or chests, or in any other way manipulate the objects that make up their gear or constitute their environment. Most such tasks require only minor actions to perform, because they're simple and quick, but a few are more complicated or time-consuming.

Depending on the object being manipulated, the Dungeon Master might require the acting creature to make a skill check or an ability check to successfully perform the desired task. In such cases, the action usually requires more time as well. For example, opening a door that's locked or stuck shut probably requires a standard action and either a Thievery check or a Strength check to open, rather than a simple minor action.

The actions listed on the table at the start of this section are examples. The Dungeon Master can extrapolate from those examples to determine what action is required for similar tasks.

Administer a Potion

+ **Action:** Standard action. The creature must be adjacent to whoever is administering the potion and must be either helpless or willing.
+ **Requires Potion in Hand:** The creature must have the potion in hand before administering it.

Drink a Potion

+ **Action:** Minor action.
+ **Requires Potion in Hand:** The creature must have the potion in hand before drinking it.

Draw or Sheathe a Weapon

✦ **Action:** Minor action.

✦ **Requires Free Hand to Draw:** The creature must have a hand free to draw a weapon.

✦ **Ready for Use:** A creature can take a sheathed or otherwise slung weapon and make it ready for use by taking this action.

✦ **Sheathed:** A sheathed weapon is in a sheath at the creature's belt or on its back, or otherwise slung out of the way so that the creature's hands are free to hold or manipulate other objects.

Drop a Held Item

✦ **Action:** Free action.

✦ **In the Creature's Space:** A creature can use this action to drop an item it is holding. The item lands in the creature's space. If the creature's space is larger than 1 square, the creature can choose what square the item lands in.

Equip or Stow a Shield

✦ **Action:** Standard action.

✦ **Requires Free Hand to Equip:** The creature must have its shield hand free to equip a shield. If the shield is a light shield, the creature can later pick up and hold another item in that hand while still using the shield, but a heavy shield requires the use of the shield hand.

✦ **Ready for Use:** A creature can take a stowed shield and make it ready for use by taking this action. Once the shield is ready for use, it grants its shield bonus to AC and Reflex (if the creature has proficiency with the shield).

✦ **Stowed:** A stowed shield is attached to a backpack or slung out of the way so that the creature's hands are free to hold or manipulate other objects.

Load a Crossbow

✦ **Action:** Minor action.

✦ **Includes Drawing Ammunition:** The minor action includes drawing a bolt from a quiver or an open case that's readily accessible.

Open or Close

✦ **Action:** Minor action.

✦ **Simple Manipulation:** A creature can use this action to open or close a door; to open or close a chest, box, drawer, or other container; to pull a lever; to open or close a book; or to perform a similar action. An object that's stuck, locked, very heavy, or otherwise difficult to manipulate probably requires a check and a standard action to open.

Pick Up an Item

+ **Action:** Minor action.

+ **Within Reach:** A creature can use this action to pick up an item that's within its reach or in its own space.

+ **Unattended:** A creature can't use this action to pick up an item in an enemy's space, unless the enemy is helpless. Similarly, the creature can't use this action to pick up an item that another creature is holding or an item on another creature's person, unless that other creature is willing or helpless.

Retrieve or Stow an Item

+ **Action:** Minor action.

+ **Easily Accessible:** A creature can use this action to retrieve an item from someplace on its own person, most commonly in a belt pouch or a backpack, or to stow an item in such a location.

Opportunity Attack

In a fight, everyone is constantly watching for enemies to drop their guard. A creature can rarely move heedlessly past its foes or use a ranged power or an area power without putting itself in danger: Such actions trigger the *opportunity attack* power. Anyone can use *opportunity attack*, regardless of class.

Triggering this power is usually referred to as provoking an opportunity attack, and using it is usually referred to as making an opportunity attack.

Opportunity Attack — Attack

Your foe drops its guard for a moment, and you exploit the opportunity.

At-Will

Opportunity Action   **Melee** 1

Trigger: An enemy that you can see either leaves a square adjacent to you or uses a ranged or an area power while adjacent to you.

Target: The triggering enemy

Effect: You make a melee basic attack against the target.

Certain types of movement don't provoke opportunity attacks, unless an effect specifies otherwise: forced movement (page 211), shifting (page 249), and teleportation (page 213).

Some powers and other effects allow a creature to enter an enemy's space. If that enemy is not helpless, entering its space still provokes an opportunity attack from that enemy, because the creature left a square adjacent to the enemy. Forced movement, shifting, and teleportation ignore this fact, as normal.

Threatening Reach Some creatures have a trait called threatening reach, which lets a creature make opportunity attacks against enemies that aren't adjacent to it. The trait specifies the extent of a creature's theatening reach.

Ready an Action

When a creature readies an action, it prepares to react to an event or to someone else's action. Readying an action is a way of saying, "As soon as *x* happens, my character does *y*." Examples include "As soon as the troll walks out from behind the corner, I shoot an arrow at it," or "If the goblin ends its movement adjacent to me, I shift away."

Ready an Action

✦ **Action:** Standard action. To ready an action, a creature follows these steps.

1. Choose Action to Ready: Choose the specific action the creature is readying (the attack it plans to use, for example), as well as the intended target, if applicable. The creature can ready a standard action, a move action, or a minor action. Whichever action is chosen, the act of readying it is a standard action.

2. Choose Trigger: Choose the circumstance that will trigger the readied action. When that trigger occurs, the creature can use the readied action. If the trigger doesn't occur or the creature chooses to ignore it, the creature can't use the readied action and instead takes its next turn as normal.

3. Immediate Reaction: Using a readied action is an immediate reaction, so it takes place right after the trigger finishes.

4. Reset Initiative: When the creature finishes the readied action, its place in the initiative order moves to directly before the creature or the event that triggered the readied action.

Triggering Opportunity Actions If a creature readies an action that normally triggers opportunity actions, it triggers them twice: when it readies the action and when it takes the action.

Example: If an adventurer readies a ranged attack while adjacent to an enemy, he provokes an opportunity attack from that enemy. If he is still adjacent to an enemy when he makes the ranged attack, he provokes an opportunity attack again.

Interrupting with a Readied Action Often a player wants his or her character to use a readied action to attack before an enemy does. In this situation, the action should be readied to respond to the enemy's movement. That way, if the enemy moves before attacking, the readied action will be triggered by a portion of that movement, allowing the character to interrupt it and attack first. Readying an action to be triggered by an enemy attack means that the readied action will occur as a reaction to the attack, so the character's attack happens only after the enemy attacks.

An enemy might use a power that lets it move and then attack with a single action. If a character readied an action to attack in response to that enemy's movement, the readied action interrupts the movement, allowing the character to attack before the enemy does.

Run

By taking the run action, a creature can use an all-out sprint when it really needs to cover ground quickly. The creature has to lower its guard to make best speed, however, and it can't attack very well.

Run

✦ **Action:** Move action.

✦ **Speed + 2:** The creature moves up to its speed plus 2 additional squares. For instance, if its speed is 6, the creature can move up to 8 squares when it runs.

✦ **-5 Penalty to Attack Rolls:** The creature takes a -5 penalty to attack rolls until the start of its next turn.

✦ **Grant Combat Advantage:** As soon as the creature begins running, it grants combat advantage until the start of its next turn.

Despite the action's name, a creature isn't always literally running when it takes this action. The action can include other movement modes such as climbing, flying, and swimming.

Second Wind

Adventurers can dig into their resolve and endurance to find an extra burst of vitality. In game terms, an adventurer focuses momentarily on self-defense and spends a healing surge to regain lost hit points. Using one's second wind is the one way that all adventurers have of healing themselves during an encounter. They must otherwise rely on other sources of healing.

Unless otherwise noted in the stat block of a monster or DM-controlled character, this action is available only to adventurers.

Use Second Wind

✦ **Action:** Standard action. A character can take this action only once per encounter, so he or she can take it again after a short or an extended rest.

A character can use his or her second wind without taking an action if another character administers first aid to him or her using the Heal skill.

✦ **Spend a Healing Surge:** The character spends a healing surge to regain hit points (see "Healing Surges," page 258).

+ **+2 Bonus to All Defenses:** The character gains a +2 bonus to all defenses until the start of his or her next turn. However, the character does not gain this bonus if he or she uses second wind as a result of someone administering first aid.

Shift

Moving through a fierce battle is dangerous; a creature must be careful to avoid a misstep that gives a foe a chance to strike a telling blow. The way to move safely when enemies are nearby is to shift. When a creature wants to flee, the safest way to do that is to first shift away from an adjacent enemy, then walk or run.

Shift

+ **Action:** Move action.
+ **Movement:** The creature moves 1 square. (Some powers and effects allow creatures to move farther than 1 square with a shift.)
+ **No Opportunity Actions Triggered:** Unless the description of an effect says otherwise, shifting doesn't trigger opportunity actions such as opportunity attacks.
+ **Special Movement Modes:** A creature can't shift when using a movement mode that requires it to make a skill check. For instance, if it is climbing, it can't shift if it has to make an Athletics check to climb. (A creature that has a climb speed can shift while climbing.)

Because a square of difficult terrain costs 1 extra square of movement to enter, a creature can't normally shift into such a square, unless it is able to shift multiple squares or ignores the effects of difficult terrain.

Squeeze

A creature can use the squeeze action to fit through an area that isn't as wide as it is. Big creatures usually use this action to move through tight corridors or to stand on narrow ledges, whereas a Medium or a Small creature can squeeze to fit into a constrained space, such as a burrow. While squeezing, a creature moves much more slowly and can't react as effectively in combat.

Squeeze

+ **Action:** Move action. A creature follows these steps when it takes this action.

1. Reduce Size: When a Large, a Huge, or a Gargantuan creature squeezes, its size category effectively decreases by one until the squeeze ends. For instance, a Large creature that squeezes is effectively Medium during the squeeze. As its size decreases, such a creature is leaving squares, so it might trigger opportunity actions such as opportunity attacks. It cannot reduce its size if it is unable to move.

When a Medium or smaller creature squeezes, the DM decides how narrow a space it can occupy.

2. Half Speed: The creature moves up to half its speed.

+ **Grant Combat Advantage:** The creature grants combat advantage until the squeeze ends.

+ **-5 Penalty to Attack Rolls:** The creature takes a -5 penalty to attack rolls until the squeeze ends.

End a Squeeze

+ **Action:** Free action.

+ **Return to Normal Size:** The creature expands to its original size. When it does so, its new space must contain the smaller space that it just occupied. It is not leaving squares when it returns to its original size, so it does not trigger opportunity actions.

Stand Up

A creature can end the prone condition on itself by standing up.

Stand Up

+ **Action:** Move action.

+ **Unoccupied Space:** If the creature's space is not occupied by another creature, the creature stands up where it is.

+ **Occupied Space:** If the creature's space is occupied by another creature, the creature can stand up and shift 1 square to an unoccupied space. It can't stand up if no unoccupied space is adjacent to it.

Even a prone creature that is limbless or amorphous can take this action, which represents the creature righting itself or regaining its balance rather than literally standing.

Talk

Talk is cheap—in fact, it's free in the game. A creature can talk as a free action, which means that it can speak even on another creature's turn and as often as it likes (within reason), as long as it's able to take free actions.

Talk

+ **Action:** Free action.
+ **No Extended Monologues:** A creature can speak freely using this action, but the Dungeon Master can limit the length of a monologue or a conversation that takes place during combat.
+ **Includes Other Communication:** Creatures that communicate using telepathy or other forms of nonverbal communication also use this action to communicate.

Total Defense

Sometimes it's more important to guard against further injury than to attack. In such circumstances, a creature focuses its attention on defense.

Use Total Defense

+ **Action:** Standard action.
+ **+2 Bonus to All Defenses:** The creature gains a +2 bonus to all defenses until the start of its next turn.

Use a Power

A creature's powers are among its most important tools in the game. All creatures have at-will powers, so a creature can potentially use a power in every round, even if it's just a basic attack. Each power specifies the type of action, if any, that is required to use it. See Chapter 3 for more about using powers.

Use a Skill

Skills have great utility both inside and outside combat. Monsters rarely use skills other than Athletics, Perception, and Stealth, but adventurers potentially have many tools at their disposal among their skills. Each skill's description specifies the type of action that is required to use it, if any.

Creative skill use can turn the tide of an encounter. Adventurers might rely on Athletics to jump over a chasm or to leap across difficult terrain, or use skills such as Arcana and Nature to learn about monsters' weaknesses. Clever use of Stealth can give a creature combat advantage. Plenty of threats provide opportunities to exploit Perception, Thievery, Endurance, and Acrobatics in the midst of combat. See Chapter 4 for more about using skills, drawing inspiration from the improvisation sidebars.

Walk

The most common way that creatures change their locations in battle is by taking the walk action.

Walk

+ **Action:** Move action.
+ **Movement:** The creature moves up to its speed.

Despite the action's name, a creature isn't always literally walking when it takes this action. The walk action can use special movement modes such as climbing, flying, and swimming.

Taking this action is safe only when no enemies are nearby. Walking through the middle of a pitched battle is dangerous, since enemies can make opportunity attacks against a walking creature. The way to move safely when enemies are nearby is to shift or teleport.

MOUNTED COMBAT

A valiant knight and her fearless warhorse charge a blue dragon. The dwarf cavalry of the Barrier Peaks takes to its hippogriffs to repel a flight of rampaging harpies. A drow scout patrol rides monstrous spiders across a cavern's ceiling, watching for surface dwellers foolish enough to blunder into its territory. From a mundane horse to a snarling dire wolf, mounts offer many options to their riders.

Mounts offer three basic advantages to riders: They are faster than most humanoids, they can offer alternative movement modes such as flight and swimming, and the more ferocious of them combine their fighting abilities with those of their riders.

The mounted combat rules define the relationship between rider and mount, specify how to mount a creature and how to dismount, and how to combine the actions and options of the two creatures, almost as though mount and rider were a single creature.

Mount Requirements

To be a mount, a creature must meet two requirements.

+ **Size:** The creature's size category must be larger than its rider's. For instance, a mount for a Medium creature must be Large or larger.
+ **Willing:** The creature must be a willing mount. The mount is considered an ally to its rider and the rider's allies.

Mounting and Dismounting

The most common ways for a rider to get on or off a mount are using the mount and dismount actions. Uncommon ways include teleportation and jumping.

Mount (Move Action): The rider mounts a creature adjacent to it and enters its space.

Dismount (Move Action): The rider dismounts, moving from the mount's space to a square adjacent to it.

Rules for the Mount and Rider

A mount and rider follow these rules while the rider is mounted.

Space: The rider and mount both occupy the mount's space and are considered adjacent to each other. However, the origin square of any of the rider's powers and other effects does not change to the mount's size. Whenever the rider uses an effect that has an origin square (such as a melee, a ranged, a close, or an area power), the rider first picks where that square is located in the mount's space, and the effect uses that origin square (the rider still shares the mount's space for the purpose of triggering effects, such as opportunity attacks). For instance, if a Medium rider uses a close burst attack power, the rider chooses a single square within the mount's space, and the burst emanates from that square. This rule means that if the burst targets each creature within it, rather than each enemy, it can hit the mount.

Initiative: The mount and rider act on the rider's initiative count, even if the mount had a different initiative before the rider mounted it. The two continue to act on the same initiative count after the rider dismounts. A monster and its mount have separate turns, whereas an adventurer and his or her mount have a single turn.

Actions (Adventurers Only): An adventurer and his or her mount have a shared set of actions: a standard action, a move action, and a minor action. However, they each have their own free actions. The player chooses how the two creatures divide up the set of actions on the adventurer's turn. Most commonly, the mount takes a move action to walk or shift, and the adventurer takes a standard action to attack. The adventurer and the mount also share a single immediate action each round and a single opportunity action each turn. If one of the creatures can't take actions, the shared set of actions is still available to the other creature. If either creature is dazed, that creature can take only one of the shared actions.

If the adventurer dismounts, the two still share one set of actions on that turn, but have separate sets of actions on subsequent turns.

Mount Attacks: The mount takes a –2 penalty to attack rolls. While not being ridden, a typical mount (such as a riding horse) rarely attacks on its own, unless it has been trained for battle, is defending itself, or feels unusually protective of its rider. Left to its own devices, a typical mount avoids combat.

Charging: When the rider charges, the rider and mount move up to the mount's speed and then the rider makes the charge attack. When the mount charges, it follows the normal rules for a charge (page 240).

Squeezing: When the mount squeezes (page 249), the rider is also considered to be squeezing.

Targeting the Mount and Rider: Even though the mount and rider occupy the same space, they are still separate creatures and are targeted separately. For instance, an attack that targets only one creature can target either the mount or the rider, not both. In contrast, area and burst attacks can affect both mount and rider, since the two are in the same space.

Provoking Opportunity Attacks: If the mount's movement provokes an opportunity attack, the attacker chooses to target either the mount or the rider, since the two of them move together. However, if the mount or the rider provokes an opportunity attack by using a ranged or an area power, the attacker must target whichever one of them provoked the opportunity attack.

Forced Movement: If the mount is pulled, pushed, or slid, the rider moves with it. If the rider is pulled, pushed, or slid and the mount isn't, the rider can have the two of them move together. Otherwise, the rider is dismounted and falls prone in the destination space of the forced movement.

Teleportation: If either the mount or the rider is teleported, the other does not teleport with it. If the mount is teleported without the rider, the rider is dismounted and falls prone.

Falling Prone: If the mount falls prone, the rider is dismounted and falls prone in an unoccupied space of the rider's choice adjacent to the now-prone mount. However, if the mount is flying when it is knocked prone, it instead falls. The rider isn't dismounted unless the mount lands and falls prone itself.

A rider who is knocked prone can immediately make a saving throw. On a roll of 9 or lower, the rider is dismounted and falls prone in an unoccupied space of the rider's choice adjacent to the mount. On a roll of 10 or higher, the rider is neither dismounted nor knocked prone.

A rider who voluntarily drops prone falls prone in an unoccupied space of the rider's choice adjacent to the mount.

AQUATIC COMBAT

Fighting underwater is tricky business for land-dwelling creatures. Water provides resistance against movement, swirling currents grab and drag a swimmer along, and tempestuous waters immobilize all but expert swimmers.

Aquatic combat refers to encounters involving combatants in water or some other liquid, not when they're aboard a vessel. The following rules apply to aquatic combat.

Swim Speed: A creature moves through the water using its swim speed. A creature that has no swim speed must use the Athletics skill to swim.

Fire Powers: Attackers take a -2 penalty to the attack rolls of fire powers used underwater.

Weapons: Attackers take a -2 penalty to attack rolls while wielding any weapon underwater that isn't from the spear or the crossbow weapon group (page 271).

UNDERWATER TERRAIN

The most important underwater terrain is the water itself, especially when the water is moving. Currents drag creatures along in their path, and difficult terrain, cover, and concealment all exist in watery realms. The ruins of a sunken ship provide cover, while dirt kicked up by powerful currents creates obscured squares. Choppy, storm-churned seas act as difficult terrain.

Underwater battles allow for up-and-down movement. Creatures can attack foes from all directions, not just along the ground. See "Movement in Three Dimensions," page 206.

Aquatic and Nonaquatic Creatures

Aquatic creatures, such as water elementals and sharks, can breathe underwater. (If a monster is aquatic, it has the aquatic keyword in its stat block.) In aquatic combat, an aquatic creature gains a +2 bonus to attack rolls against nonaquatic creatures.

Nonaquatic creatures have to hold their breath while fighting underwater. Such strenuous activity requires Endurance checks, especially if the combatant takes damage. See "Starvation, Thirst, and Suffocation" in chapter 5 for more details.

Hit Points and Healing

Over the course of a battle, adventurers and monsters take damage from attacks. Hit points measure the ability of a creature to stand up to punishment, turn deadly strikes into glancing blows, and stay on its feet throughout a battle. Hit points represent more than physical endurance. They also represent skill, luck, and resolve—all the factors that combine to help a creature stay alive in combat.

An adventurer's maximum hit points are determined during character creation and change as the character advances in level. A monster's hit points depend on its level and role and are noted in its stat block, along with its bloodied value.

RALPH HORSLEY

Whenever a creature takes damage, subtract that number from its current hit points. As long as that current hit point total is higher than 0, the creature can keep on fighting. A monster normally dies at 0 hit points; an adventurer whose current hit point total drops to 0 or lower is dying.

Powers, abilities, and actions that restore hit points are forms of healing. Characters (and some monsters) might regain hit points through rest, heroic resolve, or magic. When a creature heals, add the number of hit points regained to its current hit points. A creature can heal up to its maximum hit point total but can't exceed it.

Hit Points

Damage reduces hit points.

Maximum Hit Points: A character's class, level, and Constitution score determine his or her maximum hit points. A monster's maximum hit points are noted in its stat block. A creature's current hit points can't exceed this number.

Bloodied Value: The bloodied value of a typical creature equals one-half its maximum hit points. A creature is bloodied when its current hit points drop to its bloodied value or lower. Certain powers and effects work only against a bloodied target or work better against such a target. An object is never considered to be bloodied.

When an unbloodied creature is killed outright, the creature does not become bloodied in the process. It is just dead. This rule means a minion, which has only 1 hit point, is bloodied only if an attacker reduces the minion to 0 hit points but knocks it unconscious (see "Knocking Creatures Unconscious," page 261) instead of killing it.

Dying: When a character's current hit points drop to 0 or lower, the character is dying.

HEALING IN COMBAT

Even in a heated battle, adventurers can heal. They heal themselves by using second wind, and allies can administer first aid with the Heal skill or use healing powers on them.

When a power heals your character, he or she doesn't have to take an action to spend a healing surge. Even if he or she is unconscious, the power uses a healing surge and restores hit points. Some healing powers restore hit points without requiring your character to spend a healing surge.

Healing Surges

Most healing requires a character to spend a healing surge. When a character spends a healing surge, he or she regains lost hit points and adds them to his or her current hit point total.

Once per encounter, a character can use the second wind action to spend a healing surge and regain hit points.

A character can spend a limited number of healing surges per day. When the character takes an extended rest, his or her number of healing surges is replenished.

After a short rest, the character can spend as many healing surges as desired outside combat.

Some powers allow a character to regain hit points as if he or she had spent a healing surge. When a character receives such healing, he or she doesn't actually spend a healing surge.

Number of Healing Surges: An adventurer's class and Constitution modifier determine how many healing surges he or she can use in a day.

Healing Surge Value: When an adventurer spends a healing surge, he or she regains hit points equal to his or her healing surge value, normally one-quarter of his or her maximum hit points (rounded down).

Monsters and Other Characters: As a general rule, monsters and DM-controlled characters have a number of healing surges based on their tier: one at the heroic tier (1st-10th levels), two at the paragon tier (11th-20th levels), and three at the epic tier (21st-30th levels). However, these individuals rarely have powers that allow them to use these healing surges.

Temporary Hit Points

A variety of sources can grant temporary hit points—small reservoirs of stamina that insulate a creature from losing actual hit points.

Not Real Hit Points: Temporary hit points aren't healing, but rather a layer of "insulation" that attacks have to get through before they start dealing real damage to a target. Don't add temporary hit points to a creature's current hit points (if an adventurer has 0 hit points or fewer, he or she still has 0 or fewer after receiving temporary hit points). Keep track of them as a separate pool of hit points.

Don't Count toward Maximum: Temporary hit points don't count when comparing a creature's current hit points to its maximum hit points, when determining whether the creature is bloodied, or for other effects that depend on its current hit points.

Lose Temporary Hit Points First: When a creature takes damage, first subtract its temporary hit points from the damage. Any remaining damage reduces its current hit points.

DAMAGE AND HEALING IN ACTION

The 12th-level fighter Lyriel is locked in combat with an otyugh, keeping it busy while her allies focus on the otyugh's mind flayer master. Lyriel has 96 maximum hit points, which means she is bloodied when her current hit points drop to 48 or lower. She has eleven healing surges, which restore 24 hit points apiece.

At the start of the fight, Lyriel fell 20 feet into the otyugh's pit and took 16 damage. That brought her current hit point total to 80. Seeing her in danger, her paladin friend uses a power to grant her 5 temporary hit points. Her current hit points are still 80, but the 5 temporary hit points will soak up damage before Lyriel starts subtracting hit points again. The otyugh slams her with a tentacle, dealing 12 damage. That's enough to use up all 5 temporary hit points and deal 7 more damage to Lyriel; she now has 73 hit points. On her turn, she strikes back.

Then the otyugh scores a critical hit, dealing 22 damage. Lyriel counters with an immediate interrupt power that reduces the damage by 11. Her current hit point total is now 62. Lyriel counterattacks but misses.

The otyugh manages to score another critical hit, dealing 22 more damage and reducing Lyriel's current hit points to 40, so she is bloodied. On her turn, as insurance she uses the daily power of her *amulet of false life*, which grants her 24 temporary hit points (her healing surge value). The power is a minor action, so it doesn't interfere with her attack. Her current hit point total is still 40, though, so she is still bloodied.

The otyugh bites Lyriel and deals 16 damage, which is absorbed by Lyriel's temporary hit points. On her next turn, Lyriel uses her second wind, which restores 24 hit points, bringing her total to 64. Because using her second wind cost a healing surge, she has ten left for the day. She's not bloodied anymore, and she still has 8 temporary hit points from her amulet's power. Feeling newly invigorated, Lyriel is ready to keep fighting.

Not Cumulative: If a creature receives temporary hit points multiple times, use the highest value as its temporary hit point total. Do not add the values together. For example, a creature receives 5 temporary hit points and later receives 5 temporary hit points again before the first 5 were used. It now has 5 temporary hit points, not 10.

Likewise, if a creature's temporary hit points have been reduced and the creature receives temporary hit points again, it benefits from the higher number. For example, a creature gains 10 temporary hit points and takes 8 damage, reducing its temporary hit points to 2, then receives 5 temporary hit points. It now has 5 temporary hit points, not 7.

Until a Rest: A creature's temporary hit points last until they're reduced to 0 or until the creature takes a short rest or an extended rest.

Regeneration

Regeneration is a special form of healing that restores a fixed number of hit points every round. Regeneration doesn't rely on healing surges.

Heal Each Turn: If a creature has regeneration and at least 1 hit point, it regains a specified number of hit points at the start of its turn. However, if its current hit point total is 0 or lower, it does not regain hit points through regeneration.

Not Cumulative: If a creature gains regeneration more than once, only the largest amount of regeneration applies. For example, a wererat regenerates 5 hit points each round. If another effect grants it regeneration of 2 hit points per round, it still regenerates 5 hit points, not 7.

DYING AND DEATH

In the unending exploration of the unknown and the fight against monsters, death looms as a constant danger. Even so, death is not necessarily the end in the DUNGEONS & DRAGONS game. Some powers and magical rituals can return a dead adventurer to life.

Dying: When an adventurer's hit points drop to 0 or fewer, he or she falls unconscious and is dying. Any additional damage he or she takes continues to reduce that current hit point total until the adventurer dies.

Death Saving Throw: When an adventurer is dying, make a saving throw at the end of that character's turn each round. A death saving throw works just like any other saving throw, but the result determines how close the adventurer is to death.
+ *9 or Lower:* The adventurer slips one step closer to death. If this result comes up three times before the adventurer takes a short or an extended rest, he or she dies.
+ *10-19:* No change.
+ *20 or Higher:* The adventurer taps into his or her will to live, represented by being able to spend a healing surge. If the adventurer has at least one surge left and now spends it, he or she is considered to have 0 hit points, and then the healing surge restores hit points as normal. The adventurer is no longer dying, and he or she is conscious but still prone.

MONSTERS AND FALLEN ADVENTURERS

Most monsters don't attack enemies who are dying; they focus on any adventurers still on their feet and posing a threat. But some particularly wicked monsters might attack a dying adventurer on purpose, even using a coup de grace, and monsters make no effort to avoid including dying adventurers in an area attack or a close attack aimed at others who are still fighting.

Death: When an adventurer takes damage that reduces his or her current hit points to his or her bloodied value expressed as a negative number, the adventurer dies.

Example: Fargrim is a 6th-level dwarf fighter and has a maximum hit point total of 61. He's bloodied at 30 hit points, so he dies if his hit point total drops to -30. In a fight with an umber hulk, Fargrim has been reduced to 28 hit points and is grabbed by the monster; he is now bloodied. The umber hulk then hits him with *rending claws*, dealing 40 damage and reducing Fargrim's current hit points to -12. He's now unconscious and dying, and 18 more damage will kill him.

Knocking Creatures Unconscious

When an adventurer reduces a monster or a DM-controlled character to 0 hit points, he or she can choose to knock the creature unconscious rather than kill it. Until it regains hit points, the creature is unconscious but not dying. Any healing makes the creature conscious.

If the creature doesn't receive any healing, after a short rest it is restored to 1 hit point and becomes conscious.

Monsters and Death

Monsters and characters controlled by the Dungeon Master usually die when their hit points drop to 0, unless an adventurer chooses to knock them unconscious. Adventurers generally don't need to stalk around the battlefield after a fight, making sure all their foes are dead.

Healing the Dying

When an adventurer is dying, any healing restores him or her to at least 1 hit point. If someone has stabilized the character using the Heal skill but he or she receives no healing, he or she regains hit points after an extended rest.

Regain Hit Points: When an adventurer is dying and receives healing, he or she is considered to have 0 hit points, and then regains hit points from the healing effect. If the healing effect requires the adventurer to spend a healing surge but he or she has none left, the healing still helps a bit: The adventurer's hit point total is restored to 1.

Become Conscious: As soon as an adventurer has a current hit point total higher than 0, he or she becomes conscious and is no longer dying. (The adventurer is still prone until he or she takes an action to stand up.)

Example: Fargrim is at -12 hit points, unconscious and dying. His companion, Valenae the cleric, uses *healing word* to help him. This assistance immediately raises Fargrim's current hit points to 0 and allows him to spend a healing surge, boosted by 2d6 extra hit points from Valenae's *healing word*. Valenae gets a 6 on the dice roll, so Fargrim regains a total of 21 hit points (15 from the healing surge plus 6 from *healing word*). He is restored to consciousness with a current hit point total of 21.

CHAPTER 7

EQUIPMENT

When adventurers leave the safety of a city or a settlement and head out for the wilderness and the unknown, they must be prepared. They need protection, arms, and tools to see them through potential dangers and hardships. An unprepared adventurer can wind up injured, lost, or worse.

A Dungeon Master rarely has to consider a monster's equipment. If a monster is wearing or carrying anything noteworthy, that equipment is noted in its stat block (which also accounts for the equipment's effect). Thus, a DM doesn't have to adjust a monster's statistics based on what it picks up or wears.

Adventurers need protection: arms and tools to see them through danger and hardship.

The main relationship that monsters have to equipment is when they serve as the guardians of magic items (discussed later in this chapter). As adventurers seek ever greater power, they are constantly on the lookout for powerful items and must usually get past monsters to acquire them.

This chapter contains the following information.

✦ **Coins and Other Currency:** Adventurers start with some money to purchase equipment, and they acquire more wealth over their careers. Here's a summary of the most common sorts of currency.

✦ **Carrying, Lifting, and Dragging:** When adventurers need to haul that loot from the dungeon, they need to know how much they can carry.

✦ **Armor, Shields, and Weapons:** Basic information about these tools of the trade for adventurers.

✦ **Magic Items:** The most desirable treasures are magic weapons, armor, implements, and other wondrous items that enhance adventurers' power and survivability. This section briefly describes the categories of magic items.

COINS AND OTHER CURRENCY

Merchants and adventurers alike use the gold piece (gp) as the standard unit of currency for most transactions. The exchange of large amounts of money might be handled by letters of credit or gems and jewelry, but the value is always measured in gold pieces.

The common people of the world deal more widely in the silver piece (sp) and the copper piece (cp). A gold piece is worth 10 silver pieces, and a silver piece is worth 10 copper pieces.

People use copper, silver, and gold coins daily. Many of the world's ancient empires also minted platinum pieces, and merchants still accept them even if

WILLIAM O'CONNOR

most people never see them. They're most common in ancient treasure hoards. A platinum piece is worth 100 gold pieces.

A coin is about an inch across and weighs about one-third of an ounce (50 coins to the pound).

Gems and jewelry are more portable forms of wealth favored by adventurers. Among commoners, "portable wealth" usually means cattle (with one cow worth about 10 gp in trade).

In fantastic realms beyond the natural world—in the City of Brass in the Elemental Chaos, the Bright City in the Astral Sea, the city of Sigil, and similar markets—the astral diamond (ad) is used as currency for transactions involving staggering amounts of wealth. One astral diamond is worth 100 platinum pieces, or 10,000 gold pieces. An astral diamond weighs one-tenth as much as a coin (500 astral diamonds to the pound).

Monetary Unit	cp	sp	gp	pp	ad
Copper piece (cp)	1	1/10	1/100	1/10,000	1/1,000,000
Silver piece (sp)	10	1	1/10	1/1,000	1/100,000
Gold piece (gp)	100	10	1	1/100	1/10,000
Platinum piece (pp)	10,000	1,000	100	1	1/100
Astral diamond (ad)	1,000,000	100,000	10,000	100	1

Starting Wealth for an Adventurer

A 1st-level adventurer starts with basic clothing and 100 gold pieces to spend on armor, weapons, and adventuring gear. This number is an abstraction; the character probably doesn't walk into a store one day with a bag of coins, unless he or she just came into an inheritance or won a tournament of some sort. The items that the adventurer starts with, and any money left over, might represent gifts from family, gear used during military service, equipment issued by a patron, or even something the character made.

As an adventurer goes up in level, he or she acquires more gold that can be spent not just on mundane gear, but on common magic items as well.

MONSTERS AND EQUIPMENT

A monster's stat block notes items carried by the monster. Equipment that is not notable is left for the Dungeon Master to decide.

If an adventurer gains a monster's equipment, he or she can use it as normal gear. The adventurer does not gain any powers that a monster uses through a piece of equipment.

A piece of equipment that adventurers use does not necessarily have the same properties for monsters. For instance, a greataxe has the high crit property, but a monster using the item does not benefit from the property, unless otherwise noted in the monster's stat block.

Selling Equipment

Adventurers cannot sell mundane armor, weapons, or adventuring gear unless the Dungeon Master allows. Even then, they receive only one-fifth of an item's market price. Art objects or fine goods that have a specific value, such as a gold dagger worth 100 gp, bring their full stated price. The sale price of a magic item depends on its rarity; see "Magic Item Values," page 277.

CARRYING, LIFTING, OR DRAGGING

Adventurers carry a lot of gear. A creature's Strength score determines how heavy a load it can carry, as well as how much it can push or drag along the ground. A monster's carrying capacity comes into play only in unusual situations.

Normal Load: Multiply the creature's Strength score by 10. The result is the weight, in pounds, that the creature can carry around without penalty.

Heavy Load: Double the normal load number (that is, Strength × 20) to find a creature's heavy load, the maximum weight it can lift off the ground. While a creature is carrying more than its normal load, it is slowed. Carrying such a load requires both hands.

Maximum Drag Load: Five times a creature's normal load (that is, Strength × 50) is the most weight it can push or drag along the ground. The creature is slowed if it pushes or drags more weight than its normal load, and it can't push or drag more than its heavy load over difficult terrain.

ARMOR

Armor provides a barrier between an adventurer and attacks—or, put more bluntly, between the adventurer and death. Every class provides access to one or more armor proficiencies, and it's in an adventurer's best interest to wear the finest armor possible.

Armor Bonus: While wearing a suit of armor, an adventurer gains an armor bonus to Armor Class, determined by the type of armor. For instance, a suit of chainmail grants a +6 armor bonus to AC.

Armor Proficiency

An adventurer's class specifies the kinds of armor that he or she has proficiency with, and an adventurer can take feats to learn the proper use of other kinds of armor. If an adventurer wears armor that he or she does not have proficiency with, the armor makes the adventurer clumsy and uncoordinated: That character takes a -2 penalty to attack rolls and to Reflex.

Armor proficiency is irrelevant to a monster. If it's wearing armor, that fact is noted in its stat block, and it is able to use the armor effectively.

Donning Armor

Putting on a suit of armor takes at least 5 minutes, so it's an activity that can be undertaken only outside combat. Armor can be donned while taking a short rest.

Armor Types

Armor is grouped into categories. Each category of armor is either light armor or heavy armor.

Light Armor

Light armor is easy to act in if the wearer has proficiency with it. Cloth armor, leather armor, and hide armor are light armor. While wearing light armor, an adventurer adds either his or her Intelligence or Dexterity modifier to Armor Class, whichever is higher.

✦ **Cloth Armor:** Jackets, mantles, woven robes, and padded vests don't provide any significant protection by themselves. However, they can be imbued with protective magic. All adventurers have proficiency with cloth armor.

✦ **Leather Armor:** Leather armor is sturdier than cloth armor. It protects vital areas with multiple layers of boiled-leather plates, while covering the limbs with supple leather that provides a small amount of protection.

✦ **Hide Armor:** Thicker and heavier than leather, hide armor is composed of skin from any creature that has a tough hide, such as a bear, a griffon, or a dragon. Hide armor can bind and slightly hinder precision, but it's light enough that it doesn't affect an adventurer's speed.

Heavy Armor

Heavy armor is more restrictive than light armor, so natural agility matters less when wearing it. Chainmail, scale armor, and plate armor are heavy armor. An adventurer wearing heavy armor doesn't add an ability score modifier to his or her AC, unless directed to do so by a special effect. In addition, a typical suit of heavy armor imposes a penalty on its wearer's speed, as noted in the armor's description.

✦ **Chainmail:** Metal rings woven together into a shirt, leggings, and a hood make up a suit of chainmail. Chainmail grants good protection, but it's cumbersome, so it reduces mobility and agility.

✦ **Scale Armor:** Overlapping pieces of highly durable material, such as steel or even dragon scales, make up scale armor. Despite its heaviness, scale is easy to wear; its straps and buckles make it adjustable and able to be fit snugly to the body, allowing flexibility and agility.

✦ **Plate Armor:** The heaviest type of armor, made up of shaped plates of metal or similarly resilient material, plate provides the most armor protection. The cost for its superior fortification is mobility and agility.

Reading an Armor Description

Each type of armor is defined by a few basic characteristics that indicate how it functions in the game. These characteristics are typically specified in a table that contains the following entries.

Armor Bonus: The armor bonus to AC that a creature gains while wearing the armor.

Check: The penalty to Strength-, Dexterity-, and Constitution-based skill checks that a creature takes while wearing the armor. This penalty is called an **armor check penalty**. It does not apply to ability checks (such as a Strength check to break down a door or a Dexterity check to determine initiative in combat).

Speed: The penalty to speed that a creature takes while wearing the armor.

Price: The armor's cost in gold pieces.

Weight: The armor's weight.

SHIELDS

Shields improve an adventurer's defensive capabilities by helping to deflect attacks.

Shield Bonus: While using a shield, an adventurer gains a shield bonus to AC and Reflex, determined by the type of shield. For instance, a light shield grants a +1 shield bonus to AC and Reflex.

Shield Proficiency

An adventurer must have proficiency with a shield to gain its shield bonus. In other words, a shield provides no benefit to an adventurer who can't use it properly. Shield proficiency is irrelevant to a monster, however. If it's using a shield, that fact is noted in its stat block, and it is able to use the shield effectively.

Using a Shield

To use a shield, a creature must strap it to the forearm. Doing so is a standard action, unless otherwise noted. Removing a shield is also a standard action.

Shield Types

Each kind of shield is either a light shield or a heavy shield.

Light Shield: While using a light shield, a creature can use its shield hand for other purposes, such as holding another item or climbing, but the creature can't make attacks with that hand or with anything it is holding in that hand.

Heavy Shield: While using a heavy shield, a creature can't use its shield hand for any other task, since it must use that hand to handle the shield.

Reading a Shield Description

Each shield is defined by a few basic characteristics that indicate how it functions in the game. These characteristics are typically specified in a table that contains the following entries.

Shield Bonus: The shield bonus to AC and Reflex that a creature gains while using the shield.

Check: The penalty to Strength-, Dexterity-, and Constitution-based skill checks that a creature takes while using the shield. This penalty is called an **armor check penalty**. It does not apply to ability checks (such as a Strength check to break down a door or a Dexterity check to determine initiative in combat).

Price: The shield's cost in gold pieces.

Weight: The shield's weight.

WEAPONS

When combat breaks out, a typical adventurer or monster relies on a weapon or two. The game's weapons include things as varied as swords, maces, bows, claws, and fists.

Weapon Categories

Weapons fall into several categories:

+ **Simple Weapons:** This category includes basic weapons such as clubs, quarterstaffs, daggers, and crossbows. Most adventurers have proficiency with simple weapons.

+ **Military Weapons:** This category includes soldierly weapons such as longswords, warhammers, halberds, and longbows. Proficiency with these weapons is not as widespread as proficiency with simple weapons.

+ **Superior Weapons:** This category includes specialized weapons such as rapiers, bastard swords, and shuriken. An adventurer typically gains proficiency with a superior weapon only by taking the Weapon Proficiency feat.

+ **Improvised Weapons:** This category includes anything that was not fashioned as a weapon but that can be used as one. Examples include fists, rocks, chairs, and tankards.

Weapons in all categories are further defined as either melee or ranged and as either one-handed or two-handed.

+ **Melee:** A melee weapon is used to attack a target within the weapon's reach. Unless otherwise noted, a melee weapon has a reach of 1 square. Melee weapons are used with melee powers and with close powers that have the weapon keyword. A melee weapon cannot be used with a ranged

SILVERED WEAPONS

Some monsters, such as werewolves, are susceptible to attacks made by silvered weapons. A single weapon, 30 arrows, 10 crossbow bolts, or 20 sling bullets can be silvered at a cost of 500 gp. This cost represents not only the price of the silver, but the time and expertise needed to add silver to a weapon without making it less effective.

power or an area power that has the weapon keyword, unless the weapon has the light thrown or the heavy thrown property or the weapon is thrown as an improvised ranged weapon.

✦ **Ranged:** A ranged weapon is used to fire projectiles at a target within the weapon's range. Alternatively, the weapon is thrown at a target if the weapon has the heavy thrown or the light thrown property. Each ranged weapon has a normal range and a long range measured in squares. Ranged weapons are used with ranged powers and area powers that have the weapon keyword. A ranged weapon cannot be used with a melee power or a close power that has the weapon keyword, unless the weapon is wielded as an improvised melee weapon.

✦ **One-Handed:** A one-handed weapon is light enough or balanced enough to wield in one hand. A creature can carry a one-handed weapon in each hand, but doing so does not let the creature make extra attacks in a round. The creature must choose which of the weapons it is wielding when it makes a weapon attack. If a weapon attack power allows the use of two weapons, one of the weapons must have the off-hand property.

✦ **Two-Handed:** A two-handed weapon is too heavy or unbalanced to wield without using two hands. Bows and some other weapons require two hands because of their construction. A small creature can't use a two-handed weapon unless the weapon has the small property.

Weapon Properties

Weapon properties define additional characteristics shared by weapons that might be in different groups.

Heavy Thrown: A thrown weapon is a ranged weapon that is hurled from the hand, rather than used to launch a projectile. A ranged basic attack with a heavy thrown weapon uses the wielder's Strength modifier for the attack and damage rolls, unless otherwise noted in the description of the power used.

High Crit: A high crit weapon deals more damage when the wielder scores a critical hit with it. On a critical hit, the weapon deals 1[W] extra damage at 1st–10th levels, 2[W] extra damage at 11th–20th levels, and 3[W] extra damage at 21st–30th levels. This extra damage is in addition to any critical damage the weapon supplies if it is a magic weapon.

Light Thrown: A thrown weapon is a ranged weapon that is hurled from the hand, rather than used to launch a projectile. A ranged basic attack with a light thrown weapon uses the wielder's Dexterity modifier for the attack and damage rolls, unless otherwise noted in the description of the power used.

Load: Ranged weapons that launch projectiles, including bows, crossbows, and slings, take some time to load. Any weapon that has the load property requires two hands to load, even if only one hand is used to attack with it. (The sling, for instance, is a one-handed weapon, but it requires another free hand to load.)

When the word "free" follows a weapon's Load entry, that means the attacker draws and loads ammunition as a free action, effectively part of the action used to attack with the weapon.

When the word "minor" follows a weapon's Load entry, the weapon normally requires a minor action to draw and load ammunition. If a power allows attacks against multiple targets with a single action, the additional load time for multiple projectiles is included in the action used by the power.

Off-Hand: An off-hand weapon is light enough that the attacker can hold it and attack effectively with it while also holding a weapon in his or her main hand. An adventurer can't attack with both weapons in the same turn, unless he or she has a power that allows such an attack, but he or she can attack with either weapon.

Reach: With a reach weapon, a creature can make melee attacks against enemies that are 2 squares away from it as well as adjacent enemies. Even so, the wielder can make opportunity attacks only against enemies adjacent to it and can flank only enemies adjacent to it.

Small: This property describes a two-handed or a versatile weapon that a Small character can use in the same way a Medium character can. A halfling can use a shortbow, for instance, even though halflings can't normally wield two-handed weapons.

Versatile: Versatile weapons are one-handed, but creatures can use them two-handed. An attacker that does so gains a +1 bonus to the weapon's damage rolls.

A Small creature, such as a halfling, must use a versatile weapon two-handed and doesn't gain the bonus to damage rolls.

Weapons and Size

The statistics given for a weapon assume a Medium wielder, which includes most adventurers. Creatures that are smaller or larger than Medium have special rules.

Small creatures use the same weapons that Medium creatures do. However, a Small creature (such as a halfling) can't use a two-handed weapon. When a

Small character uses a versatile weapon, he or she must wield it two-handed and doesn't deal any extra damage for doing so.

Large, Huge, and Gargantuan creatures use weapons that are specially sized for them, and a monster's stat block accounts for how the monster's size interacts with any weapons it wields.

If it's necessary to figure out the damage of a larger-than-normal weapon, use this rule of thumb: Each size category larger than Medium increases the weapon's damage die by one size, as shown below.

One-Handed							
1d4 →	1d6 →	1d8 →	1d10 →	1d12 →	2d6 →	2d8 →	2d10

Two-Handed							
1d8 →	2d4 →	1d10 →	1d12 →	2d6 →	2d8 →	2d10	

Thus, a longsword sized for a Large fire giant deals 1d10 weapon damage instead of 1d8, and a Large quarterstaff deals 2d4 weapon damage instead of 1d8.

Large creatures can use two-handed weapons intended for creatures one size category smaller than themselves and treat the weapons as one-handed weapons. For instance, a fire giant (Large) can use a human's greatsword with one hand, and a fire titan (Huge) can use a fire giant's greatsword with one hand. A creature can't use an undersized one-handed weapon at all; its hand is too large to effectively hold the weapon's small grip.

Creatures can't use weapons designed for creatures larger than themselves. A human adventurer can't fit his or her hands properly around the hilt of a fire giant's dagger, let alone use it as an effective weapon.

Weapon Groups

Weapon groups are families of weapons that share certain physical aspects. They are wielded similarly and are equally suited to certain kinds of attacks. In game terms, some powers and feats work only when attacking with a weapon in a specific group.

If a weapon falls into more than one group, an adventurer can use it with powers that require a weapon from any of its groups.

Axe: These weapons have bladed, heavy heads and deal vicious cuts. An axe's weight makes it fine for delivering crushing blows.

Bow: A bow is a shaft of strong, supple material with a string stretched between its two ends. It's a projectile weapon used to fire arrows.

Crossbow: Essentially a small metal bow mounted on a stock and equipped with a mechanical trigger, a crossbow is a point-and-shoot projectile weapon. Crossbows are popular because they require little training to master, yet the heavy pull of the metal bow gives them substantial power.

Hammer: A hammer has a blunt, heavy head with one or more flat striking surfaces attached to a haft.

Heavy Blade: Blades are balanced edged weapons. Heavy blades share some of the precision of light blades and some of the mass of axes. They are used primarily for slashing cuts rather than stabs and thrusts.

Light Blade: Light blades reward accuracy as much as force. Pinpoint attacks, lunges, and agile defenses are the strong points of these weapons.

Mace: Much like hammers, maces are blunt weapons that have a heavier head than handle, but they're more balanced than hammers. They are useful for delivering crushing blows.

Polearm: Polearms are reach weapons (see above) mounted at the end of long hafts. A polearm typically also belongs to a second weapon group, such as axe or spear.

Sling: A sling is a leather strap used to hurl stones or metal pellets. Slings are projectile weapons.

Spear: Consisting of a stabbing head on the end of a long shaft, a spear is great for lunging attacks.

Staff: In its most basic form, a staff is a long piece of wood or some other hard substance, roughly the same diameter along its whole length.

Unarmed: When a creature punches, kicks, elbows, or head-butts an opponent, it's making an unarmed strike.

Improvised Weapons

Sometimes an attacker doesn't have a proper weapon available and makes do with something else. The attacker might punch or head-butt a foe, smash a chair over the foe's head, hurl a rock at it, or clobber it with a tankard.

Unless the Dungeon Master says otherwise, an improvised weapon has the statistics noted here.

IMPROVISED MELEE WEAPONS

Weapon	Prof.	Damage	Range	Weight	Prop.	Group
One-handed	—	1d4	—	5 lb. or less	—	None or unarmed
Two-handed	—	1d8	—	6 lb. or more	—	—

IMPROVISED RANGED WEAPONS

Weapon	Prof.	Damage	Range	Weight	Prop.	Group
Any	—	1d4	5/10	Varies	—	—

When a weapon is used as an improvised weapon, the weapon's normal characteristics (such as properties, powers, bonuses, and critical hit effects) do not apply. For instance, if an adventurer smacks an adjacent monster with his or her magic bow and scores a critical hit, the bow's critical hit effect does not apply, since the adventurer is using the bow as an improvised melee weapon.

Reading a Weapon Entry

Each weapon is defined by a few basic characteristics that indicate how it functions in the game. These characteristics are typically specified in a table that contains the following entries.

Proficiency: Proficiency with a weapon means that the adventurer is trained in the use of that weapon, which gives him or her a proficiency bonus to attack rolls. The bonus appears in this column if applicable. Some weapons are more accurate than others, as reflected by their bonus. If an adventurer does not have proficiency with the weapon, he or she doesn't gain this bonus.

Damage: The weapon's damage die. When a power deals a number of weapon damage dice (such as 1[W] or 4[W]), the wielder rolls the number of dice indicated by this entry. If the weapon's damage die is an expression of multiple dice, roll that number of dice the indicated number of times. For instance, a greatclub (which has a damage die of 2d4) deals 8d4 damage when used with a power that deals 4[W] damage on a hit.

Range: Weapons that can strike at a distance have a range. The number before the slash in this entry indicates the normal range (in squares) for an attack. The number after the slash indicates the long range for an attack; an attack at long range takes a -2 penalty to the attack roll. Squares beyond the second number are considered to be out of range and can't be targeted with this weapon.

If a melee weapon has a range entry, it can be thrown and has either the light thrown or the heavy thrown property.

An entry of "−" indicates that the weapon can't be used at range.

Price: The weapon's cost in gold pieces. An entry of "−" indicates that the item has no cost.

Weight: The weapon's weight in pounds. An entry of "−" indicates that the weapon's weight is negligible.

Properties: A weapon's properties.

Group: A weapon's group.

Implements

Some creatures use implements to channel the magical energy that fuels their powers. Members of certain classes, such as wizards, rely so heavily on implements that their members rarely use weapons, unleashing attacks through implements instead.

An implement is different from a weapon in many ways. It doesn't typically have a damage die, a range, or properties. In fact, nonmagical implements are little more than symbols of their users' magic. See "Magic Implements," page 283, for how magic implements work.

Proficiency

Unlike weapons, an implement doesn't grant a proficiency bonus. Instead, an adventurer must have proficiency with an implement to use it at all. In the hands of a nonproficient user, an implement—magical or nonmagical—is effectively a bauble.

Using an Implement

Implements are used with powers that have the implement keyword. A creature must be holding an implement to use it, unless otherwise noted.

An implement cannot be used to make a weapon attack. Some types of implements, such as staffs, expressly break this rule.

Implement Groups

Implement groups are families of implements that share certain physical qualities. Some groups are associated with certain power sources. The following groups are the most common.

Holy Symbol: Associated with the divine power source, a holy symbol represents a deity and bears an emblem or an image of the god. Unlike other implements, a holy symbol can be used whether it is held or worn. If a creature wears or holds more than one holy symbol, none of these symbols function until only one remains (this rule is usually relevant only to magic holy symbols).

Orb: An orb is a heavy, round object, usually made of glass or crystal, of a size that fits comfortably in the palm of the hand.

Rod: A rod is a short, heavy cylinder, typically covered in mystic runes or inscribed crystals.

Staff: A staff is a shaft, usually of wood, that is typically as tall as or slightly taller than its wielder. Staffs are sometimes crowned with decorative crystals or other symbols of magical power.

This implement also counts as a quarterstaff. Even a creature who doesn't have proficiency with the staff as an implement can use it as a weapon, but if the staff is magical, the creature cannot use its properties or powers, only its enhancement bonus and critical hit effect.

WEAPONS AS IMPLEMENTS AND VICE VERSA

Some adventurers have the ability to use a weapon as an implement or an implement as a weapon, and some magic items grant this ability. For example, the *holy avenger* weapon can be used as a holy symbol, which is a type of implement. The following rules govern such uses.

Using a Weapon as an Implement: If an adventurer is able to use a weapon as an implement, the weapon works like a normal implement, but the adventurer uses neither the weapon's proficiency bonus nor its nonmagical weapon properties with his or her implement powers. For example, if a weapon has the high crit property, that property does not work with implement powers if the weapon can be used as an implement.

When an adventurer uses a magic version of the weapon as an implement, he or she can use the magic weapon's enhancement bonus, critical hit effects, properties, and powers. However, some magic weapons have properties and powers that work only with weapon powers. Also, a weapon's range and damage dice are usually irrelevant to an implement power, since such a power has its own range and damage expression.

Using an Implement as a Weapon: Most implements cannot be used as weapons, but a few, such as staffs, are expressly usable as both implements and weapons. When an adventurer wields such an implement as a weapon, follow the normal rules for using a weapon.

When an adventurer uses a magic version of the implement as a weapon, he or she can use the magic implement's enhancement bonus and critical hit effects. To use the implement's properties and powers, the adventurer must have proficiency with the implement. Also, some magic implements have properties and powers that work only with implement powers.

Totem: Associated with the primal power source, a totem is a short length of wood or bone carved to resemble a patron animal or nature spirit. One end is typically adorned with feathers, teeth, small bones, scraps of hide, leaves, or other symbols of primal power.

Wand: Associated with the arcane power source, a wand is a slender, tapered piece of wood, crafted to channel magical energy.

MAGIC ITEMS

Magic items have a wide variety of powers and properties that are useful to adventurers. They fall into several broad categories: armor, weapons, implements, clothing and jewelry, wondrous items, and potions. Items in a particular category have similar effects or share certain themes. For instance, magic weapons grant bonuses to attack rolls and damage rolls with them, and magic boots typically have powers or properties related to movement. Wondrous items encompass a broad spectrum of handy tools, from a *bag of holding* to a *flying carpet*.

Magic items are primarily the domain of adventurers. Monsters can use them, but aside from some intelligent humanoids, they rarely do so. If a monster does use a magic item, this fact is noted in its stat block, and the effects are already incorporated into the monster's statistics and powers. The DM does not need to keep track of the item's effects separately from the monster's other capabilities.

Whatever an item's effects, properties, or powers, the item's description indicates how a character uses them.

Item Slots

Within the broad category of clothing and jewelry, items are grouped by kind— whether the item is worn on the head or the feet, for instance. These groups, called item slots, are as follows.

- ✦ Arms
- ✦ Feet
- ✦ Hands
- ✦ Head
- ✦ Neck
- ✦ Rings (two slots)
- ✦ Waist

Item slots represent a practical limit to the number of magic items a character can wear and use. A character can benefit from only one magic item worn in the arms slot even if the character can physically wear bracers and carry a shield at the same time. Sometimes physical limitations exist as well; a character can't wear two pairs of boots at the same time, for instance.

The character benefits from the item that was put on first; any other item put in the same item slot doesn't function until the character takes off the first one.

Magic Item Level and Rarity

Two aspects of a magic item control when it is likely to become available to adventurers: its level and its rarity.

Level A magic item's level is a general measure of its power and corresponds to the average level of characters using that item. An item's level doesn't limit who can acquire or use the item, though it's unusual for an adventurer to find magic items more than a few levels above his or her own level.

If an adventurer finds some means of creating a magic item, such as a magical ritual, the adventurer cannot create a magic item above his or her level, unless otherwise noted.

Rarity

A magic item's rarity indicates how easy it is to obtain in the DUNGEONS & DRAGONS world.

Common magic items are the sort that the most advanced dwarf smiths and elf weavers create in their workshops. These items are generally simple, often having only a single special property: a bonus to certain skill checks or attacks, enhanced effects on a critical hit, and so on.

Adventurers can purchase these common magic items just as they can buy mundane equipment, though few shops or bazaars routinely sell them. Some fantastic locales, such as the legendary City of Brass in the heart of the Elemental Chaos, have such markets, but those are the exception rather than the rule. Adventurers must usually seek out the artisans who create common magic items, though they are not too difficult to find. In most situations—particularly with a little free time to spend—adventurers can buy any common magic item they can afford without the shopping trip becoming an adventure in its own right.

Uncommon and **rare** magic items are not normally created in the current age of the world. These items were crafted in the distant past, some even during the Dawn War, and the techniques for their creation have been lost to the ravages of time. Now they are found only as part of treasure hoards in ancient ruins and dangerous dungeons. Uncommon items are more complicated and potent than common items, though they usually carry a single property, a single power, or one of each. Rare items are even more complex and wondrous, frequently having multiple properties or powers. Such a marvelous possession can help define a character's identity.

Identifying Magic Items

Most of the time, an adventurer can determine the properties and powers of a magic item during a short rest. In the course of handling the item for a few minutes, he or she discovers what the item is and what it does. An adventurer can identify one magic item per short rest.

Rare magic items could be harder to identify. The Dungeon Master might ask an adventurer to make a hard Arcana check to identify the properties and powers of a such an item. Perhaps a special quest is required to identify or to unlock the powers of an especially powerful magic item.

Magic Item Values

The gold piece value of a magic item depends on its level, as shown on the table below. The value of a consumable item (such as a potion) is much lower than the value of a nonconsumable item of the same level. The sale price of a magic item (the amount a character gets from selling an item) depends on the rarity of the item, as shown on the table. A common item's sale price is 20 percent of its gold piece value; an uncommon item's sale price is 50 percent of its gold piece value; and a rare item's sale price is its full gold piece value.

MAGIC ITEM VALUES

Level	Gold Piece Value	Sale Price (gp) Common	Uncommon	Rare
1	360	72	180	360
2	520	104	260	520
3	680	136	340	680
4	840	168	420	840
5	1,000	200	500	1,000
6	1,800	360	900	1,800
7	2,600	520	1,300	2,600
8	3,400	680	1,700	3,400
9	4,200	840	2,100	4,200
10	5,000	1,000	2,500	5,000
11	9,000	1,800	4,500	9,000
12	13,000	2,600	6,500	13,000
13	17,000	3,400	8,500	17,000
14	21,000	4,200	10,500	21,000
15	25,000	5,000	12,500	25,000
16	45,000	9,000	22,500	45,000
17	65,000	13,000	32,500	65,000
18	85,000	17,000	42,500	85,000
19	105,000	21,000	52,500	105,000
20	125,000	25,000	62,500	125,000
21	225,000	45,000	112,500	225,000
22	325,000	65,000	162,500	325,000
23	425,000	85,000	212,500	425,000
24	525,000	105,000	262,500	525,000
25	625,000	125,000	312,500	625,000
26	1,125,000	225,000	562,500	1,125,000
27	1,625,000	325,000	812,500	1,625,000
28	2,125,000	425,000	1,062,500	2,125,000
29	2,625,000	525,000	1,312,500	2,625,000
30	3,125,000	625,000	1,562,500	3,125,000

Reading a Magic Item Description

Here's a sample magic item, the *dragonslayer weapon*.

Dragonslayer Weapon · Level 9+ Uncommon

The bane of dragonkind.

Lvl 9	+2	4,200 gp	Lvl 24	+5	525,000 gp
Lvl 14	+3	21,000 gp	Lvl 29	+6	2,625,000 gp
Lvl 19	+4	105,000 gp			

Weapon: Any

Enhancement: Attack rolls and damage rolls

Critical: +1d8 damage per point of enhancement bonus, or +1d12 damage per point of enhancement bonus against dragons

Property: This weapon provides resistance against a dragon's *breath weapon* power, as shown below.
Level 9: Resist 10
Level 14 or 19: Resist 20
Level 24 or 29: Resist 30

Power (Daily): Minor Action. Your next attack with this weapon against a dragon, if made before the end of your turn, gains a +5 power bonus to the attack roll and automatically ignores any resistance the dragon has.

Name, Level, and Rarity

The name of the magic item, the item's level, and its rarity (common, uncommon, or rare) appear on the first line of the description.

If an item's level entry ends with a plus sign (+), that item is available at more than one level, with higher-level versions having a greater enhancement bonus or more potent powers and properties, as described later in the item's description.

Example: A *dragonslayer weapon* is available as a level 9 item and also comes in four higher-level versions. It's an uncommon item, carrying magical power beyond that possessed by common items.

Flavor Text

The next entry gives a brief description of the item, sometimes explaining what it does in plain language, other times offering flavorful information about its appearance, origin, effect, or place in the world. This material isn't rules text; the item's exact effect is described in the entries that follow.

Category and Value

The next line or lines indicate the magic item's various levels and enhancement bonuses (if applicable) and the gold piece value for each version of the item. For weapons, the line beneath this information lists which weapon groups can be enchanted with that set of qualities, and for armor, it notes the same for the five types of armor (plus clothing). For implements, it shows the specific kind of implement. For clothing items, the entry appears as "Item Slot" followed by the appropriate slot.

The magic item's gold piece value is either a single number (for an item with a fixed level) or a list of values.

Example: The price of a *dragonslayer weapon* (as well as its enhancement bonus) depends on its level. The level 14 version is a +3 weapon and costs 21,000 gp, and the level 29 version is a +6 weapon and costs 2,625,000 gp. It's a weapon, and it can be a weapon from any group.

Enhancement For items that give an enhancement bonus, this entry specifies what that bonus applies to: AC, other defenses, or attack rolls and damage rolls.

Magic weapons and magic implements grant their enhancement bonus to attack rolls and damage rolls only when the wielder uses powers through the weapon or the implement (or directly from the weapon or the implement, for items that have attack powers). A power's description indicates if it functions through the use of a weapon or an implement.

Example: Because a *dragonslayer weapon* is a magic weapon, its enhancement bonus applies to the wielder's attack rolls and damage rolls with the weapon.

Critical For magic weapons and implements, this entry describes what happens when a creature scores a critical hit using that item. Just as with an enhancement bonus, this effect applies only for attacks that are delivered through the weapon or the implement. (A wizard who uses an arcane power can't benefit from the critical hit effect noted for the magic dagger on his or her belt, for instance.)

Unless otherwise noted, this extra damage has the same damage type as the normal damage type for the weapon. An attack that does not normally deal damage still does not deal damage on a critical hit.

Example: A *dragonslayer weapon* deals 1d8 or 1d12 extra damage (depending on whether the target is a dragon or some other creature) on a critical hit.

Property Many magic items have a special property that is constantly active, or active in certain circumstances. A property doesn't normally require any action to use, although some properties allow the user to turn them off (or on again). Unless otherwise noted, a magic item's property remains active for a creature only while it wears the item (in the case of a wearable item such as a suit of armor) or wields the item.

Example: When a character wields a *dragonslayer weapon*, he or she gains resistance against a dragon's breath weapon. The amount of resistance depends on the level of the weapon. This property is always in effect; it isn't turned on or off.

Power

Some uncommon and most rare magic items have a special power. This entry, when present in an item description, includes the action required to use the power and the effect of the power. In some cases, it might also specify the circumstances in which the power can be used (for instance, only if the wielder is bloodied). In general, magic item powers follow the same rules as other powers.

Like other powers, magic item powers often have keywords, which indicate the powers' damage or effect types. When using a magic item as part of a racial power or a class power, all the keywords of the item's power and the other power apply.

Like other powers, magic item powers are sometimes at-will powers, sometimes encounter powers, and sometimes daily powers. Magic item powers have two other categories as well: healing surge powers and consumable powers. The power's category appears in parentheses following "Power" in the entry.

Example: Once per day, the wielder of a *dragonslayer weapon* can take a minor action to make his or her next attack against a dragon more likely to hit and more likely to deal appreciable damage (because the attack ignores the dragon's resistance). The wielder regains the use of this power when he or she takes an extended rest.

At-Will: These powers can be used as often as their action types allow.

Encounter: These powers can be used once per encounter and are recharged when their user takes a short rest.

Daily: A magic item's daily power can be used once per day and is recharged when its user takes an extended rest.

Healing Surge: The character begins with one use of the power per day, as with a daily power. He or she can recharge this item's power by taking a standard action to funnel vitality into the item, spending a healing surge in the process. Spending a healing surge in this way doesn't restore hit points, and this standard action is separate from the action required to activate the item's power.

Consumable: Some items, particularly potions, contain one-use powers that are expended when used.

Special

If any special rules or restrictions on the item's use exist, they're described in a "Special" entry in the item's stat block.

Magic Item Categories

The following sections provide rules and notes about the main categories of magic items.

Magic Armor

Magic armor adds an enhancement bonus to AC, so a set of *+5 black iron plate* adds a total of 13 to the wearer's Armor Class (8 from the plate armor and 5 from the enhancement bonus). If an adventurer does not have proficiency with the armor's type, he or she takes a –2 penalty to attack rolls and to Reflex, as normal, but still gains the enhancement bonus of the magic armor.

The description of a type of magic armor indicates what categories of armor can be enchanted with that particular set of qualities. "Any" includes armor of all categories: cloth, leather, hide, chainmail, scale, and plate.

Masterwork Armor Certain kinds of armor are made according to esoteric methods that involve weaving magic into the substance of the armor. Masterwork armor never appears except as magic armor, and even then only at higher levels. The various kinds of masterwork armor fall into the same categories as mundane armor and have similar statistics, but they grant higher armor bonuses than their mundane counterparts do. The cost of masterwork armor is included in the cost of magic armor.

Magic Weapons
A magic weapon adds an enhancement bonus to attack rolls and damage rolls of attacks made with the weapon. The bonus does not apply to any ongoing damage dealt by those powers.

A magic weapon's category determines the sorts of weapons that can be enchanted with that particular set of qualities. "Any ranged" includes projectile weapons and weapons with the heavy thrown or the light thrown property. "Any" or "Any melee" includes all applicable categories.

Thrown Weapons Any magic light thrown or heavy thrown weapon, from the lowly *+1 dagger* to a *+6 dragonslayer javelin*, automatically returns to its wielder's hand after a ranged attack with the weapon is resolved.

WILLIAM O'CONNOR

Catching a returning thrown weapon is a free action; if the wielder does not wish (or is unable) to catch the weapon, it drops in his or her space.

Ammunition Magic projectile weapons, such as magic bows and slings, impart their magic to appropriate ammunition fired from them. For instance, an arrow shot from a *+1 longbow* delivers the bow's +1 enhancement bonus to attack rolls and damage rolls. If a piece of ammunition is itself magical, the ammunition's enhancement bonus is used in place of the weapon's bonus, but the items' other characteristics, such as properties and powers, are combined.

Magic Implements A magic implement adds an enhancement bonus to the attack rolls and damage rolls of attack powers used with the implement. The bonus does not apply to any ongoing damage dealt by those powers.

Because an adventurer must have proficiency with an implement to use it, an adventurer cannot gain an implement's enhancement bonus or benefit from any of the implement's other characteristics (such as properties, powers, and critical hit effects) unless he or she has proficiency with the implement.

Arms Slot Items Shields
and bracers often contain powers that protect the wearer from harm. Some magic shields are always light shields, others are always heavy shields, but most can be found as either kind of shield.

Feet Slot Items Boots and greaves typically contain powers that enhance the wearer's speed, provide additional movement, or otherwise assist in movement-related situations.

Hands Slot Items Gloves and gauntlets contain powers that assist with skill checks, increase attack rolls and damage rolls, and even allow rerolls in some situations.

Head Slot Items These items typically contain powers that improve Intelligence-based and Wisdom-based skills, increase damage, and enhance senses.

EVA WIDERMANN

Neck Slot Items Amulets and cloaks grant an enhancement bonus to Fortitude, Reflex, and Will. Many of them provide other benefits as well.

Rings Magic rings provide properties and powers that aid users in a variety of ways, from healing and skill use to flying and teleportation. Rings are almost always rare, magic items of wonder and legend forged during the Dawn War or the early ages of the world.

A character can wear and gain the benefit of up to two magic rings (one on each hand). If a character is wearing more than two magic rings at once, none of them function until the character is wearing no more than two.

Waist Slot Items Belts contain powers that improve Strength-based skills, healing, and resistances.

Wondrous Items This category includes some of the most useful and interesting items in the game. They don't take up item slots. Examples include crystal balls, flying carpets, bags that can hold extraordinary loads, and figurines that animate to aid their owners.

JASON A. ENGLE

BUILDING A COMBAT ENCOUNTER

Dungeon Masters sometimes use published combat encounters, and other times they build combat encounters of their own for their group's adventurers to face. This appendix summarizes how to build a combat encounter. The *Dungeon Master's Kit* contains detailed advice on encounter design.

1. **Choose an encounter level.**

   An *easy* encounter is one or two levels lower than the group's level.

   A *standard* encounter is of the group's level or one level higher.

   A *hard* encounter is two to four levels higher than the group's level.

2. **Determine the XP budget.** Multiply the number of characters in the group by the XP value of a standard threat of the encounter's level, as shown on the Encounter XP Budget table. If the group includes any DM-controlled characters who can contribute significantly in combat, count those characters as members of the group when determining the XP budget.

3. **Spend the XP budget.** Choose threats that are within three levels of the encounter level. Keep choosing threats until the sum of their XP values equals the XP budget or slightly exceeds it. Threats can include monsters, traps, hazards, and skill challenges.

ENCOUNTER XP BUDGET

Encounter Level	XP per Character	Encounter Level	XP per Character	Encounter Level	XP per Character
1	100	15	1,200	29	15,000
2	125	16	1,400	30	19,000
3	150	17	1,600	31	23,000
4	175	18	2,000	32	27,000
5	200	19	2,400	33	31,000
6	250	20	2,800	34	39,000
7	300	21	3,200	35	47,000
8	350	22	4,150	36	55,000
9	400	23	5,100	37	63,000
10	500	24	6,050	38	79,000
11	600	25	7,000	39	95,000
12	700	26	9,000	40	111,000
13	800	27	11,000		
14	1,000	28	13,000		

Monster Roles

Each monster's role appears in the monster's stat block. Most combat encounters involve groups of monsters occupying different roles. A group of varied monsters makes for a more interesting and challenging encounter than a group of identical foes.

A good rule of thumb is to include two or three brutes or soldiers and then spice up the encounter with other roles.

Artillery

+ Specializes in high-accuracy ranged and area attacks
+ Often has good defenses against ranged or area attacks
+ Low hit points
+ Best paired with brutes or soldiers

Tip: Use artillery monsters to harry the adventurers from afar.

Brute

+ Specializes in high-damage melee attacks
+ High hit points
+ Often simpler to run than other monsters
+ Good at protecting artillery or controllers

Tip: Use multiple brutes to form a front line.

Controller

+ Specializes in forced movement and other forms of manipulation
+ Often more complex to run than other monsters
+ Benefits from brutes or soldiers for protection

Tip: Use a single controller as the centerpiece of an encounter.

Leader

+ A subrole that can be combined with other roles (a soldier leader or a solo controller leader, for instance)
+ Grants its allies bonuses to attack rolls, damage rolls, defenses, or other statistics
+ Sometimes allows its allies to heal

Tip: Use a leader to reinforce a particular theme (such as confronting an evil cleric).

Lurker

+ Usually alternates high-damage attacks with an ability to escape counterattacks
+ Low hit points
+ Tricky to oppose effectively
+ Benefits from brutes or soldiers that draw the adventurers' attention

Tip: Use a single lurker as a surprise addition to an encounter.

Skirmisher

+ Specializes in mobility and clever positioning during battle
+ Prefers to attack on the move or with combat advantage
+ Benefits from brutes or soldiers that draw the adventurers' attention

Tip: Use one or two skirmishers to keep the adventurers on their toes.

Soldier

+ Specializes in melee attacks and close-range control effects
+ Punishes foes for attacking its allies
+ High defenses
+ Good at protecting artillery or controllers

Tip: Use multiple soldiers to form a front line.

Specialty Roles

Three particular roles can help bring variety to an encounter: elite, solo, and minion. Elite monsters and solo monsters are tougher than standard monsters, and minions are weaker. For the purpose of encounter building, an elite monster counts as two standard monsters of its level, a solo monster counts as five, and four to six minions count as one (four at heroic tier, five at paragon tier, and six at epic tier).

Elite

+ Combined with another role (an elite brute, for instance)
+ Deals twice the damage of a standard monster
+ Lasts twice as long as a standard monster

Tip: Use one elite monster as a "mini-boss" or an otherwise notable foe.

Minion

+ Combined with another role (a minion skirmisher, for instance)
+ Has only 1 hit point
+ Simple to run
+ Almost always appears in a group of others of its kind

Tip: Use four or more minions at a time to create waves of enemies or to build a short-lived wall between the adventurers and other foes.

Solo

+ Combined with another role (a solo lurker, for instance) but contains elements of other roles
+ Deals five times the damage of a standard monster
+ Lasts five times as long as a standard monster

Tip: Use one solo monster as an entire encounter, or pair one with minions or one or two standard monsters.

WILLIAM O'CONNOR

REWARDS

Although encounters involve risk, they also hold the promise of great rewards. Every successful encounter brings experience, measured in experience points. As the adventure continues, adventurers also gain action points, treasure, and perhaps rewards of reputation, status, or other intangibles.

Experience Points

Experience points are a measure of each adventurer's learning and growth. When the adventurers complete an encounter or a quest, the DM awards them experience points (XP). The amount of XP depends on the difficulty of the encounter or the quest. Completing a major quest is comparable to completing an encounter, while minor quests bring smaller rewards. See "Experience Point Rewards" later in this appendix for details on how to assign these rewards.

A 1st-level adventurer starts with 0 experience points. Each adventurer accumulates XP from each encounter and quest, always adding to his or her XP total. Adventurers never lose XP, and an adventurer's XP total never resets to 0.

As an adventurer accumulates experience points, he or she gains levels. The amount of XP an adventurer needs for each level varies. For instance, an adventurer needs 1,000 XP to reach 2nd level but an additional 1,250 to get from 2nd to 3rd level. When an adventurer has gained 1,000,000 XP, he or she reaches 30th level, the pinnacle of accomplishment.

Action Points

Action points are a special resource that each adventurer can spend during combat to take an extra action or gain other special benefits. See "Action Points," page 235, for rules on how this resource works.

Treasure

Treasure comes in a variety of forms, but it falls into two basic categories: magic items that adventurers can use, and money that they can spend to acquire items and services. Money can be coins, gemstones, fine art, or even magic items that adventurers decide to sell instead of use.

Adventurers don't necessarily receive treasure at the completion of each encounter. Treasure is usually a reward for completing several encounters, a quest, or even an entire adventure. Some creatures might carry—and use—magic items that become treasure after adventurers defeat the creatures. Other creatures might keep chests of gold, or adventurers might find treasure suspended in the slimy body of a gelatinous cube. Sometimes adventurers find treasure locked in a vault, stockpiled in an armory, or heaped in a dragon's hoard.

Intangible Rewards

Intangible rewards include noble titles, medals and honors, favors, and reputation. Such rewards appear most often as quest rewards, as recognition of the adventurers' work in completing a quest. If adventurers save the baron's son from kidnappers, the baron might reward each of them with a medal or even a minor noble title, in addition to granting some monetary reward to them. If adventurers retrieve a magic orb from the bleak ruins of Havoc Hall and bring it to the mysterious wizard who sent them there, she might promise them a later favor, along with the money she promised them up front. When the adventurers save a village from goblin raiders, the village honors them as local heroes, and word of their deeds begins to spread.

Adventurers can't buy anything with intangible rewards, and they don't grant any combat bonuses. But they can be important in the campaign's story, and they can help adventurers out in social interactions. Don't overlook the importance of contacts, favors, and fame, even if they don't translate directly into fortune.

GAINING REWARDS

This table summarizes when adventurers typically gain rewards.

When	What
After an encounter	XP, maybe treasure
After a milestone	Action point
After a completed quest	XP, treasure, other
After a session of play	XP, treasure

After an Encounter

At the end of each encounter, the Dungeon Master adds up the XP rewards for each of the monsters, traps, and hazards that the adventurers overcame during the encounter (see "Experience Point Rewards," below). Divide this total by the number of characters in the adventuring group, and add that value to each character's XP total.

Some groups think it's easier to wait until the end of a gaming session to award XP. In that case, the DM just jots down a note of how many experience points each encounter is worth so that he or she can easily total them later.

Some encounters include a treasure reward. If the adventurers found treasure during the encounter, they can either divide it among themselves immediately or wait until the end of the session. If the adventurers choose to divide treasure infrequently, one player should take the responsibility of tracking all the treasure found by the group.

Even if the adventurers normally divide treasure only at the end of a session, any magic item found should be assigned to a particular character so that he or she can use it during the session.

After a Milestone

When adventurers complete two consecutive encounters without stopping for an extended rest, they reach a milestone. Whenever they reach a milestone, each of them gains an action point (page 235).

A few other things, particularly magic items such as rings, interact with milestones as well. A magic ring's power often has a greater effect if its wearer has reached at least one milestone since the last extended rest. In addition, the DM might choose to provide other rewards when adventurers reach a milestone, depending on the adventure and the style of campaign. For instance, after an exceptionally grueling pair of encounters, the DM might allow each adventurer to regain a healing surge. Such a reward should be rare.

After a Completed Quest

When a group of adventurers completes a quest, the DM awards each adventurer the appropriate XP for that quest (see "Experience Point Rewards," below).

If the quest has other rewards, those should be awarded as appropriate for the story. For example, if a guildmaster offered the adventurers 100 gp to rescue a missing merchant, they receive that reward only when they can prove to the guildmaster that the merchant is safe and sound (which probably means waiting until they get back to town with the merchant in their custody).

After a Session of Play

At the end of a session of play, the DM normally awards any experience points that haven't already been passed out. If the adventurers have any treasure left to divide, they should do that now.

EXPERIENCE POINT REWARDS

Experience points are the fundamental reward of the game, just as encounters are the building blocks of adventures and campaigns. Every encounter comes with an experience point reward to match its difficulty. Any encounter that includes a reasonable risk of failure—and some tangible cost to the adventurers for that failure—should have an XP reward associated with it. Conversely, situations that don't include a risk of failure, or in which failure has no significant resource costs or story ramifications, should usually have no XP reward.

The Experience Point Rewards table presents the standard XP value for threats of different levels and types (standard, minion, elite, and solo). Monsters are the most typical threats in the game, but traps, hazards, skill challenges, and quests are also considered threats for the purpose of awarding experience points.

EXPERIENCE POINT REWARDS

Threat Level	Standard	Minion	Elite	Solo
1	100	25	200	500
2	125	31	250	625
3	150	38	300	750
4	175	44	350	875
5	200	50	400	1,000
6	250	63	500	1,250
7	300	75	600	1,500
8	350	88	700	1,750
9	400	100	800	2,000
10	500	125	1,000	2,500
11	600	150	1,200	3,000
12	700	175	1,400	3,500
13	800	200	1,600	4,000
14	1,000	250	2,000	5,000
15	1,200	300	2,400	6,000
16	1,400	350	2,800	7,000
17	1,600	400	3,200	8,000
18	2,000	500	4,000	10,000
19	2,400	600	4,800	12,000
20	2,800	700	5,600	14,000
21	3,200	800	6,400	16,000
22	4,150	1,038	8,300	20,750
23	5,100	1,275	10,200	25,500
24	6,050	1,513	12,100	30,250
25	7,000	1,750	14,000	35,000
26	9,000	2,250	18,000	45,000
27	11,000	2,750	22,000	55,000
28	13,000	3,250	26,000	65,000
29	15,000	3,750	30,000	75,000
30	19,000	4,750	38,000	95,000
31	23,000	5,750	46,000	115,000
32	27,000	6,750	54,000	135,000
33	31,000	7,750	62,000	155,000
34	39,000	9,750	78,000	195,000
35	47,000	11,750	94,000	235,000
36	55,000	13,750	110,000	275,000
37	63,000	15,750	126,000	315,000
38	79,000	19,750	158,000	395,000
39	95,000	23,750	190,000	475,000
40	111,000	27,750	222,000	555,000

Monster XP Rewards

Each time the adventurers overcome an enemy monster, the group gains experience points for that foe. A monster's stat block indicates the XP reward the monster is worth. That number comes from the Experience Point Rewards table. A standard monster counts as a single threat of its level. As shown in the table, a minion is worth one-quarter of the XP of a standard monster of its level. An elite monster is worth twice as much XP, and a solo monster is worth five times as much XP.

What counts as overcoming a monster? Killing, routing, or capturing an enemy in a combat encounter certainly counts. Adventurers don't get XP for overcoming creatures that aren't threats, such as harmless shopkeepers or innocent bystanders. Adventurers also usually don't get XP for overcoming monsters that don't represent a challenge, even if those monsters are enemies. Remember that XP rewards come only from encounters that feature risk.

For instance, the adventurers avoid encountering a hydra before getting into the treasure vault it guards. Do they get XP for overcoming the hydra? No. If the treasure was the object of a quest, they get the reward for completing the quest, which should include XP as well as the treasure. But because they didn't have an encounter with the hydra, they didn't overcome the challenge. In contrast, if they engage in a skill challenge to sneak past or trick the hydra, they should earn XP for succeeding on that skill challenge.

Trap/Hazard XP Rewards

Traps and hazards that serve as combat complications have levels just as monsters do. If the adventurers encounter a trap or a hazard that presents a threat, they get XP for the trap or hazard, whether they disable it, neutralize it in some other way, avoid it altogether, or suffer its effects.

Overcoming a trap or hazard earns the same amount of XP as overcoming a monster of the same level, so use the Experience Point Rewards table. Unless otherwise noted, a trap or a hazard counts as a single threat of its level. Minion, elite, and solo traps are very rare.

Skill Challenge XP Rewards

Skill challenges and other noncombat encounters that carry risk also carry reward. A skill challenge has a level and a complexity that combine to determine the XP the adventurers earn for successfully completing the challenge. A skill challenge counts as a number of threats of its level equal to its complexity. For instance, a 7th-level challenge that has a complexity of 3 counts as three 7th-level threats, for a reward of 900 XP.

The Skill Challenge XP Rewards table summarizes the XP values of skill challenges of various levels and complexities.

SKILL CHALLENGE XP REWARDS

Level	Complexity 1	Complexity 2	Complexity 3	Complexity 4	Complexity 5
1	100	200	300	400	500
2	125	250	375	500	625
3	150	300	450	600	750
4	175	350	525	700	875
5	200	400	600	800	1,000
6	250	500	750	1,000	1,250
7	300	600	900	1,200	1,500
8	350	700	1,050	1,400	1,750
9	400	800	1,200	1,600	2,000
10	500	1,000	1,500	2,000	2,500
11	600	1,200	1,800	2,400	3,000
12	700	1,400	2,100	2,800	3,500
13	800	1,600	2,400	3,200	4,000
14	1,000	2,000	3,000	4,000	5,000
15	1,200	2,400	3,600	4,800	6,000
16	1,400	2,800	4,200	5,600	7,000
17	1,600	3,200	4,800	6,400	8,000
18	2,000	4,000	6,000	8,000	10,000
19	2,400	4,800	7,200	9,600	12,000
20	2,800	5,600	8,400	11,200	14,000
21	3,200	6,400	9,600	12,800	16,000
22	4,150	8,300	12,450	16,600	20,750
23	5,100	10,200	15,300	20,400	25,500
24	6,050	12,100	18,150	24,200	30,250
25	7,000	14,000	21,000	28,000	35,000
26	9,000	18,000	27,000	36,000	45,000
27	11,000	22,000	33,000	44,000	55,000
28	13,000	26,000	39,000	52,000	65,000
29	15,000	30,000	45,000	60,000	75,000
30	19,000	38,000	57,000	76,000	95,000

Quest XP Rewards

When a group of adventurers completes a major quest, each character receives an XP reward equal to the value for a single threat of the quest's level. This is an exception to the general rule that characters divide all XP rewards evenly among themselves. For instance, each adventurer receives 125 XP for completing a 2nd-level major quest.

A minor quest typically counts as a single threat of the quest's level, which is divided among the adventurers as normal. For instance, each adventurer in a group of five receives 20 XP for completing a 1st-level minor quest. If the DM wants a minor quest to carry more weight, he or she can award XP to each adventurer equal to as much as one-half the value of a single threat of the quest's level. Using this alternative awards 50 XP to each adventurer for that 1st-level minor quest.

A quest's level is typically equal to the level of the characters in the adventuring group when they complete the quest, but the DM can decide to adjust its level (and thus the XP reward characters gain for completing it) upward or downward to reflect its difficulty and significance.

The Quest XP Rewards table summarizes the XP value of major quests. It also includes a range of XP values for minor quests.

QUEST XP REWARDS

Character Level	Major Quest	Minor Quest	Character Level	Major Quest	Minor Quest
1	100	20-50	16	1,400	280-700
2	125	25-60	17	1,600	320-800
3	150	30-75	18	2,000	400-1,000
4	175	35-85	19	2,400	480-1,200
5	200	40-100	20	2,800	560-1,400
6	250	50-125	21	3,200	640-1,600
7	300	60-150	22	4,150	830-2,075
8	350	70-175	23	5,100	1,020-2,550
9	400	80-200	24	6,050	1,210-3,025
10	500	100-250	25	7,000	1,400-3,500
11	600	120-300	26	9,000	1,800-4,500
12	700	140-350	27	11,000	2,200-5,500
13	800	160-400	28	13,000	2,600-6,500
14	1,000	200-500	29	15,000	3,000-7,500
15	1,200	240-600	30	19,000	3,800-9,500

TREASURE

Treasure rewards come in two basic flavors: magic items and monetary treasure. Magic items include magic weapons, armor, clothing, jewelry, and wondrous items. Monetary treasure includes coins (silver pieces, gold pieces, and platinum pieces), precious gems, and valuable objects of art. Over the course of an adventure, characters might acquire treasure of many kinds.

Monetary Treasure

Monetary treasure doesn't have a level, but it has a similar economy. Gold pieces are the standard coins of treasure hoards from 1st level through the paragon tier. At the lowest levels, characters might find silver pieces as well, but that mundane coinage disappears from hoards after about 5th level.

In the mid-paragon tier, platinum pieces start appearing in treasures. One platinum piece (pp) is worth 100 gp and weighs the same as 1 gold piece, so it's a much easier way to transport the quantities of wealth that high-level characters possess. By the time characters reach epic level, they rarely see gold any more. Platinum is the new standard.

In the mid-epic tier, a new currency comes into play: astral diamonds. These precious gems are used as currency in the Elemental Chaos and in any divine dominions that have currency. One astral diamond (ad) is worth 100 pp or 10,000 gp, and 10 ad weigh as much as one gold or platinum coin—so 500 ad weigh 1 pound. Astral diamonds never completely replace platinum, but they're a useful measure of wealth in the high epic tier. Astral diamonds are most commonly found in strings of five or ten, linked together in settings of precious metal.

Gems

Precious gems are as good as currency. Characters can cash them out at full value or use them to purchase expensive items. Gemstones come in four standard values: 100 gp, 500 gp, 1,000 gp, and 5,000 gp. The most common examples of each value are given below. (Numerous other kinds of gems exist.) Astral diamonds are technically gemstones worth 10,000 gp apiece, but they are more often used as currency in their own right.

Gemstones by Value

100 gp: amber, amethyst, garnet, moonstone, jade, pearl, peridot, turquoise

500 gp: alexandrite, aquamarine, black pearl, topaz

1,000 gp: emerald, fire opal, sapphire

5,000 gp: diamond, jacinth, ruby

Gems appear in treasures beginning at 1st level. In the paragon tier, 100 gp gems are rare. Gems worth 500 gp start appearing in 5th-level treasures and fade out in the paragon tier. Gems worth 1,000 gp appear from the middle of the heroic tier to the high end of the paragon tier. The most precious gems are found only in paragon and epic treasures.

DAVID MARTIN

Art Objects

Art objects include idols of solid gold, necklaces dripping with gems, old paintings of ancient monarchs, bejeweled golden chalices, and more. Art objects found as treasure are at least reasonably portable, as opposed to enormous statues (even if they are made of solid platinum) or tapestries woven with gold thread. Many of the most precious art objects include material from the Elemental Chaos or the Astral Sea.

In the heroic tier, characters commonly find art objects worth 250 gp or 1,500 gp. At paragon levels, items worth 2,500 gp or 7,500 gp appear. At high paragon and epic levels, items worth 15,000 gp or 50,000 gp appear in treasures as well. Examples of each category of item are given below.

Art Objects by Value

250 gp: gold ring with 100 gp gem, bone or ivory statuette, gold bracelet, silver necklace, bronze crown, silver-plated sword, silk robe

1,500 gp: gold ring with 1,000 gp gem, gold or silver statuette, gold bracelet with 500 gp gems, gold necklace with 100 gp gems, silver tiara or crown with 100 gp gems, ivory comb with 500 gp gems, cloth of gold vestments

2,500 gp: gold or platinum ring with 1,000 gp gems, gold or silver statuette with 500 gp gems, gold necklace with 500 gp gems, gold crown with 500 gp gems, gold chalice with 100 gp gems, ceremonial gold breastplate

7,500 gp: platinum ring with 5,000 gp gem, gold statuette with 1,000 gp gems, mithral necklace with 1,000 gp gems, adamantine crown with 1,000 gp gems, adamantine box containing elemental flame, black tunic woven of pure shadow

15,000 gp: mithral ring with an astral diamond, gold statuette with 5,000 gp gems, gold necklace with 5,000 gp gems, mithral tiara with 5,000 gp gems, cup of celestial gold that glows with a soft inner light, silvery cloak of astral thread, enormous emerald or sapphire

50,000 gp: bracelet formed of cold elemental lightning, gown woven of elemental water, brass ring with bound elemental fire, celestial gold statuette with astral diamonds, royal attire of astral thread with 5,000 gp gems, enormous diamond or ruby

Magic Items

As adventurers gain levels, the mundane equipment they use at the start of their careers is quickly supplanted by the magic items they acquire on their adventures. Magic armor that can cloak them in shadow, magic weapons that burst into flame, magic rings that turn them invisible, or *Ioun stones* that orbit their heads to grant them great capabilities—these items enhance and supplement the powers they gain from their classes and enhance their attacks and defenses.

Two aspects of a magic item control when it is likely to become available to adventurers: its level and its rarity.

Magic items have levels, just as characters, powers, and monsters do. An item's level is a general measure of its power and translates to the average level of character using that item. There's no restriction on using or acquiring items based on their level. If a creature is able to make magic items, it normally cannot create an item above its level.

Some magic items are easier to obtain than others. Adventurers can purchase common items just as they can buy mundane equipment, though few shops routinely sell them. Uncommon and rare magic items were created in the distant past and now are found only as part of treasure hoards. Uncommon items are more complicated than common items, and rare magic items are even more complex and wondrous. See "Magic Items" in Chapter 7 for more information about magic item levels and rarity.

On average, about half the magic items that characters find as treasure are common. Most of the rest are uncommon. About one magic item in eight is rare, so these items show up only about once every other level the adventurers gain. That means that any given character will acquire one rare item per tier of play, and no one is likely to own more than three.

If the adventurers find a magic item they don't want to keep, or they find an item that replaces an item they already have, they might end up trying to sell the item. This usually isn't a favorable transaction for them, though. See "Magic Item Values," page 277, for more information about selling magic items.

Awarding Treasure

Experience points are fundamentally an encounter-based (or quest-based) reward, whereas treasure is a larger-scale reward doled out over the course of an adventure. Characters typically find some treasure when they complete encounters (collecting the hoard of the dragon they've slain, for instance), find other treasure in secret rooms or trapped vaults, and acquire still more as rewards for completing quests. Over the course of the eight to ten encounters it takes characters to advance from one level to the next, they should acquire about ten treasures. The DM can award treasure after each encounter or save it up and award several treasures at once. The dragon's hoard might consist of three treasures while other encounters offer no treasure reward.

To generate a single treasure for the characters in your game, you make a series of die rolls on the Treasure by Party Level table. Roll a d20 once for each line of the part of the table that corresponds to the level of the party (not the level of the encounter). Typically, you'll roll once for coins, once for gems, once for art objects, and once for magic items. If the d20 roll falls within the range shown on the table, the hoard includes that kind of treasure.

For instance, the treasure table for 6th-level characters looks like this:

6	(11+) 8d8 × 10 gp
	(14-19) 1d4 gems worth 100 gp; (20+) one gem worth 500 gp
	(18+) 1d3 art objects worth 250 gp
	(13+) one magic item of level 1d4 + 6

To generate a treasure for five 6th-level characters, the DM rolls a d20 four times. If the first roll is 11 or higher, the treasure includes gold, so roll 8d8 and multiply the result by 10 to determine how many gold pieces are in the treasure. If the second roll is 14 or higher, the treasure includes gems; if the roll is 20, it's a particularly valuable gem. If the third roll is 18 or higher, the treasure includes art objects. If the fourth roll is 13 or higher, the treasure includes a magic item.

Group Size: If the adventuring group has more or fewer than five characters, apply a modifier to rolls on the table. The modifier is +2 for each character more than five, or –2 for each character fewer than five. A roll of a natural 20 for a treasure always produces the best result, unless the modified result would not normally indicate any treasure of a given type. In that case, the treasure includes the lesser result.

Example: When generating treasure for a party of three 6th-level characters, the DM applies a –4 modifier to the level 6 lines of the Treasure by Party Level table. If the DM rolls a natural 20 for art objects, the treasure includes 1d3 art objects worth 250 gp each, even though the adjusted roll of 16 would normally be insufficient to generate any art objects. If the DM rolls a natural 20 for gems, the treasure includes one gem worth 500 gp, even though the adjusted roll of 16 would normally indicate gems of lesser value.

Magic Items: Special rules apply to the roll for magic items as part of a treasure. If the number on the die (before any adjustments for group size) is odd, the item is a common item. If the number on the die is even, but not a natural 20, the item is uncommon. On a roll of a natural 20, the item is rare. Group size doesn't affect the likelihood of finding common or rare items.

The trickiest part of awarding treasure is determining what magic items to give out. The DM should tailor these items to the party of characters in his or her game. These items are supposed to excite the characters, so they should be things the characters want to use rather than discard. For instance, if none of the characters in a 6th-level party uses a longbow, don't put a 10th-level longbow in the dungeon as treasure.

One way to make sure that adventurers receive magic items they'll be excited about is to ask the players for wish lists. At the start of each level, each player writes down a list of three to five uncommon items that he or she is intrigued by and that are no more than four levels above his or her character's level. The DM can choose treasure from those lists (making sure to place an item from a different character's list each time), crossing the items off as the characters find them.

Don't use wish lists for rare items. These items are completely in the DM's purview, and they should advance the story of the campaign and provide unexpected delights to the players.

Combining Treasures: It's possible to combine treasures to make larger hoards. Try to find a balance between the excitement of finding a large treasure and the regular reward of finding several smaller treasures. As a rule of thumb, over the course of eight to ten encounters, one hoard should contain three treasures, two should contain two treasures each, and three should consist of a single treasure each. That leaves two to four encounters with no treasure reward.

TREASURE BY PARTY LEVEL (HEROIC TIER)

Party Level	Treasure
1	(11-14) 2d6 × 100 sp; (15+) 2d6 × 10 gp (18+) 1d2 gems worth 100 gp (20+) one art object worth 250 gp (13+) one magic item of level 1d4 + 1
2	(11-13) 3d6 × 100 sp; (14+) 3d6 × 10 gp (18+) 1d3 gems worth 100 gp (19+) one art object worth 250 gp (13+) one magic item of level 1d4 + 2
3	(11-12) 3d8 × 100 sp; (13+) 3d8 × 10 gp (17+) 1d3 gems worth 100 gp (19+) one art object worth 250 gp (13+) one magic item of level 1d4 + 3
4	(11) 5d6 × 100 sp; (12+) 5d6 × 10 gp (16+) 1d3 gems worth 100 gp (19+) 1d2 art objects worth 250 gp (13+) one magic item of level 1d4 + 4
5	(11+) 4d8 × 10 gp (16+) 1d4 gems worth 100 gp (19+) 1d3 art objects worth 250 gp (13+) one magic item of level 1d4 + 5
6	(11+) 8d8 × 10 gp (14-19) 1d4 gems worth 100 gp; (20+) one gem worth 500 gp (18+) 1d3 art objects worth 250 gp (13+) one magic item of level 1d4 + 6
7	(11+) 2d4 × 100 gp (14-19) one gem worth 500 gp; (20+) one gem worth 1,000 gp (18+) 1d3 art objects worth 250 gp (13+) one magic item of level 1d4 + 7
8	(11+) 2d6 × 100 gp (13-19) one gem worth 500 gp; (20+) one gem worth 1,000 gp (18-19) 1d3 art objects worth 250 gp; (20+) one art object worth 1,500 gp (13+) one magic item of level 1d4 + 8
9	(11+) 2d8 × 100 gp (13-19) one gem worth 500 gp; (20+) one gem worth 1,000 gp (18-19) 1d4 art objects worth 250 gp; (20+) one art object worth 1,500 gp (13+) one magic item of level 1d4 + 9
10	(11+) 2d10 × 100 gp (13-19) one gem worth 500 gp; (20+) one gem worth 1,000 gp (18-19) one art object worth 1,500 gp; (20+) one art object worth 2,500 gp (13+) one magic item of level 1d4 + 10

TREASURE BY PARTY LEVEL (PARAGON TIER)

Party Level	Treasure
11	(11+) 4d8 × 100 gp (13-19) one gem worth 1,000 gp; (20+) one gem worth 5,000 gp (18-19) one art object worth 1,500 gp; (20+) one art object worth 2,500 gp (13+) one magic item of level 1d4 + 11
12	(11+) 4d12 × 100 gp (13-19) 1d2 gems worth 1,000 gp; (20+) one gem worth 5,000 gp (17-18) 1d3 art objects worth 1,500 gp; (19+) one art object worth 2,500 gp (13+) one magic item of level 1d4 + 12
13	(11+) 1d6 × 1,000 gp (13-19) 1d3 gems worth 1,000 gp; (20+) one gem worth 5,000 gp (17-19) one art object worth 2,500 gp; (20+) one art object worth 7,500 gp (13+) one magic item of level 1d4 + 13
14	(11-19) 1d8 × 1,000 gp; (20+) 1d6 × 10 pp (13-18) 1d4 gems worth 1,000 gp; (19+) one gem worth 5,000 gp (17-19) 1d2 art objects worth 2,500 gp; (20+) one art object worth 7,500 gp (13+) one magic item of level 1d4 + 14
15	(11-18) 1d10 × 1,000 gp; (19+) 1d8 × 10 pp (13-17) 1d4 gems worth 1,000 gp; (18+) one gem worth 5,000 gp (17-18) 1d2 art objects worth 2,500 gp; (19+) one art object worth 7,500 gp (13+) one magic item of level 1d4 + 15
16	(11-17) 2d8 × 1,000 gp; (18+) 2d8 × 10 pp (13+) 1d2 gems worth 5,000 gp (17-18) 1d6 art objects worth 1,500 gp; (19+) one art object worth 7,500 gp (13+) one magic item of level 1d4 + 16
17	(11-16) 4d6 × 1,000 gp; (17+) 4d6 × 10 pp (13+) 1d3 gems worth 5,000 gp (17-19) one art object worth 7,500 gp; (20+) one art object worth 15,000 gp (13+) one magic item of level 1d4 + 17
18	(11-14) 4d8 × 1,000 gp; (15+) 4d8 × 10 pp (13+) 1d4 gems worth 5,000 gp (17-19) 1d3 art objects worth 7,500 gp; (20+) one art object worth 15,000 gp (13+) one magic item of level 1d4 + 18
19	(11-12) 4d10 × 1,000 gp; (13+) 4d10 × 10 pp (13+) 1d6 gems worth 5,000 gp (17-19) 1d3 art objects worth 7,500 gp; (20+) one art object worth 15,000 gp (13+) one magic item of level 1d4 + 19
20	(11-11) 4d12 × 1,000 gp; (12+) 4d12 × 10 pp (13+) 1d8 gems worth 5,000 gp (17-19) 1d3 art objects worth 7,500 gp; (20+) one art object worth 15,000 gp (13+) one magic item of level 1d4 + 20

TREASURE BY PARTY LEVEL (EPIC TIER)

Party Level	Treasure
21	(11-20) 1d8 × 100 pp
	(13+) 2d6 gems worth 5,000 gp
	(16-18) 1d3 art objects worth 15,000 gp; (19+) one object worth 50,000 gp
	(13+) one magic item of level 1d4 + 21
22	(11-20) 1d12 × 100 pp
	(13+) 2d8 gems worth 5,000 gp
	(16-18) 1d6 art objects worth 15,000 gp; (19+) 1d2 objects worth 50,000 gp
	(13+) one magic item of level 1d4 + 22
23	(11-20) 2d8 × 100 pp
	(13+) 2d8 gems worth 5,000 gp
	(16-17) 1d8 art objects worth 15,000 gp; (18+) 1d3 objects worth 50,000 gp
	(13+) one magic item of level 1d4 + 23
24	(11-19) 2d10 × 100 pp; (20+) 1d3 × 5 ad
	(13+) 2d6 gems worth 5,000 gp
	(16-17) 1d10 art objects worth 15,000 gp; (18+) 1d6 objects worth 50,000 gp
	(13+) one magic item of level 1d4 + 24
25	(11-19) 2d12 × 100 pp; (20+) 1d4 × 5 ad
	(13+) 2d4 gems worth 5,000 gp
	(15-16) 2d8 art objects worth 15,000 gp; (17+) 1d6 objects worth 50,000 gp
	(13+) one magic item of level 1d4 + 25
26	(11-18) 1d4 × 1,000 pp; (19+) 1d6 × 5 ad
	(13+) 2d6 gems worth 5,000 gp
	(15-16) 3d6 art objects worth 15,000 gp; (17+) 1d12 objects worth 50,000 gp
	(13+) one magic item of level 1d4 + 26
27	(11-18) 1d6 × 1,000 pp; (19+) 2d6 × 5 ad
	(13+) 2d8 gems worth 5,000 gp
	(15-16) 3d6 art objects worth 15000 gp; (17+) 3d6 objects worth 50,000 gp
	(13+) one magic item of level 1d3 + 27
28	(11-17) 1d8 × 1,000 pp; (18+) 2d8 × 5 ad
	(13+) 3d6 art objects worth 50,000 gp
	(13+) one magic item of level 1d2 + 28
29	(11-17) 1d10 × 1,000 pp; (18+) 3d6 × 5 ad
	(13+) 2d12 art objects worth 50,000 gp
	(13+) one magic item of level 30
30	(11-16) 1d12 × 1,000 pp; (17+) 2d12 × 5 ad
	(13+) 4d6 art objects worth 50,000 gp
	(13-18) one magic item of level 30; (19+) two items of level 30

TERRAIN FEATURES

Whether the adventurers are exploring an ancient vault, a bustling marketplace, a trackless desert, or some other environment, they must deal with terrain. Certain terrain features appear again and again over the course of a campaign: walls, doors, statues, trees, fey circles, and so on. These features can affect exploration, combat, or both.

This appendix provides rules for the most common terrain features, both mundane and fantastic. The information here relies on the rules for interacting with the environment (Chapter 5), skill checks and ability checks (Chapter 4), and movement and terrain (Chapter 6).

MUNDANE TERRAIN

Most of the terrain that adventurers face is the same sort found on Earth, particularly during the Middle Ages and earlier. Even when terrain is mundane, it often bears the marks of a fantastic world: statues of magical beasts that really exist, flowers growing in mysterious patterns, or trees taller than Earth's tallest redwoods.

Each kind of mundane terrain falls into one of two categories, either constructed or natural.

Constructed Terrain Features

Arrow Slits: These small openings are designed to provide archers with maximum protection while they fire. An arrow slit grants a ranged attacker superior cover while granting him or her a view of the battlefield. The attacker determines the target's cover as if the attacker were in the square just outside the slit.

Catwalks: A narrow catwalk is difficult terrain. An exceptionally narrow catwalk might require Acrobatics checks to cross.

Doors: Opening a door takes a minor action, or a standard action if the door is stuck and requires a Strength check. A door could have a window in it that provides superior cover to anyone firing through it. Doors might be locked, and creatures can try to open them by using the Thievery skill.

Furniture: It costs 1 extra square of movement to move on top of a table or a chair, but no extra movement to move off. A creature can also crawl beneath a table to gain cover.

Ladders: A creature can normally climb a ladder without making Athletics checks, but the creature must spend 1 extra square of movement for each square it enters on the ladder.

Ledges and Platforms: Low ledges or platforms (lower than waist-high) are difficult terrain. Higher ones require Athletics checks to jump or climb onto.

Murder Holes: Murder holes use the same rules as arrow slits, except that they are placed in the ceiling of a chamber to allow archers above to rain fire on attackers below.

Pools: A shallow pool (waist-deep or shallower) is difficult terrain. A creature that doesn't have a swim speed must make Athletics checks to swim through a deeper pool.

Portcullises: A portcullis is a metal gate that swings shut or drops down from the ceiling. It provides partial cover, and a Strength check allows a creature to lift it or pull it open.

Secret Doors and Trapdoors: Some doors are disguised as part of a wall, floor, or ceiling. A successful Perception check (usually against a hard DC) allows a creature to spot an average version of one of these portals. They make great ambush points for monsters or hiding places for treasure.

Stairs: A set of stairs is difficult terrain, unless the steps are sufficiently broad or the slope of their ascent is gentle.

Statues and Pillars: A big statue or pillar that completely fills 1 square or more is blocking terrain. A statue or pillar that doesn't fill its square is difficult terrain. Statues and pillars of any size normally provide cover.

WILLIAM O'CONNOR

Streets: The best maintained streets are normal terrain, but potholes and poor maintenance in the rough parts of town can make the streets there difficult terrain.

Tapestries and Curtains: It costs 1 square of movement to move through a tapestry or a curtain hung to partition a room or hallway. Tapestries and curtains normally block line of sight.

Walls: Most dungeon walls are masonry or carved out of solid rock. A creature that doesn't have a climb speed uses Athletics checks to climb walls.

Windows: Opening a window is a minor action, and moving through one large enough for a creature to fit itself through costs 1 extra square of movement.

Natural Terrain Features

Foliage, Leaves, and Vines: Screening foliage, leaves, and vines provide concealment if the plant material hangs down low enough or projects outward enough to interfere with sight. Such plant matter might also be difficult terrain if the branches are thick or difficult to move through.

Hills: A slope is difficult terrain, although shallow or gentle slopes are normal terrain.

Ice: A slick ice patch is difficult terrain. An exceptionally slippery patch might require Acrobatics checks to cross.

Lakes and Ponds: See "Pools," above.

Sand and Dirt: Soft, shifting sand or dirt is difficult terrain. Hard-packed sand and dirt is normal terrain.

Swamp: Swampy squares are difficult terrain.

Trees: A tree that is large enough to have a trunk that fills 1 square or more is blocking terrain. Smaller trees are difficult terrain. Trees of any size normally provide cover.

Undergrowth: Shrubs and other undergrowth are difficult terrain.

FANTASTIC TERRAIN

The DUNGEONS & DRAGONS game world is rife with magic, and this power spawns wondrous terrain. Enormous spiderwebs choke ancient passages. Elemental energy surges through a cavern, granting strength to fire-based spells. This section provides rules for some of the most prevalent types of fantastic terrain.

Tier and Terrain Effects: Throughout these examples, the term "per tier" is used to show how an effect scales. Multiply the per tier value by 1 for heroic tier, 2 for paragon, and 3 for epic. For instance, if a terrain feature grants a

+1 bonus to attack rolls per tier, the bonus is +1 at heroic tier, +2 at paragon tier, and +3 at epic tier. Similarly, some terrain effects call for skill or ability checks. The DM usually chooses an easy DC from the Difficulty Class by Level table (page 126) to set a DC that's appropriate to the creature's level.

Terrain effects are scaled in this way scales so that the terrain stays challenging as adventurers and monsters gain higher skill modifiers and more hit points. For instance, the cave slime found in the deeper reaches of the Underdark is thicker and more slippery than the thin sheen found in higher dungeon levels, so the Acrobatics DC to avoid falling prone is higher.

Blood Rock

This terrain occurs at the site of a ceremonial sacrifice, a great slaughter, or some other calamity. The spirit of death hovers over blood rock.

Effect: A creature standing in a square of blood rock can score a critical hit on a natural die roll of 19–20.

Bolt Stone

In some areas, lightning energy fuses with rock to form a highly unstable, dangerous mixture. In various regions of the Elemental Chaos, and in dungeons located near the conflux of different types of elemental energy, blue-tinged areas of bolt stone appear.

Effect: When a creature enters a square of bolt stone, the creature takes 5 lightning damage per tier. The DM also rolls a d20. On a 10 or higher, the bolt stone's energy is discharged, and the stone becomes inert. Otherwise, the lightning energy is transferred to all unoccupied squares adjacent to the original square of bolt stone, and those squares become bolt stone.

Cave Slime

This thin, blue slime is harmless but extremely slick.

Effect: A creature that enters a square filled with cave slime must succeed on an Acrobatics check or fall prone.

Defiled Ground

The dead do not always rest in peace. Some cemeteries are darker than others, and ancient events leave unseen traces of their former presence. Defiled ground sometimes attracts undead.

Effect: Undead gain a +1 bonus to rolls to recharge their powers while on defiled ground. In addition, if an undead creature is reduced to 0 hit points while on defiled ground, the DM rolls a d20. On a 10 or higher, the undead creature revives with 1 hit point at the start of its next turn. If radiant damage reduces an undead creature to 0 hit points, it can't revive in this manner.

Fey Circle

Often distinguished by the presence of tangled vines or large toadstools, this kind of location is empowered with the extraordinary energy of the Feywild.

Effect: A creature can spend a minor action while in a fey circle's square to teleport 5 squares.

Illusions

Illusions can mimic terrain, creatures, or both. Creatures that realize that something is an illusion ignore its effects; those that do not realize the truth behind the illusion react to it as appropriate.

The DM uses a creature's passive Perception (for illusory objects and terrain) or passive Insight (for illusory creatures) to determine whether the creature notices that something is awry. Once a creature has reason to be suspicious, it can make an Insight check as a minor action to attempt to disbelieve an illusion.

Unless otherwise noted, an illusion doesn't deal any actual damage, and interacting with it might reveal its true nature. For instance, an adventurer who walks over an illusory pit doesn't fall. At that point, the character realizes the pit is fake.

Illusory Wall: An illusory wall blocks line of sight. Creatures can move through it without restriction, although a creature that believes the illusion isn't likely to try doing so. Some illusory walls are similar to one-way mirrors, in that they are transparent from one side and opaque from the other.

Mirror Crystal

Mirror crystal causes strange twists and turns in space.

Effect: A creature standing on mirror crystal can look down and see all the other mirror crystal squares within 20 squares of it. That creature can use ranged attack powers against targets on those squares or adjacent to them. The distance to such a target is 1 square.

Spiderwebs

Enormous spiders haunt the underground regions of the world, sometimes leaving sticky webs behind long after they themselves are gone.

Effect: The webs of giant spiders are difficult terrain, and a spiderweb square is lightly obscured. A creature that enters such a square must make an Athletics or an Acrobatics check. On a failure, the creature is immobilized until it uses the escape action successfully (usually against a moderate DC of the creature's level).

Glossary

This glossary defines many of the terms in the DUNGEONS & DRAGONS game. The material here assumes you're familiar with the basic rules of the game. Consult the index for terms that don't appear here.

aberrant [origin]: Aberrant creatures are native to or shaped by the Far Realm.

acid [keyword]: A damage type. See also **damage type**.

adventurer: The character controlled by a player other than the Dungeon Master. An adventurer is sometimes called a player character. See also **character**.

air [keyword]: An air creature is strongly connected to the element of air.

angel [keyword]: Angels are immortal creatures native to the Astral Sea. They don't need to breathe, eat, or sleep.

animate [type]: Animate creatures are given life through magic. They don't need to breathe, eat, or sleep.

augmentable [keyword]: An effect type. A power that has the augmentable keyword has optional augmentations, which a character can use at the cost of power points. Only certain characters have such points. Augmentable powers follow special rules given in Chapter 3.

aquatic [keyword]: Aquatic creatures can breathe underwater. In aquatic combat, an aquatic creature gains a +2 bonus to attack rolls against non-aquatic creatures.

area of effect: An area of a specific size where a particular effect takes place. An area of effect usually has one of three types: blast, burst, or wall. Area powers and close powers almost always involve an area of effect.

attack: An attack roll and its effects, including any damage rolls. The word "attack" is sometimes used as shorthand for "attack power." Some attack powers include multiple attacks, and some powers, such as *magic missile*, are designated as attacks yet lack attack rolls (using such a power counts as making an attack if the power has a target).

aura [keyword]: An effect type. An aura is a continuous effect that emanates from a creature. Auras follow special rules given in Chapter 3.

battle grid: The network of 1-inch squares that represents an encounter area.

beast [keyword]: An effect type. A beast power can be used only in conjunction with a beast companion.

beast [type]: Beasts are either ordinary animals or creatures akin to them. They behave instinctively.

beast form [keyword]: An effect type. A character can use a beast form power only while in beast form. Only certain characters can assume a beast form.

blind [keyword]: A blind creature relies on special senses, such as blindsight or tremorsense, to see within a specified range, beyond which the creature can't see. The creature is immune to gaze attacks and cannot be blinded.

blinded [condition]: While a creature is blinded, it can't see, which means its targets have total concealment against it, and it takes a -10 penalty to Perception checks. It also grants combat advantage and can't flank.

blindsight: A creature that has blindsight can clearly see creatures or objects within a specified radius and within line of effect, even if they are invisible or in obscured squares. The creature otherwise relies on its other senses.

blocking terrain: A type of terrain that blocks squares, often by filling them. *Examples:* Walls, doors, and large pillars. Blocking terrain provides cover, interferes with movement around it, and blocks line of effect. It also blocks line of sight, unless it's transparent.

bonus: A number added to a die roll. If a bonus has a type (such as a power or a feat bonus), the bonus is not cumulative with bonuses of the same type; only the highest bonus applies. Bonuses that have no type are called untyped bonuses. Such bonuses are cumulative. However, untyped bonuses from the same named game element (such as a power or a feat) are not cumulative; only the highest applies.

burrow speed: A creature that has a burrow speed can move through loose earth at a specified speed, and the creature can move through solid stone at half that speed. The creature can't shift or charge while burrowing.

channel divinity [keyword]: An effect type. A channel divinity power allows a creature to harness the magic of the gods. A creature can use no more than one channel divinity power per encounter.

character: Another term for a creature. The term is usually used to refer to a person who is not monstrous: either an adventurer or a DM-controlled person (sometimes called a nonplayer character, or NPC).

charm [keyword]: An effect type. A charm power controls a creature's actions in some way.

climb speed: A creature that has a climb speed moves on vertical surfaces at that speed without having to make Athletics checks to climb. While climbing, the creature ignores difficult terrain, and climbing doesn't cause it to grant combat advantage.

clumsy: Some creatures are clumsy while using a specific movement mode (noted next to that mode in the creature's stat block), and others are clumsy while on the ground (noted next to the creature's speed). While a creature is clumsy, it takes a -4 penalty to attack rolls and all defenses.

cold [keyword]: A damage type. A creature that has this keyword is strongly connected to cold. See also **damage type**.

combat advantage: An advantageous state that a creature can gain in a variety of ways. When a creature has combat advantage against a target, the creature gains a +2 bonus to attack rolls against the target.

conjuration [keyword]: An effect type. A conjuration power produces a conjuration, which is a creation of magical energy that resembles a creature, an object, or some other phenomenon. Conjurations follow special rules given in Chapter 3.

construct [keyword]: Constructs are not living creatures, so effects that specifically target living creatures do not work against them. They don't need to breathe, eat, or sleep.

creature: A being in the game world. Both adventurers and monsters are creatures. See also **adventurer** and **monster**.

damage roll: A roll of a die or dice to determine damage dealt by a power or some other effect. Modifiers to a damage roll apply to the entire roll, not to each die rolled.

damage type: A specific type of damage: acid, cold, fire, force, lightning, necrotic, poison, psychic, radiant, or thunder. Each damage type has a keyword associated with it. If a power has such a keyword, the power deals that type of damage (the exception is poison, the keyword for which refers to damage, a nondamaging effect, or both).

darkvision: A creature that has darkvision can see normally regardless of light. The creature therefore ignores concealment that is a result of dim light or darkness.

dazed [condition]: While a creature is dazed, it doesn't get its normal complement of actions on its turn; it can take either a standard, a move, or a minor action. The creature can still take free actions, but it can't take immediate or opportunity actions. It also grants combat advantage and can't flank.

deafened [condition]: While a creature is deafened, it can't hear, and it takes a –10 penalty to Perception checks.

demon [keyword]: Demons are chaotic evil elemental creatures native to the Abyss. They don't need to sleep.

devil [keyword]: Devils are evil immortal creatures native to the Nine Hells. They don't need to sleep.

difficult terrain: Rubble, undergrowth, shallow bogs, steep stairs, and other impediments are difficult terrain, which hampers movement. Each square of difficult terrain costs 1 extra square of movement to enter. Because difficult terrain costs that extra square of movement to enter, a creature can't normally shift into it.

disease [keyword]: Some powers expose a creature to a disease. If a creature is exposed to a disease one or more times during an encounter, it makes one saving throw at the end of the encounter to determine if it contracts that disease. If the saving throw fails, the creature is infected.

dominated [condition]: While a creature is dominated, it can't take actions. Instead, the dominator chooses a single action for the creature to take on the creature's turn: a standard, a move, a minor, or a free action. The only powers and other game features that the dominator can make the creature use are ones that can be used at will, such as at-will powers. The creature also grants combat advantage and can't flank.

dragon [keyword]: Dragons are reptilian creatures. Most of them have wings as well as a breath weapon.

dying [condition]: A dying creature is unconscious and must make death saving throws. This condition ends immediately on the creature when it regains hit points.

earth [keyword]: An earth creature is strongly connected to earth.

earth walk: A type of terrain walk. A creature that has earth walk ignores difficult terrain that is rubble, uneven stone, or an earthen construction.

effect: The result of a game element's use. The damage and conditions caused by an attack power are the power's effects, for instance. Some powers have "Effect" entries, which contain some but not necessarily all of the powers' effects. In an attack power, the effects of such an entry are not contingent on a hit or a miss.

elemental [origin]: Elemental creatures are native to the Elemental Chaos.

extra damage: Many powers and other effects grant the ability to deal extra damage. Extra damage is always in addition to other damage and is of the same type or types as that damage, unless otherwise noted. An effect that deals no damage cannot deal extra damage.

fear [keyword]: An effect type. A fear power inspires fright.

fey [origin]: Fey creatures are native to the Feywild.

fire [keyword]: A damage type. A creature that has this keyword is strongly connected to fire. See also **damage type**.

fly speed: A creature that has a fly speed can fly a number of squares up to that speed as a move action. If the creature is stunned or knocked prone while flying, it falls. See also **hover**.

force [keyword]: A damage type. See also **damage type**.

forced movement: Movement that a creature is compelled to do, specifically a pull, a push, or a slide. A creature can be moved in other ways, such as through teleportation, but only pulls, pushes, and slides are technically forced movement.

forest walk: A type of terrain walk. A creature that has forest walk ignores difficult terrain that is part of a tree, underbrush, or some other forest growth.

full discipline [keyword]: An effect type. A full discipline power contains what are effectively two mini-powers, an attack technique and a movement technique. Full disciplines follow special rules given in Chapter 3.

gaze [keyword]: A kind of attack. Blind or blinded creatures are immune to gaze attacks, and a creature cannot make a gaze attack while blinded.

giant [keyword]: Giants are Large or larger humanoid creatures that trace their origin back to the primordials and the Elemental Chaos.

grabbed [condition]: While a creature is grabbed, it is immobilized.

Maintaining this condition on the creature occupies whatever appendage, object, or effect the grabber used to initiate the grab. This condition ends immediately on the creature if the grabber is subjected to an effect that prevents it from taking actions, or if the creature ends up outside the range of the grabbing power or effect.

half damage: When a power or another effect deals half damage, apply all modifiers to the damage, including resistances and vulnerabilities, and then divide the damage in half (round down).

healing [keyword]: An effect type. A healing power restores hit points, usually either by restoring hit points immediately or by granting regeneration.

heavily obscured: A measure of visibility. A creature has total concealment when it is in a heavily obscured square, although it has only partial concealment against an enemy adjacent to it. *Examples:* Heavy fog, smoke, or foliage. Contrast with **lightly obscured** and **totally obscured**.

helpless [condition]: While a creature is helpless, it grants combat advantage.

hidden: When a creature is hidden from an enemy, the creature is silent and invisible to that enemy. A creature normally uses the Stealth skill to become hidden. See also **invisible**.

hindering terrain: A type of terrain that hinders creatures, usually by damaging them. *Examples:* Pits, lava, and deep water. A creature can make a saving throw when it is pulled, pushed, slid, or teleported into hindering terrain. See also **teleportation**.

homunculus [keyword]: Homunculi are animate constructs tasked with guarding a creature, an area, or an object.

hover: If a creature can hover, it can remain in the air if it is stunned. See also **fly speed**.

humanoid [type]: Humanoid creatures either are human or resemble humans in form, behavior, facial features, or all three. Most are bipedal.

ice walk: A type of terrain walk. A creature that has ice walk ignores difficult terrain that is ice or snow.

illusion [keyword]: An effect type. An illusion power deceives the mind or the senses. If an illusion power deals damage, the damage itself is not an illusion.

immobilized [condition]: When a creature is immobilized, it can't move, unless it teleports or is pulled, pushed, or slid.

immortal [origin]: Immortal creatures are native to the Astral Sea. Unless they are killed, they live forever.

implement [keyword]: An accessory type. This keyword identifies a power that can be used with an implement, an item, such as a wand, that certain creatures can wield to channel powers. An adventurer must have proficiency with an implement to use it with his or her powers.

insubstantial: When a creature is insubstantial, it takes half damage from any damage source, including ongoing damage. See also **half damage**.

invigorating [keyword]: An effect type. Invigorating powers grant temporary hit points to their users. Such powers follow special rules given in Chapter 3.

invisible: If a creature is invisible, it has several advantages against creatures that can't see it: It has total concealment against them, it doesn't provoke opportunity attacks from them, and they grant combat advantage to it.

knowledge check: A skill check used to remember a useful bit of information in a particular field of knowledge. Arcana, Dungeoneering, History, Nature, and Religion are the skills most commonly used to make knowledge checks.

lightly obscured: A measure of visibility. A creature has partial concealment when it is in a lightly obscured square. *Examples:* Dim light, foliage, fog, smoke, and heavy rain or falling snow. Contrast with **heavily obscured** and **totally obscured**.

lightning [keyword]: A damage type. See also **damage type**.

line of effect: A clear line from one point to another point in an encounter that doesn't pass through or touch blocking terrain. Unless noted otherwise, there must be line of effect between the origin square of an effect and its intended target for that target to be affected.

line of sight: A clear line from one point to another point in an encounter that doesn't pass through or touch an object or an effect—such as a stone wall, a thick curtain, or a cloud of fog—that blocks the vision of the viewer.

living construct [keyword]: Unlike other constructs, living constructs are living creatures.

low-light vision: A creature that has low-light vision can see in dim light without penalty.

magical beast [type]: Magical beasts resemble beasts but often possess magical abilities, behave like people, or both.

marked [condition]: When a creature marks a target, the target takes a -2 penalty to attack rolls for any attack that doesn't include the marking creature as a target. A creature can be subjected to only one mark at a time, and a new mark supersedes an old one. A mark ends immediately when its creator dies or falls unconscious.

minion [role]: A minion is destroyed when it takes any damage. If a minion is missed by an attack that deals damage on a miss, the minion doesn't take that damage.

modifier: A bonus or a penalty applied to a die roll. See **bonus** and **penalty**.

monster: A creature controlled by the Dungeon Master. The term is usually used to refer to creatures that are hostile to the adventurers (often including DM-controlled characters). See also **adventurer**, **character**, and **creature**.

mount [keyword]: A creature that has the mount keyword has at least one mount trait or mount power.

move: Any instance of movement, whether it is done willingly or unwillingly. Whenever a creature, an object, or an effect leaves a square to enter another, it is moving. Shifting, teleporting, and being pushed are all examples of moves.

natural [origin]: Natural creatures are native to the natural world.

necrotic [keyword]: A damage type. See also **damage type**.

occupied square: A square occupied by a creature.

once per round: Some effects can occur only once per round. When a creature uses such an effect, the creature can't use the effect again until the start of its next turn.

once per turn: Some effects can occur only once per turn. When a creature uses such an effect, the creature can use the effect on each turn, not only during its turn.

ooze [keyword]: Oozes are amorphous creatures.

origin square: The square where an effect originates. Every power has an origin square. A power's attack or utility type determines the origin square's location. Some exceptional powers place the origin square elsewhere.

penalty: A number subtracted from a die roll. Unlike bonuses, penalties don't have types. Penalties add together, unless they're from the same named game element (such as a power or a trait).

petrified [condition]: While a creature is petrified, it is unconscious. In addition, it has resist 20 to all damage and doesn't age.

phasing: While phasing, a creature ignores difficult terrain, and it can enter squares containing enemies, blocking terrain, or other obstacles. The creature follows the normal rules for where it must end its movement (normally an unoccupied space).

plant [keyword]: Plant creatures are composed of vegetable matter. They don't need to sleep.

poison [keyword]: A damage and effect type. A poison power delivers a non-damaging poisonous effect, deals poison damage, or both. See also **damage type**.

polymorph [keyword]: An effect type. Polymorph powers change a creature's physical form in some way. Such powers follow special rules given in Chapter 3.

prone [condition]: When a creature is prone, it is lying down. If the creature is climbing or flying when it is knocked prone, it falls instead. A prone creature takes a -2 penalty to attack rolls, and the only way it can move is by crawling, teleporting, or being pulled, pushed, or slid. In addition, it grants combat advantage to enemies making melee attacks against it, but it gains a +2 bonus to all defenses against ranged attacks from enemies that aren't adjacent to it. A creature can end this condition on itself by standing up. A creature can drop prone as a minor action.

psychic [keyword]: A damage type. See also **damage type**.

radiant [keyword]: A damage type. See also **damage type**.

rage [keyword]: An effect type. A rage power allows the user to enter a rage specified in the power. Rages follow special rules given in Chapter 3.

range: The maximum distance that an effect can reach. Range is often expressed as a number of squares.

rattling [keyword]: An effect type. A rattling power typically penalizes a target's attack rolls. Such powers follow special rules given in Chapter 3.

reliable [keyword]: An effect type. If a reliable power misses every target, the power is not expended.

removed from play [condition]: Some effects can temporarily remove a creature from play. While a creature is removed from play, its turns start and end as normal, but it can't take actions. In addition, it has neither line of sight nor line of effect to anything, and nothing has line of sight or line of effect to it.

reptile [keyword]: Reptiles are cold-blooded creatures that have scaly skin.

restrained [condition]: While a creature is restrained, it can't move, unless it teleports. It can't even be pulled, pushed, or slid. It also takes a –2 penalty to attack rolls, and it grants combat advantage.

round: A round represents about 6 seconds in the game world. In a round, every combatant takes a turn. See also **turn** and **once per round**.

runic [keyword]: An effect type. A runic power channels the magic of runes that are specified in the power. Runic powers follow special rules given in Chapter 3.

save: A successful saving throw. A save ends an effect that includes one of the following notations in parentheses: "save ends," "save ends both," or "save ends all."

shadow [origin]: Shadow creatures are native to the Shadowfell.

shapechanger [keyword]: A shapechanger has the ability to alter its form, whether freely or into specific forms.

sleep [keyword]: An effect type. Sleep powers knock creatures unconscious. A creature that has fallen asleep naturally (as opposed to being knocked unconscious by a power or other effect) is unconscious, but not totally deprived of awareness; it can use its passive Perception to hear things, but with a –5 penalty. See also **unconscious**.

slowed [condition]: When a creature is slowed, its speed becomes 2 if it was higher than that. This speed applies to all of the creature's movement modes (walking, flying, and so on), but it does not apply to forced movement against it, teleportation, or any other movement that doesn't use the creature's speed. The creature also cannot benefit from bonuses to speed, although it can take actions, such as the run action, that allow it to move farther than its speed.

solid obstacle: See **blocking terrain**.

space: The square area that a creature occupies or the squares where an object or a phenomenon is located. A typical adventurer's space is a single square.

speed: The distance (in squares) that a creature can move using the walk action.

spider [keyword]: Spider creatures include spiders as well as creatures that have spiderlike features: eight legs, web spinning, and so forth.

spider climb: A creature that can spider climb can use its climb speed to move across overhanging horizontal surfaces (such as ceilings) without making Athletics checks. See also **climb speed**.

spirit [keyword]: An effect type. A spirit power can be used only in conjunction with a spirit companion. Such powers follow special rules given in Chapter 3.

square: A 1-inch square on the battle grid, which is equivalent to a 5-foot square in the game world. The square is the main unit of measurement in the game.

stance [keyword]: An effect type. When a character uses a stance power, the character assumes a stance of some kind. Stances follow special rules given in Chapter 3.

stunned [condition]: While a creature is stunned, it can't take actions. It also grants combat advantage and can't flank. The creature falls if it is flying, unless it can hover.

summoning [keyword]: An effect type. Powers that have the summoning keyword bring creatures magically from elsewhere—often from other planes of existence—to serve the summoner. Summoning powers follow special rules given in Chapter 3.

surprised [condition]: While a creature is surprised, it can't take actions. It also grants combat advantage and can't flank.

swamp walk: A type of terrain walk. A creature that has swamp walk ignores difficult terrain that is mud or shallow water.

swarm [keyword]: A swarm is composed of multiple creatures but functions as a single creature. A swarm can occupy the same space as another creature, and an enemy can enter a swarm's space, which is difficult terrain. A swarm cannot be pulled, pushed, or slid by melee or ranged attacks.

    A swarm can squeeze through any opening large enough for even one of its constituent creatures. For example, a swarm of bats can squeeze through an opening large enough for one of the bats to squeeze through.

swim speed: A creature that has a swim speed moves through water at that speed without having to make Athletics checks to swim.

telepathy: A creature that has telepathy can communicate mentally with any creature that has a language, even if they don't share the language. The other creature must be within line of effect and within a specified range. Telepathy allows for two-way communication.

teleportation [keyword]: An effect type. A teleportation power transports creatures or objects instantaneously from one location to another. Teleportation follows special rules given in Chapter 6.

threatening reach: A creature that has threatening reach can make an opportunity attack against any enemy within its reach that provokes an opportunity attack.

thunder [keyword]: A damage type. See also **damage type**.

totally obscured: A measure of visibility. A creature has total concealment when it is in a totally obscured square. *Example:* Total darkness. Contrast with **heavily obscured** and **lightly obscured**.

tremorsense: A creature that has tremorsense can clearly see creatures or objects within a specified radius, even if they are invisible, obscured, or outside line of effect, but both they and the creature must be in contact with the ground or the same substance, such as water or a web. The creature otherwise relies on its other senses.

truesight: See **blindsight**.

tunneling: A creature that has tunneling leaves tunnels behind it as it burrows. The creature, as well as smaller creatures, can move through these tunnels without any reduction in speed. Creatures of the same size as the tunneling creature must squeeze through these tunnels, and larger creatures cannot move through them at all. See also **burrow speed**.

turn: On a creature's turn, it takes actions: a standard action, a move action, a minor action, and any number of free actions, in any order it wishes. See also **once per turn**.

unconscious [condition]: While a creature is unconscious, it is helpless, it can't take actions, and it takes a –5 penalty to all defenses. It also can't flank and is unaware of its surroundings. When a creature is subjected to this condition, it falls prone, if possible. See also **helpless** and **prone**.

undead [keyword]: Undead are not living creatures, so effects that specifically target living creatures don't work against them. They don't need to breathe or sleep.

unoccupied square: A square that is neither occupied by a creature nor filled by an object.

water [keyword]: A water creature is strongly connected to water.

weakened [condition]: While a creature is weakened, its attacks deal half damage. However, two kinds of damage that it deals are not affected: ongoing damage and damage that isn't generated by an attack roll. See also **half damage**.

weapon [keyword]: An accessory type. This keyword identifies a power that is used with a weapon, which can be an unarmed strike.

zone [keyword]: An effect type. Powers that have the zone keyword create zones, magical areas that last for a round or more. Zones follow special rules given in Chapter 3.

Index

EVERY ADVENTURER
SHOULD BE EQUIPPED
WITH THE ESSENTIA[L]

FOR PLAYERS

FOR DMs

Whether you're new to the game or a veteran, a player or Dungeon Master, the D&D Esse[ntial]
line of products gathers all the rules you need—and all the options you'll want—for buildi[ng]
characters, creating encounters, and running the game.

Pick them up and bring even more to the table.

DUNGEON[S]
&DRAGON[S]

NEVER SPLIT THE PA[RTY]

DUNGEONSANDDRAGONS.COM